D1599575

# The Future Faces
of War

**Recent Titles in**
**The Changing Face of War**

# The Future Faces of War

## Population and National Security

Jennifer Dabbs Sciubba

The Changing Face of War
James Jay Carafano, Series Editor

 PRAEGER

AN IMPRINT OF ABC-CLIO, LLC
Santa Barbara, California • Denver, Colorado • Oxford, England

**Library of Congress Cataloging-in-Publication Data**

Sciubba, Jennifer Dabbs.
   The future faces of war : population and national security / Jennifer Dabbs Sciubba.
     p. cm. — (The changing face of war)
   Includes bibliographical references and index.
   ISBN 978-0-313-36494-5 (hbk. : alk. paper) — ISBN 978-0-313-36495-2 (ebook)
1. Demographic transition—Political aspects. 2. Population—Political aspects. 3.
Population geography—Political aspects. 4. National security—Social aspects. 5.
Revolutions—Demographic aspects. I. Title.
   HB887.S37    2011
   355'.033—dc22    2010039424

ISBN: 978-0-313-36494-5
EISBN: 978-0-313-36495-2

15  14  13  12  11   1  2  3  4  5

This book is also available on the World Wide Web as an eBook.
Visit www.abc-clio.com for details.

Praeger
An Imprint of ABC-CLIO, LLC

ABC-CLIO, LLC
130 Cremona Drive, P.O. Box 1911
Santa Barbara, California 93116-1911

This book is printed on acid-free paper ∞

Manufactured in the United States of America

# Contents

# Acknowledgments

This book project grew out of an article originally published in *Joint Forces Quarterly* in January/February 2008 that benefited greatly from the help of Thomas Mahnken, Alisa Stack, and Robert Lamb. Thanks also to Kathleen Hicks, Barry Pavel, and Amanda Dory for guiding me as I learned to integrate my scholarship into policy.

I am indebted to many readers for helpful comments, particularly David Romano, Andrew Michta, Elizabeth Leahy Madsen, Richard Cincotta, Eric Kaufmann, Allison Garland, John Sewell, Lauren Herzer, Dennis Dimick, Kent Butts, and Geoff Dabelko. Jennifer Taylor very patiently gave comments on each chapter and helped me with editing.

I owe a special thanks to the Environmental Change and Security Program (ECSP) of the Woodrow Wilson International Center for Scholars for hosting a review of several chapters. The staff of ECSP, Kayly Ober, Sean Peoples, Meaghan Parker, and Geoff Dabelko, are always so supportive of political demography and my work in this field. At Rhodes College, Emma Redden, Derek Washam, and Kimberly Stevenson were a tremendous help with research.

I am also very grateful for the team at ABC-CLIO. Though many helped with this project, any and all shortcomings are my own.

Finally, thank you to my wonderful husband, Paul, for his patience and his help with everything from the chapters to the dishes.

# 1
## Chapter

# A Framework for Demography and National Security

Without people there would be no power and no politics.
Sprout and Sprout (1945, p. 29)

Demographers often say that population change is like a glacier; it moves slowly, but has a big impact. For decision makers faced with immediate concerns, such as avoiding a terrorist attack in a major city or stemming the flow of illegal drugs, turning attention to the challenges and opportunities of age structure or urbanization can seem peripheral, because these changes take place over decades and are more often underlying causes of insecurity than immediate ones. From a practical standpoint, the positive or negative consequences of population issues may not come to fruition until long after policy makers have vacated their positions. However, far from peripheral, population issues of fertility, mortality, and migration are central to all facets of national security, whether it is the ability of the state to defend itself from external threats, avoid collapse, or provide for the individual needs of its citizens. Demographic trends mean that the 21st century will undoubtedly include interstate wars, civil conflict, and millions of deaths from poverty and disease, but policy plays a large role in determining who will be the future faces of war.

Statesmen from Thucydides to Kissinger have warned about the grave implications of population trends during their time. As historical writings show, the challenges of the present always seem daunting, but a combination of forces, including globalization and technology, have created an environment of increasing complexity that arguably makes today's challenges to states greater than ever before. Not only is the security environment more complex today—with a larger number of empowered actors, more advanced technology, higher demand to react quickly, and more lethal weapons—but the demographic situation is also more complex. Although world population did not reach 2 billion until about 1930, it now stands at nearly 7 billion and, if current population trends continue, there will be more than 11 billion people on the planet by 2050.[1] What we once thought of as "young countries" hardly compare with today's young and growing states, some of which have nearly 50 percent of their population younger than the age of 15 years, because death rates are so much lower today but fertility remains high. Population aging and decline, which seemed improbable during the heyday of baby booms, is now firmly entrenched among advanced industrial democracies, which have unprecedented proportions of retirees and increasingly empty school desks. Thanks, in part, to international family planning efforts, the next wave of aging countries will age even faster than Europe and Japan have, yet with far lower levels of development. The combination of population and environmental trends will exacerbate many demographic problems, particularly for the world's weakest states, where drought threatens to lower agricultural yield at the same time that lack of freshwater and food demands increase.[2] So, too, has population created greater prospects for prosperity and peace. The biggest cities are bigger than we have ever seen before, and there are more of them. These cities concentrate services like health care and education, and provide income opportunities unavailable in rural areas. Globalization has empowered migrants to seek political and economic opportunities in new places. Population density is unmatched, especially for some of the fastest growing countries, bringing together people of different backgrounds and ambitions. Whether creating security or insecurity, all these trends mean that states will have to continue to plan for the spectrum of warfare, and respond to civil conflict, instability, and humanitarian disasters. A complex problem means that we need a comprehensive vision of national security, one that will encompass a state's ability to survive and thrive by the absence of threat at the system, state, and individual levels of analysis.

The main purpose of this book is to describe the national security implications of demographic trends. Specifically, I will

1. Recommend an approach for systematically including population variables in assessments of national security
2. Identify and describe the trends most likely to pose challenges and opportunities for national security
3. Forecast how these trends are likely to develop in tandem with other political, economic, and social trends

The chapters show that population has real and measurable effects on national security, but numbers carry little information on their own; they need context. Population trends themselves, no matter how headline grabbing they may be, are not enough to create meaningful political change. In fact, the security implications of demographic trends will depend on political capacity, especially the institutions, governance, and leadership that attempt to address demographic challenges. Although demography is important, leaders—whether government or civil society—have points of leverage to shape its effects. Evidence for this is everywhere. States with similar age structures often have very different levels of economic growth; one multiethnic state may be at peace whereas another with similar ethnic composition is embroiled in war. In fact, analyzing demography by itself would greatly overpredict conflict.[3] Links between population trends, particularly growth in youth cohorts or differential growth among ethnic groups, are logically sound, but our theories need to systematically include political variables, like institutions and the geopolitical context, between population on one side of the equation and security outcomes on the other. There are many factors that could either trump or at least temper the effects of demography. This viewpoint is empowering for states, because it means they can harness their demographic potential and overcome challenges. It also places responsibility on states to do so or face major consequences, including civil strife, extreme poverty, and systemic challenges to power. Population trends by themselves are neither inherently good nor bad, but they do create conditions for peace or conflict within which states must respond. Depending on a state's ability to draw on its population resources, any population trend—including growth, decline, or migration–could be either a challenge or an opportunity.

A framework is important for helping us understand the complex relationships between demography and security, and how to defeat challenges and harness opportunities. When I was working on demographic issues at the Department of Defense in the mid 2000s, I found that the leadership—under both secretaries Rumsfeld and Gates in the United States and in defense ministries abroad—was very receptive to the idea that demography influences national security. Yet, policy makers were often hesitant to act on these findings and felt limited in their ability to do so because of the overwhelming number of ways demography seemed to matter. Overload of information is always a risk in assessments that define security broadly, making a clear framework all the more important.

To address the multiple connections between population and security, this book disaggregates national security and frames the discussion according to three realms: military, regime, and structural security or, more generally, external defense, internal stability, and the relation of human security to the state.[4] There are both theoretical and practical reasons for defining national security in broad terms. In general, the field of security studies has increasingly come to recognize that merely defining security in terms of the military is insufficient, because military security gives a state the ability to respond to some threats, but does not encompass the multitude of threats to national goals. States have, among others, three objectives: (1) to project power in the international system, (2) to protect their interests, and (3) to secure access to resources. Demography—in particular, the number of people in a population and those who make up the population—can affect a state's ability to pursue each of these goals. The ability to project power is one of the most direct links. Demography affects a state's strength through manpower and economic growth, and thus can tell us something about long-term competition among great powers like the United States, the European Union (EU), and Russia. States also want competent partners. However, how can a poorly governed Pakistan with a population of 400 million provide the security and support to deal with extremism? Demographic trends also drive global competition for resources. China has increased its presence in Africa in part because they need access to resources to support their population; their pursuit of port access in the Indian Ocean and South China Sea is an outcome of that quest. Demography plays an integral role in risk assessment and foresight, informs assessments of alliances and partnerships, and indicates potential hotspots for instability. Strategy has to account for demography as one of the forces that will shape the world over the planning horizon.

## THEORETICAL LINKS

Thanks to attention by the National Intelligence Council in their series of *Global Trends* reports, and to a number of well-received articles, momentum for synergy between the security and demography communities has been building. During the past several decades, security practitioners have begun to consider seriously the roles of demography, identity, and environmental issues in disrupting state stability and instigating conflict, and how they can help us better understand a variety of security issues, from irregular challenges to great-power politics. Although its popularity has grown throughout recent years, demography is no passing fad among leaders. Millennia ago, most of the world's major monotheistic religions exhorted their followers to "increase and multiply" to spread the faith, not unlike the calls of leaders like Russia's Vladimir Putin and Iran's Mahmoud Ahmadinejad today.[5] Ancient and modern thinkers alike understand the potential power of demography, and along the way have identified important demographic issues and their relationship to multiple forms of security.

The demographic security literature provides many theoretical links among fertility, mortality, and migration on the one hand, and security on the other. We can parse this literature into two main camps. The first is mostly concerned with interstate conflict and sees population as part of an index of power. The second category describes theories, like that of the famous Reverend

Thomas Malthus, that draw our attention to the consequences of imbalance between population and resources, including the effects on civil conflict. Looking at demographic trends alone, we can see how population issues create conditions conducive to conflict, but theory is necessary to understand the mechanisms by which conflict or peace actually result. Because this book provides a broad overview of population and national security, it does not test one theory; rather, it draws liberally from the literature to understand dynamics of specific trends in particular places and times.

## Population as Power

The first way to think about the relationship between population and conflict echoes a realist view of national security that argues states seek power to defend or deter potential threats. This literature points our attention to two important connections between population and national security. The first is the contribution of population to capabilities and the second is how relative differences in capabilities can create conditions for conflict. This is the literature that brought demography into the political science fold and continues to be one of the most influential. Early scholars focused on ways that population trends, as a means to power, might contribute to yet another world war. Many of them had seen connections between population trends and both wars of that early century, and were especially disturbed by Hitler and the Nazi Party's obsession with eugenics and population growth as a means to international power. To the realist, the distribution of power within the international system or one state's power relative to an adversary can be the primary determinant of political outcomes such as war. Population contributes to power primarily through providing military manpower and labor for economic production under certain conditions. In particular, some argue that a large population is an asset; a young and growing population is favorable, because a youthful age structure provides a continuous flow of young men (in particular) to serve in the military.[6] Such simplistic assessments of the relationship between population and power have mostly been discarded, as scholars have realized that a large and growing population can sometimes be as much of a burden as a boon. Harold and Margaret Sprout were two of the first to emphasize that "quality"—productivity, education, and so forth—matters as much as "quantity."[7] A large and growing population is not sufficient for military power, nor is it always necessary when technology is taken into account, as nuclear weapons have shown. Still, there is a relationship between population and capabilities, and understanding this relationship is useful for assessing the relative power of states. In particular, the population sizes of China and India are important in terms of potential size of their armed forces and labor forces, but characteristics like the level of education and health of their populations must also be taken into consideration. Likewise, assessments of aging populations must complicate the links between age structure and military power, and not over-simplify the relationship by too quickly writing off aging states.

Katherine and A. F. K. Organski add another dimension by emphasiz-ing that political capacity, or how the state mobilizes its population, matters as well:

> Population is, indeed, a nation's greatest resource, though like other resources it may be squandered or misused. What greater asset can a nation have than a multitude of able-bodied citizens, ready to stoke its furnaces, work its mines, run its machinery, harvest its crops, build its cities, raise its children, produce its art, and provide the vast array of goods and services that make a nation prosperous and content? On the other hand, what greater liability can a nation have than a mass of surplus people, living in hunger and poverty, scratching at tiny plots of land whose produce will not feed them all, swarming into cities where there are no more jobs, living in huts or dying in the street, sitting in apathy or smoldering with discontent, and ever begetting more children to share their misery? The rela-tionship between numbers and wealth and power is not simple, but surely it is significant.[8]

One of the major arguments of this book is that any population trend can be an opportunity or a challenge. Ethnic diversity, age structure, or migration can contribute positively to a state's power and security, or can set the stage for insecurity and conflict. As the Organskis argue, demography is important for national security, but it is essential to emphasize the state's role in making the most of their population.

The multiple connections between population and power are useful in comparing capabilities of states, but how do these differences turn into inter-national conflict? Many prominent theories point out that population, as an indicator of power, raises or lowers the potential of conflict through perceptions of a state's own capabilities and of its capabilities relative to its competitors. One way that power increases the likelihood of conflict is through expansion-ism. Some argue that the quest for material power may lead to expansionism as states try to meet the needs of their populations. The *lebensraum* thesis is relevant here, because it assumes that countries with large populations will need to expand to obtain resources, including land for agriculture, to satisfy the needs of their population.[9] Though it was once popular, this theory fails to account for the international norms of sovereignty that have only grown more entrenched since World War II, and displays little faith in states' abilities to gain resources through trade. More plausible is the argument that increased capabilities can lead to the desire to expand when rising powers are discontent with the status quo and want to have a greater international presence.

Many theories have explored the links between population, power, and conflict. Offensive realists tend to argue that more power increases the likelihood of conflict.[10] To them, power may take the form of size of armed forces or economic growth, both of which population can affect. Another way that power increases the likelihood of conflict is that more powerful states tend to be more active internationally, and thus have greater chances of becoming embroiled in arguments and clashes that could turn violent.[11] Several of these ideas are reflected in the lateral pressure theory advanced by Nazli Choucri and Robert North.[12] They argue that stronger actors (defined as having more capabilities and resolve) will have a greater presence on the international scene than weaker actors. Both capabilities and demand are derived from population, technology, and access to resources. Conflict results from the inevitability that expanding states will collide with other actors. Choucri and North argue that lateral pressure by itself may not trigger a war, but it will if the states are already adversaries or if one perceives the other's activities as threatening. Offensive realism and lateral pressure theory direct us to consider the distribution of power across the international system and see population variables in light of the geopolitical context. These theories focus our attention on states with increasing capabilities and favorable population trends.

Defensive realists, on the other hand, argue that insecurity leads states to expand, and insecurity can often result from a state's decreasing capabilities, especially when an adversary's capabilities are increasing. Population variables are applicable here as well, insofar as they relate to capabilities. According to this theory, those states, particularly aging ones, that have a decreased ability to fund defense may have a higher likelihood of going to war with an adversary. But capabilities alone do not lead to war; preferences of the leadership are also relevant. Assessments of propensity to wage war on states with declining populations, like Russia's, or growing ones, like China's, must also take preferences into account. Likewise, power transition theorists argue that power is shaped by a state's population size, productivity, and political capacity. The theory tries to take into account how changes in these variables change state power and, when combined with preferences, affect the hierarchy of states in the international system.[13] What we learn from defensive realism and power transition theory is that perception of power may matter as much as actual measures.

## Population and Resources

The relationship between population and power illuminates how demography can set the context for or exacerbate conditions that lead to international conflict. To understand the relationship between population and civil conflict, many scholars have focused on the role of resources, particularly the balance between population and resources. The most widely cited arguments are those that see a negative relationship between population and resources on the one hand and conflict on the other. The work of Thomas Malthus and the neo-Malthusian arguments of the 20th century are similar to those of other classical economists like Adam Smith and David Ricardo, who were afraid that population growth would outpace the planet's ability to provide resources and would lead to widespread poverty. According to Malthus, population growth, because it expands exponentially, would eventually outstrip the resources needed to sustain it, because food resources expand geometrically.[14] Thus, population eventually strains the land's carrying capacity and becomes problematic. Following this logic, contemporary neo-Malthusians argue that the strains population places on the environment threaten political stability. Neo-Malthusians still argue for a relationship between population growth and environmental degradation, but move away from Malthus by giving a more prominent place to intermediate variables such as consumption habits and technology. The deprivation caused by imbalance can motivate certain factions to rebel against the state out of frustration. Likewise, competition for resources can increase the likelihood of intergroup violence.[15] These theories are relevant to assessments of youthful age structures and youth bulges, which essentially describe crowded youth cohorts in which individuals compete for jobs and other resources. However, the motive literature only tells part of the story, and political opportunity attempts to fill in the rest by explaining how the weakness of the state can open space for aggrieved groups to rebel.

The motive and opportunity perspectives are closely related as connecting individual and structural explanations of how demography turns into conflict. The concept of state failure is one example of how these two perspectives come together. According to the state failure hypothesis, conflict erupts when social grievances combine with eroding state authority and escalating intraelite competition.[16] In some ways, this returns us to the idea of political capacity, mentioned previously in relation to power transition theory. Stronger states may not experience civil conflict even in situations when population and resource strains create the motivations for rebellion. Strongly authoritarian regimes with a lot of political capacity and strong democracies that provide for peaceful resolution of grievances are less likely than weaker states to see violent conflict.

Neoclassical economists take a different tack than neo-Malthusians and argue that there are military and economic advantages of larger populations, and that economic growth leads to increased security. Their faith that markets, governments, and institutions will adapt to the changes brought by population growth points us to the need to recognize the role of governance and warns us against being overly deterministic with regard to population.

The population as power literature has been politically influential in informing assessments of relative capabilities, particularly among great powers. The population-resource literature has arguably had an even greater impact in terms of policy. Particularly influential were the population and security scholars of the 1960s who focused on the dangers of growth, specifically the population–resource balance. Such arguments were most notably encompassed in Paul Ehrlich's *The Population Bomb.*[17] Work like Ehrlich's directly influenced U.S. National Security Study Memorandum 200, which called for studying the impact of world population growth on U.S. security and overseas interests.[18] In the wake of the population "crisis" the United States Agency for International Development (USAID) budget for population jumped from $6 million in 1966 to $120 million in 1972 (mainly for research).[19] Including demography in assessments of the future security environment is something we see echoed today. For example, the 2008 U.S. National Defense Strategy (NDS) was groundbreaking because it recognized the security risks posed by both population growth and deficit—resulting from aging, shrinking, or disease—the role of climate pressures, and the connections between population and the environment.[20] One of the aims of this book is to provide policy-relevant analysis of population trends, firmly grounded in political science. The framework outlined in the following section is a tool to make the numerous connections between population and national security clearer and thus make demographic projections more valuable to policy makers.

## FRAMEWORK

Although there is a distinction between risk of interstate conflict and risk of civil conflict, both are manifestations of insecurity with connections to population. If we define national security as the absence of threat, we must take into account external threats and internal threats at the system, state, and individual levels of analysis. A systematic way of including these levels and characteristics is to see national security as a function of military security (*MS*), regime security (*RS*), and structural security (*SS*)[21]:

$$NS = f(MS, RS, SS)$$

Even as population trends change, this framework is useful, because it provides a *way* to think about the effects that are not solely dependent on particular countries.

The category of military security encompasses conventional defense concerns about securing state borders and states' ability to pursue their objectives.

The second category, regime security, describes the government's ability to prevent civil conflict that could threaten their legitimacy or position of power. As an illustration, consider that some European states may be primarily concerned about military strikes conducted by an external foe (military security), whereas others may be more concerned about subversion from within resulting from the differential growth of ethnic groups (regime security). The third category is structural security, which refers to the state's ability to meet the demands of its population given the availability of resources and technology.[22] Although there are many similarities between this category and what others call "human security," there is one major difference. The referent for most human security theorists is not the state. Instead, they see individuals or humanity, as a collective unit, as the entity that is ultimately to be secured.[23] The idea of structural security recognizes that humankind should be secured from poverty, disease, or other threats, as human security scholars point out, but individual insecurity creates conditions for state failure and collapse, ultimately an issue of national security.

As this last example points out, these three pieces come together in a meaningful way. As Nazli Choucri says, "*A state is secure to the extent that all three dimensions or conditions for security are in place*; and it is insecure to the extent that one or more conditions (or dimensions) of security are threatened or eroded [emphasis in original]."[24] The three components—military, regime, and structural security—are highly interdependent and causally connected, so it is important to consider all three realms in a comprehensive assessment of national security. A lack of structural security can provide the motive for rebellion and create regime insecurity. Lack of regime security can provide the political opportunity for those motives to turn to action, and can even spill over into military security threats when conflict crosses borders. One state's regime insecurity is another state's military insecurity, if the former's inability to maintain a monopoly on the legitimate use of force allows terrorists, organized criminals, or other actors to flourish and become transnational threats. As U.S. Secretary of Defense Robert Gates has said: "In the decades to come, the most lethal threats to the United States' safety and security—a city poisoned or reduced to rubble by a terrorist attack—are likely to emanate from states that cannot adequately govern themselves or secure their own territory."[25]

The three realms of national security are theoretically connected, but sorting national security in this way also increases its utility to policy makers. As most recent defense strategies—including the United States's, Russia's, and the EU's—recognize, there is value in comprehensive assessment.[26] Although many theorists and policy makers, especially those from the realist tradition, have resisted a broadening of the definition of national security from its traditional military/power focus, there is increasing recognition among policy makers that a multitude of threats emanating from a variety of sources affects national security. There is also increasing recognition that greater structural security—health, education, development—can foster stability. For example, demographic pressures play a major role in the annual failed states ranking compiled by The Fund for Peace and *Foreign Policy Magazine*. The index of failed states includes rankings based on pressures deriving from group settlement patterns; pressures from skewed population distributions, such as a youth bulge age structure or from divergent rates of population growth among competing groups; and massive movement of refugees or internally displaced persons (IDPs).[27] Somalia and Sudan, numbers one and three on the 2010 list, clearly demonstrate how such population factors play a role in civil conflict and disarray.

Another reason for including all three factors is that militaries are being called upon to provide order when individuals are in danger from structural failures, as U.S. and Canadian military responses to Haiti's natural disaster in January 2010 illustrate. The interesting connection among these kinds of security is that if demography affects military security in a way that weakens it (not enough military-age people, too many fiscal constraints), then the military will be unable to continue its "human security" missions (in other words, delivering aid and building schools).

In a situation of limited time and resources—one likely familiar to policy makers—how should we prioritize these three dimensions and the multiple demographic trends? It depends. Various actors will weigh these variables in different ways depending on their goals. European states, for example, have often placed high regard on humanitarian missions. Fragile African states have focused on gaining and maintaining sovereignty and legitimacy, and on suppressing rebellion. The United States and Russia have often made preparing for interstate war a priority. Rather than deem one aspect of national security more important than the other, this book points out the different ways each element is affected by demography.

There are problems with focusing on just one demographic issue at a time, as each of the following chapters does, or even with focusing purely on demography while marginalizing technology, economics, or environmental issues. Colin Gray points out that future conflict will not have a purely political dimension, a purely economic one, or a purely social one: "[R]ather it will have one mega-context that combines all elements to produce outcomes unpredictable from single-trend analyses."[28] Wherever possible in this book, I suggest areas where demographic trends could combine with trends in the other contexts, such as political and economic, but a full and thorough understanding of context is best left to case studies of particular times and places, not an overview book on demography and security.

## OUTLINE OF THE BOOK

There have been several excellent books on the links between demography and security, but most focus on a specific demographic trend, region, or consequence (such as ethnic conflict). Although each chapter in this book is organized around a different demographic issue, together they paint a comprehensive picture of demography and national security. Some demographic issues have obvious implications for all three aspects of national security—military, regime, and structural—whereas others are more specifically tied to one or two realms; chapters focus on the most relevant aspects. Each of the chapters answers two key questions: What challenges and opportunities do demographic trends pose for states? And what strategies and military capabilities will be beneficial for states to respond to demographic developments? The bottom line is a need for flexible and responsive institutions, not rigid ones—a trend in defense thinking as laid out in the U.S. 2010 Quadrennial Defense Review.[29] Although the role of the state is always limited when it comes to demography, states can adapt to changing circumstances, like new security threats or new age structures.

One of the most important trends during the next several decades will be the growing divide in age structure between the aging industrialized great powers and the youthful industrializing powers. Most of the world's expected future population growth, which could be anywhere from two to four billion by 2050, will take place in developing states.[30] Chapter 2 discusses how the youthful age structures of these states and their continued high population growth are a regime security risk. Large numbers of youthful dependents often impede development and undermine efforts to combat terrorism and to foster stability and governance. There is a robust correlation between youth bulges and armed conflict, especially under conditions of economic stagnation, and states with an abundance of youth face many problems with civil conflict, rebellion, and crime. In many Middle Eastern and African states, between 40 percent and 50 percent of the population is younger than 18 years of age; the populations of these two regions are the fastest growing in the world. Many of the approximately 120 million youth there are without employment or political opportunities.[31] Although the region has seen a slight upswing in economic growth, current rates are not robust enough to put the region on track for creating an adequate number of jobs. Economic structures have invariably been constructed for smaller populations; thus, youth bulges and youthful age structures, both cases when youth generations are larger than the preceding generations, generate a mismatch between the pool of labor and the economy's capacity to absorb it. With so few ways to earn an honest living and support their families, young men are more willing to accept a couple hundred dollars—or less—to plant a roadside bomb or take up arms for warring factions.

On the other side of the demographic divide, the world's most developed countries are rapidly aging—and in some cases shrinking—as a result of decades of low fertility. Although these states have historically been some of the world's most peaceful and their citizens have high standards of living, there may be major military security implications as this unprecedented shift in age structure challenges military funding and manpower; these topics are the subject of Chapter 3. Japan, the North Atlantic Treaty Organization (NATO), the European Union, and South Korea are highlighted to describe the future of recruitment, willingness to intervene, strength of alliances, and new trends in technology to replace ground forces. This chapter assesses the likelihood that population aging could affect the willingness and ability of allies and partners to support global security efforts. If aging states do not act to mitigate the effects of aging, budget and manpower strains may undermine the ability of aging states to respond to global crises and wield influence, which not only disrupts the pursuit of their own goals, but also tests their ability to intervene in crises around the world, regardless of whether the challenge is about civil conflict or humanitarian disasters.

The North–South divide describes those states with age structures at two extremes—young and old—but there are many states in the middle, as Chapter 4 illustrates. These states, which demographers often refer to as those in the "window of opportunity," have age structures with higher numbers of laborers relative to older and younger dependents. Today, India, China, and many countries in Latin America have lowered fertility and mortality, and the boost of potential workers means that these states have the ability to experience a demographic "bonus" of productivity and economic growth, if they harness their resources. From a national security standpoint, these states could become stable and productive partners in fostering global peace and security, and could see increasing democratization and increasing standards of living for their populations. Population momentum, which is the tendency for a population to continue growing even after fertility has declined because there are still a high number of reproductive age women, means that most states with a transitional age structure are still growing. From a national security perspective, population growth can be the impetus for new strategic relationships. As groups try to secure access to scarce resources, those that cooperate could form strategic alliances that challenge the Western great powers. For example, to meet the needs of its growing population and developing economy, China is establishing relations with Russia and many states in Africa, South America, and Central Asia.

Age structure is only one demographic issue. International migration, the subject of Chapter 5, is a security challenge because large-scale movements of people can change the composition of a country's population within days or weeks—much quicker than the years associated with fertility and mortality trends. Movements between countries or regions can affect the composition of a region or locale, and this effect is often larger than the national impact that tends to be disguised in large-scale data sets. When people move, so do their politics; clashes of identity and interests may lead to conflict or, at a minimum, may create deep social divisions. In the Middle East and Africa, migration—including internal displacement—itself is often conflict driven. The millions displaced by troubles in Sudan, Iraq, and elsewhere potentially carry their domestic political skirmishes across borders and threaten to disrupt these regions further. In Central Asia and the Middle East, movement of people is upsetting a delicate demographic balance among tribes and religious sects. Even the Global North is not immune to the challenges to identity that migration poses. These challenges relate to military security because controversies and tensions over migration are becoming factors in discussions about the future existence and expansion of the EU and NATO. Tensions between immigrants and native-born citizens over representation, resources, and identity have sometimes erupted into violence. The pressures aging places on military resources, combined with political skirmishes over migration, may cause Europe to focus more on inward stability than an outward projection of power.

Chapter 6 examines how urbanization, defined as the movement of people from urban to rural areas, and the growth of urban areas themselves provide both challenges and opportunities for national security. The number of urban residents worldwide is expected to increase from about 50 percent of world population in 2010 to 59 percent by 2030, with virtually all growth occurring in developing countries.[32] For some states, urbanization will bring technology, education, and health care to the masses, and is a positive step toward increasing potential for economic development. For others, urbanization will take the form of ever-increasing slums around city centers. Humanitarian disasters associated with or exacerbated by urbanization, particularly of coastal regions, can result in disarray and are particularly devastating in fragile states. Climate change will only make these areas more vulnerable. Population distribution problems, especially the disparity between rural and urban populations, may have a major effect on violence, decay, rebellion, and revolution. Finally, some of sub-Saharan Africa's urban slums are becoming safe havens for terrorists and are potential sites of peacekeeping engagements.

Chapter 7 examines four additional challenges with demographic composition: the age structure changes that come from high mortality; sex ratio imbalance; and differential growth among ethnic and religious groups. While early chapters cover a number of the links between age structure and national security, they focus on the consequences of shifts in fertility. Age structure changes can also result from high mortality, raising new issues for security.

High mortality from disease in Russia and in many African states can affect military preparedness, economic growth, and governance. Gender imbalances, particularly high proportions of unmarried males, may be correlated with higher crime rates and pose a risk to regime security. Differential growth among ethnic and religious groups can create regime security issues in democracies as changing compositions of the electorate alter the political leadership, whereas in authoritarian states, differential growth, especially when resources are scarce, can be the impetus for rebellion.

The final chapter summarizes the general relationship of demography to the three areas of national security, suggests policy responses that can mediate the effects, and raises questions for future research. The conclusion also introduces a different way of viewing the relationship between demography and national security by focusing on particular regions of the world, instead of individual trends. Most regions and states experience multiple demographic issues at any given time; shifting the lens gives greater insight into how demography informs the strategic calculus of these regions and states. Finally, the chapter also discusses some of the pitfalls of securitizing population.

Primarily, this book is aimed at policy makers and those tasked with strategic planning, particularly in the military or national security communities, but I also hope this book will make a modest contribution to the field of political demography within international relations by reconnecting to the early literature on demography as a component of power, advanced by such pillars as Harold and Margaret Sprout, A. F. K. Organski, and Nazli Choucri. This book is also relevant for students of demography and security. Although there are currently few places in higher education where these connections are considered as part of courses, their number is growing, and I believe inclusion of demography in security studies will be facilitated by a comprehensive volume on the connections.

Though it can illuminate the past and present, demography cannot predict the future. Indeed, this book will actually emphasize the factors most likely to change contingencies. However, demography is the most predictable of the social sciences and a useful tool for policy makers because demographic projections are reasonably reliable for 15 to 20 years out. Uncertainty increases along with the time horizon, but momentum for change—growth, decline—during the next several decades is already built into a state's age structure. Current age structures say far more about what the world will look like 10 or 20 years from now than economic models, weather forecasts, or indices that try to predict a coup. And we can still use the past to explore the future. There is virtue in identifying what should be avoided; this is one of the ways demographic projections can be most useful. As the editors of *Population and Development Review* once commented, demographic projections "are, in short, stylized futures, serving as often to show what ought if possible to be avoided as to indicate what is actually expected to happen."[33] Policy makers can use analysis of demography to draw conclusions about how to shape the future. Like investing in infrastructure, benefits from policies that seriously consider demographic trends may only be reaped a decade or more into the future; then they pay dividends, albeit uncertain, for decades.

# 2
Chapter

# Youth and Youthful Age Structures

Paul Ehrlich famously wrote of a hot, crowded night in Delhi in his 1968 book *The Population Bomb:* "The streets seemed alive with people. People eating, people washing, people sleeping. People visiting, arguing, and screaming. People thrusting their hands through the taxi window, begging. People defecating and urinating. People clinging to buses. People herding animals. People, people, people."[1]

Although Ehrlich has received a fair share of criticism throughout the years for his portrayal of the people of India and other developing countries, no one else has so vividly captured the scale of population growth. The increase in world population from 1.6 billion in 1900 to 6 billion in 2000 was the defining population trend of the 20th century.[2] This is a huge leap, considering that it took all of human history to reach the 1.6 billion mark but less than 100 years to add five and half more. The size of the planet has remained the same, but the number of inhabitants continues to increase; growth is concentrated in the world's least developed countries, most of which are already straining to meet the needs of their populations. Population growth and size are important because of their connection to resources, but a population's age structure—the distribution of the population across different age groups—also has links to national security. Ehrlich neglects one crucial detail in his opening paragraphs: the vast majority of the faces of these multitudes of "people" he describes are likely young. A population grows rapidly when the number of children born to each woman exceeds the replacement of her and her partner. For populations with child and maternal mortality rates at industry-country levels, replacement fertility is around 2.1 children per woman: one each to replace the mother and her partner, plus a margin of error to account for those female children who don't make it to reproductive age. At the time *The Population*

*Bomb* debuted, the average Indian woman could expect to have at least five children during her lifetime, and India's population growth rate was about 2.1 percent per year, meaning that the country's population was on track to double every 30 years. India's population was large, growing, and extremely young. In 1965, almost 42 percent of the population was younger than the age of 15; almost 60 percent was younger than the age of 25.[3]

Since Ehrlich's time—and perhaps because he scared a generation of policy makers into action— fertility has declined for most of the world. In 2005, the average Indian woman had around three children fewer than her peer in 1965—India's total fertility rate (TFR) was down to 2.8. India's population has undergone major changes during the past half century that have positioned the country for economic growth and more influence in international affairs. However, many other states have failed to achieve lower fertility and mortality. What kind of impact does a median age of 19 years, like Iraq's, have on national security? If 46 percent of the population is younger than 15 years old, as in Afghanistan, what kind of challenges and opportunities does this pose for military and economic power, governance, and development?[4]

This chapter introduces a discussion of age structure and national security. Subsequent chapters will focus on the implications of structures with an abundance of people of working age and of the elderly, but this chapter examines age structures with an abundance of youth, like Afghanistan's today and India's in the 1960s. Most important for national security, countries with youthful age structures are generally the least developed and least democratic in the world, and tend to have the highest risk of civil conflict.[5] Six out of nine new outbreaks of civil conflict between 2000 and 2006 occurred in countries with very young or youthful age structures.[6] There is little doubt that a correlation between youth and conflict exists. Henrik Urdal, one of the foremost researchers on the subject, found that "when youth make up more than 35 percent of the adult population, which they do in many developing countries, the risk of armed conflict is 150 percent higher than in countries with an age structure similar to most developed countries."[7] However, armed conflict is not the only regime security threat faced by states with youthful age structures. The category of regime security can encompass a range of domestic disorder that threatens to undermine the ability of the regime to govern, including terrorism, riots, crime, and other forms of unrest, such as protest. Depending on your perspective, this could be either a challenge or an opportunity. Naturally, if you are the regime in charge, you want to stay in power. However, if you are the leader of a rival state or a citizen living under what you see as an oppressive regime, you would likely be glad to see some unrest.

This chapter draws on examples of each of these forms of regime insecurity and describes connections with structural security to illustrate how a youthful age structure becomes a national security issue. To understand fully why a youthful age structure creates insecurity for the state, we must also understand the condition of individuals. Youth face and pose a unique set of challenges, and one of the factors that seems to be present in cases of youth and regime insecurity is marginalization in the economic, social, and political realms. Although there are still many questions about the ways that youth actually cause violence within or between societies, there is much more certainty about their role as victims. These two perspectives may be related. Even though they are often considered at odds, both the motive and opportunity literature for causes of civil violence argue that youth who are marginalized and are victims of violence or exclusion are more likely to carry out violence against the state or other groups. The United Nations (UN) describes this reciprocal relationship: "Those most likely to suffer from violence are between the ages of 16 and 19. [However,] an overwhelming majority of those who participate in violence against young people in developed countries are about the same age and sex as their victims."[8] This chapter describes some of the links between motive and opportunity on the one hand, and insecurity on the other.

In addition to national security challenges, youthful age structures also present opportunities to create greater security and prosperity for the state. The exclusion of youth from social, economic, and political opportunities prevents their individual fulfillment and wastes their potential to contribute to society. If governments establish institutions and policies that give youth positive opportunities when they enter their working years, by encouraging education, skills training, jobs, and political participation, they can decrease their risk of conflict, harness the potential energy of youth, and reap the benefits of increased human capital.

The following sections first describe the attributes of a youthful age structure. The chapter then describes the security challenges most often associated with young populations and discusses what factors may lead youth to pursue different forms of conflict, including protest, rebellion, and more organized and violent forms like civil war. The chapter then moves to a discussion of the links between demography and democracy. Finally, the chapter concludes with a series of policy recommendations that aim to address the challenges faced by youth in political, social, and economic exclusion.

## DEFINING YOUTH

In general, there are stark differences in age structure between developed countries and less developed countries. About 98 percent of the growth in world population during the next several decades will take place in less developed countries, meaning that these populations are the youngest in the world. In 2009, there were 237 births per minute in less developed countries whereas there were only 27 per minute in developed countries.[9] In some less

**Figure 2.1** Population tree for Afghanistan, 2005. (Population Action International)

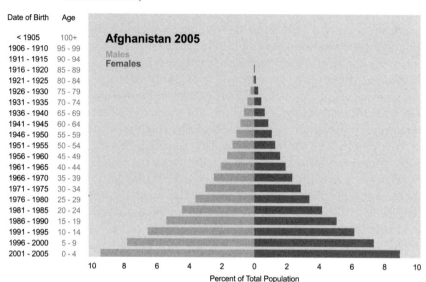

developed countries, as much as two-thirds of the population is younger than the age of 30. These populations have a classic pyramid-shaped age structure, like Afghanistan's. Most of the states with youthful age structures are located in Central Asia, North Africa, and parts of the Middle East, with the youngest age structures in sub-Saharan Africa. A population with a youthful age structure generally has high fertility, a low median age, high proportions of young dependents, and a rapidly growing population. For example, Bolivia and Pakistan, although in different regions, both have youthful age structures, median ages of 21 years, and about six child dependents for every 10 working-age adults (Fig. 2.1).[10]

Total fertility has been declining for both of these countries, since the early 1960s for Bolivia and the late 1970s for Pakistan, as it has been for most areas of the world.[11] To some degree, worldwide reduction in fertility illustrates the acceptability of smaller families across different cultures and religions. In the Arab countries of the Middle East and North Africa, with the exception of the Palestinian territories, growth has slowed in recent decades because of changes in marriage and childbearing, but declines are uneven. Although some areas, such as Lebanon, Egypt, Iran, and Tunisia, have made tremendous progress in reducing fertility, and their age structures are clearly maturing away from the classic pyramid shape (Fig. 2.2), others have not.[12] The regions with the highest fertility and the youngest populations are in Africa and Asia. For

**Figure 2.2** Population tree for Egypt, 2005. (Population Action International)

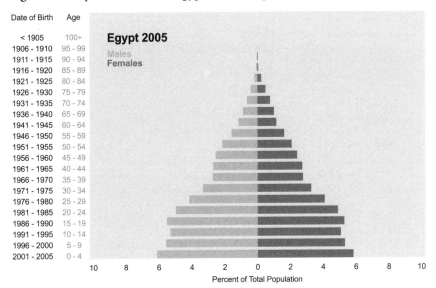

all of Africa, the total fertility rate is almost five children per woman, meaning that the population of the continent is likely to double from one billion to two billion during the next four decades.[13]

Countries like Uganda often make headlines for their high fertility—more than six children per woman on average—but fertility does not have to be very high for a population to grow tremendously.[14] Even a fertility rate of three children per woman means that the next generation will be 50 percent larger than their parents, assuming most children live to adulthood. As a way to compare the difference fertility and age structure can make in a country's economic and political situations, we can take a cue from Egyptian President Hosni Mubarak and compare Egypt and South Korea. As he noted in a 2008 speech, "in 1960 . . . both Egypt and South Korea had each a population of about 26 million people, but now South Korea has a population of about 48 million and we have about 80 million."[15] These countries both had high fertility in the middle of the past century, but by 1985, South Korea's TFR was well below replacement at 1.6 whereas Egypt's was still about 5.5.[16] The economic and political paths of the two countries have diverged along with their population patterns. Table 2.1 illustrates the more general patterns that Egypt and South Korea represent. Researchers at Population Action International studied the relationship between age structure, risk of civil conflict, likelihood of democratic governance, and economic growth between 1970 and 1999. They found that countries with 67 percent or more of the population younger than 30 years of age

**Table 2.1** Age Structure, Conflict, Governance, and Economic Growth between 1970 and 1999

| Percent Population 0–29 Years | Percent Likely to Have Civil Conflict | Percent Likely to Be Fully Democratic | Median Average GDP Growth |
|:---:|:---:|:---:|:---:|
| 67+ | 26 | 13 | 3.6 |
| 60–67 | 15 | 21 | 3.1 |
| 45–60 | 9 | 74 | 3.6 |
| 30–45 | 6 | 83 | 2.4 |

GDP, gross domestic product.

*Source:* Leahy, Elizabeth, Robert Engelman, Carolyn Gibb Vogel, Sarah Haddock, and Tod Preston. *The Shape of Things to Come: Why Age Structure Matters to a Safer, More Equitable World.* Washington, DC: Population Action International, 2007, pp. 23, 35, 43, and 55.

were 26 percent more likely to experience civil conflict between 1970 and 1999. There is also a clear relationship between democracy and age structure, one that will be examined in more detail in a following section.

The policy implications of their findings are immense. The most important takeaway for our purposes is that government and civil society actors working to foster development, peace, and democracy in countries with youthful age structures may face grim prospects. Egypt's Mubarak has said of his country's population that "increase is continually devouring any returns resulting from economic development and growth; we have to admit that the demographic dilemma is the cornerstone in the gap between the ceiling of our ambition and our limited resources."[17] Children, as dependents, have limited ability to contribute to their family's economic well-being and even less to their country's. To flourish, they require care for their basic needs, education, and the hope of employment as they enter working ages. However, when these children become young adults they can play an essential role in their country's economy, and thus its development and security in a broader sense. For this reason, we need to consider in particular the experiences of adolescents and young adults, which have some commonalities across developed and developing countries.

A youthful age structure generally describes a population with large proportions of both children and young adults, but sometimes we are more interested in zeroing in on youth ages 15 to 29 years, because they are potentially socially, economically, and politically active and thus have a unique relationship to national security in a way those of younger ages do not. This time of young adulthood is a crucial one, when most hope to find a partner and start their own family, get a job, and have some say in the way they are governed. Either a youthful or youth bulge age structure can limit these opportunities.

A population experiences a youth bulge when its cohort of 15 to 29 years is significantly larger than the ones preceding and following it—a true bulge. Youth bulge countries have been about two-and-a-half times more likely to experience onset of political violence or civil conflict than countries with a more mature age structure.[18] Why is that the case? One of the most instructive theories is Richard Easterlin's theory of relative cohort size. According to this theory, a cohort's economic and social prospects tend to have an inverse relationship to the cohort's size relative to those around it, other things being constant.[19] Youth are assumed to engage in violence because they experience "crowding" compared with other generations; they may be crowded out of the labor market or out of political opportunities. A large youth cohort lowers the cost of recruitment, because potential soldiers are abundant and the opportunity cost of joining a rebel group is low for a young person when there are no other opportunities available in the society.[20] As Finer and Fekeiki described in *The Washington Post:* "U.S. and Iraqi officials acknowledge that every young man without work is a potential recruit for insurgents who pay as little as $50 to people who plant explosives on a highway or shoot a policeman."[21] In a way, conflict represents missed opportunity to capitalize on the energy of youth. The state benefits from ensuring that young people have social, economic, and political opportunities, because these young people will eventually be the producers, civil servants, and citizens that make the country run. For example, if young people are building their skills during youth, the dividends when they enter working ages are higher because the state can collect taxes and potentially build a competitive economy. A large youth cohort can also provide states with large pools from which to draw military recruits. Youth can also be a force for positive political change as they demand representation and inclusion in the political process. Although it is treated as an example of regime insecurity for countries with youthful age structures, social protest is not always a bad thing, even if it does threaten a country's stability, because it may lead to more representative governance or other benefits. Each of the following sections describes the connections between youthful age structures and national security, drawing on examples from countries with youthful age structures, but also from countries where youth have been engaged in conflict resulting from marginalization, even if they are in a country with a more mature age structure.

## REGIME INSECURITY

The ability of the government to stay in power and remain the sovereign, legitimate authority can be questioned by a variety of disruptions—rebellion, revolt, and even protest. At the bottom rung is low-intensity, nonviolent conflict. There are many historical incidents of youth, particularly student movements, leading protests that challenge the authority of the government. Extrapolating from particular moments in history when youth have led movements, like the student movements in the United States during the 1960s or Iranian student protests in 2009, though, could be misleading. Those generations may have had particular experiences that led them to protest, especially because there are generations of youth who do not revolt. Assuming that the connection between youth and conflict is straightforward would lead us to overpredict conflict. Yet, the instances when youth play the decisive role in movements against the state warrant a deeper look at why some movements turn violent and others remain peaceful.

Many researchers believe that there is something particular about young ages that makes people more willing to protest, rebel, or revolt. Psychologists argue that the brain's prefrontal cortex is one of the last parts of the brain to develop. This part regulates risky behavior, meaning that teenagers actually have fewer inhibitions than adults.[22] When impressionable and rebellious youth are mobilized by a leader, it can create regime security or insecurity, depending on your perspective. China and Russia provide two examples of state-sponsored youth movements that create security for those two states, but insecurity for other states. Protests over lack of economic and political opportunities in states like Greece and Iran are other examples of youth checking the power of the state.

China has had a long history of mobilizing youth to further the interests of the state. During the Cultural Revolution, *fenqing* was the term used to describe the millions of urban-dwelling students the government sent to the countryside to work alongside the peasants. These "angry youth," as the term is often translated, became "embittered towards a society that had stolen their futures." During the 1980s, the term was applied to the students and intellectuals who were active in the movement for political freedom leading up to the Tiananmen Square massacre of June 4, 1989. Although in prior eras youth directed their anger at the government, since the mid 1990s, urban educated youth in China have focused their anger externally. Today, these "angry youth" are much more nationalistic and blame the West for trying to suppress China's rise.[23] The role of Chinese leadership in redirecting that anger is unclear, but such a move takes something that should be a regime security threat to China and turns it into a military security threat for the West.

Engaging youth in organized activity is one way to quell potential unrest, but youth cadres can also be potentially mobilized as arms of the state or to create unrest purposefully. In Russia, the youth group *Nashi* is the largest of the movements created in 2005 by Vladimir Putin to win over the country's youth. This one group claims 10,000 active members and as many as 200,000 participants in its events, including organized marches of tens of thousands of youth in support of the regime. Other groups include the Youth Guard, which is part of the pro-Putin party United Russia, and the *Grigorevtsy*, which is affiliated with the Russian Orthodox Church.

The security implications of such movements are major. Leaders can use these movements to secure their position or to create insecurity and division within society. For example, the group Locals, created by the Moscow regional government, launched an anti-immigrant campaign several years ago. Certainly, youth who participate in these movements are being conditioned to have strong nationalist and xenophobic feelings, which can boost the power of the government, but the indoctrination of these groups also has implications for foreign policy. According to an article in *The New York Times:* "'Putin's Generation' is growing up with a diet of anti-European and anti-American sentiment that could deepen the social and political divides between Russia and the West for decades to come."[24] At the same time, Mr. Yashin, the leader of liberal party *Yabloko,* points out the susceptibility of these groups and the rapidity with which they could be mobilized against the state: "Today they are loyal, but tomorrow they may become the opposition."[25] Indeed, youth in both China and Iran have been responsible for anti-government, pro-democracy protests. In a *Foreign Policy* Web exclusive, written in response to the summer 2009 protests in Iran, Richard Cincotta compares Iran's youth bulge age structure with China's from 1989, right around the time of the Tiananmen Square uprising. The age structures are nearly identical and reflect the correlation between youth bulge countries and uprising. As Cincotta notes, youth bulge countries "have been, on average, two-and-a-half times more vulnerable to the onset of political violence or civil conflict than relatively mature populations."[26] Yet, youth protests and uprisings have not led to democracy in those places, perhaps *because* these countries are too youthful. As a following section will demonstrate, youthful age structures are correlated with rebellion but they are also correlated with a lack of democracy.

In addition to political exclusion, economic marginalization may also be an impetus for unrest, as has been the case with protests in Greece, Iran, France, and China throughout the first decade of the millennium.[27] For example, in Greece in 2008, riots broke out when youth protested the lack of employment opportunities. Young Greek graduates face an unemployment rate of 21 percent, compared with eight percent for the workforce as a whole.[28] Depending on the rigidity of the labor market, youth may be the first ones let go in an economic downturn, or have a hard time competing for scarce jobs when their skills and experience fall short of those of older generations. Job shortage and competition are also problems in most countries in the Pacific Islands, which have high population growth rates as a result of high fertility and low to very low levels of out migration.[29] High fertility in Kiribati, the Marshall Islands, Papua New Guinea, the Solomon Islands, Vanuatu, and Timor-Leste means that these populations are likely to grow by more than two percent annually during at least the next decade. According to a World Bank–commissioned study, less than 10 percent of job seekers in the Solomon Islands and Vanuatu are likely to find paid work at home.[30] How might this translate to regime insecurity? In Greece, protests resulted because the expectations of the population for employment were not met. If youth of the Pacific Islands don't have the same expectations, then the motive to act out against the regime may not be there. Or, rather than protesting, youth may engage in activities, such as crime, that challenge the government's monopoly on violence.

Although crime is often not included in national security assessments, it should be because of its ability to pose a transnational threat. Piracy and organized crime are just two examples. In a study of 150 years worth of data from England, Wales, France, and the United States, Hirschi and Gottfredson found that the frequency of criminal acts rises during the teen years, peaks around age 20, and then declines throughout the adult ages.[31] Men are more prone to violent crime than women. Ninety percent of arrests for homicide in almost all the countries they surveyed were committed by men, mostly ages 15 to 34.[32] According to one UN report on youth: "In most cases the offenders are males acting in groups. Police records indicate that the crime rates of juvenile and young adult male offenders are more than double those of females, and conviction rates are six or seven times higher."[33] Richard Easterlin's theory is relevant here: when young people are part of a larger cohort than preceding ones, they will tend to have lower relative income because they are crowded out of benefits in the family, school, and labor markets. One study of Tunisians looking for work reported that many of these dynamics were at play. In particular, "family and marital problems were common. They became poorer, lost confidence, and became fatalistic and submissive. Over the long run, the majority saw unemployment as a source of disequilibrium, humiliation, and even oppression."[34] Relative male income, the standard of living a man's income can buy relative to his father's, matters because younger generations will expect to meet or exceed the standard of living of their parents. When those expectations go unmet, youth have the motive for pursuing that income however necessary, including illegally.[35]

Another example of connections between youth and crime is Somali piracy. Somali pirates are generally young, uneducated, and unemployed. Raymond Gilpin describes three broad categories of pirates: "battle-hardened clan-based militia, youth looking for quick money to finance plans (like marriage or emigration) and fishermen who are forcibly recruited for their navigational skills."[36] Somalia has unemployment rates of 66 percent for urban areas and 41 percent for rural areas. Unemployment is exacerbated by lack of governance, including naval patrols, which creates perfect conditions for youth to turn to crime.[37] Piracy in Somalia creates national security challenges for many stakeholders. The regime in Somalia itself is obviously threatened by the activities of the pirates.

Their very existence demonstrates that the government is too weak to shut down the practice. Piracy also creates insecurity for countries trying to shuttle their goods and citizens through the Gulf of Aden, where the pirates operate. States with capable navies have had to redirect resources to the region to monitor crime in the area.

In Afghanistan, a very youthful state with limited legitimate economic opportunities, the drug trade facilitates insurgency. Afghanistan is the principal source of heroin that goes into a global market, primarily to Western Europe and Russia, worth about $55 billion annually. According to the UN Office on Drugs and Crime, the primary beneficiaries are organized crime groups along the drug route, but some of the profits fund Afghan insurgents.[38] Crime is certainly a threat to regime instability, as "countries can become locked in a vicious circle where social trust is lost and economic growth undermined."[39] The problem is not unique to Afghanistan. In Southwest Asia, Southeast Asia, and the Andean region, insurgent groups draw resources from taxing or managing organized criminal activities, like drug trafficking.[40] Groups like the Revolutionary Armed Forces of Colombia, the National Liberation Army, and successor organizations, such as the United Self-Defense Forces of Colombia and the Shining Path in Peru, are all involved.[41] In addition to trafficking drugs, rebels can also finance their activities by trafficking other goods. In the Democratic Republic of the Congo, insurgents harvest and traffic the natural resources in areas under their control. This kind of organized crime brings income opportunities that would be impossible in peacetime.[42] Diamonds in Angola and Sierra Leone, and oil in the Niger Delta are additional examples of trafficking natural resources to finance rebellion. Consequently, those countries' age structures are extraordinarily young. The median age in Angola is only 17, and is 18 in Sierra Leone and Nigeria. In all three states the average woman can expect to have five to six children in her lifetime, based on TFRs for 2005 to 2010.[43] Therefore, each of these countries has an abundance of youth to recruit into conflict, plus the presence of natural resources to finance that conflict and lure the youth—a toxic brew of insecurity.

## The Middle East and North Africa

To illustrate in greater detail how youth and youthful age structures can create challenges to national security, this section examines the experiences of youth in the Middle East and North Africa (MENA), one of the fastest growing and youngest regions in the world. MENA is a region that highlights the interactions between military, regime, and structural security. One of the most prevalent problems is lack of employment opportunities. In many Middle Eastern countries, decades of free and open admission to university, rent control, progressive taxation, and universal health care led to a bloated public sector and created barriers to growth in the private sector. Egypt's system of guaranteed public employment for all college graduates encouraged education but also led to a glut of well-educated job seekers.[44] Oil revenues, remittances from migrants, and foreign aid kept this system in place until the 1980s. Declining revenues and demographic pressure weakened the government's ability to keep the system afloat.[45] In Iran, on the other hand, there is a foundation for human capital development because the average years of schooling have increased greatly during the past couple of decades. However, youth face a "highly competitive and exclusionary education system, where students compete to win the 'university lottery'" and those fortunate enough to graduate still face massive unemployment.[46] In some cases, there is a mismatch between graduates' degrees, which may be in humanities, education, or Islamic studies, and the skills needed for available jobs.[47]

In Iraq, 28 percent of the male labor force age 15 to 29 is unemployed, which is 10 percent higher than the national rate. Certainly, the war has impeded regular economic activity and reduced the number of employment opportunities for all, but the higher rate for youths means they are relatively disadvantaged compared with other age groups. Given the many social restrictions in Iraq, only 17 percent of women participate in the labor force. One reason economic opportunities are limited is that the public sector dominates; this arena provides 43 percent of all jobs and 60 percent of all full-time employment. In fact, public-sector salaries took up one-third of planned government expenditure in 2009.[48] In a broad sense, there is little industrial investment; only 47 percent of employment is in services and 26 percent is in agriculture. Because wages can be up to one-third higher in the public sector, sometimes young graduates will reject private-sector jobs and hold out for an opening in the public sector.[49]

A second problem is sheer numbers. Although Iraq's fertility has been declining since the 1960s, the population still has a large proportion of youth.[50] About 450,000 youth were expected to enter the labor market in 2009. A third issue is that there is too much reliance on oil revenues, which face unsteady pricing. When oil revenues fall to less than $52 per barrel, spending will have to be diverted from investment to financing public salaries. And as the UN assesses, in the long run, reduced spending on investments will translate to fewer new jobs.[51] Labor market rigidities are also a major problem. In the Middle East and North Africa, the well trained are disproportionately unemployed, whereas in Europe, low-skilled workers are more disadvantaged. Young workers in the Middle East and North Africa not only face labor market crowding because of their large cohort sizes, but the ones that are employed are not as well protected as older workers. For example, 69 percent of youth in Egypt work without a contract. In Egypt and Syria, about half of employed youth are in temporary, noncareer jobs.[52] A survey of Arab youth by the Right Start Foundation found that unemployment is a major concern, and 88 percent of young people believe they will not find a job easily.[53] Finally, there are not enough business protections through government regulation, and, of course, there are tremendous security issues, which dissuade capital investment.

Religious extremism has clearly been a problem in the region. Providing economic opportunities may help dissuade potential extremists from choosing that route and instead provide them with more legitimate opportunities. Hilary Silver, in her work on Arab social exclusion, says that there is some indication that religious extremism among some young men will moderate with military service and marriage.[54] However, the lack of economic opportunities can close out social opportunities as well. Marriage continues to be one of the most important foundations of social life in many cultures, but even that institution is being shaped and shifted by larger economic changes. As Dhillon and Yousef note, "social norms in the Middle East make the transition to family formation critical to full social inclusion."[55] The problem is that increasing youth unemployment, costly housing, and opportunities to continue education have become barriers to marriage. Because the cost of marriage is so prohibitive, less than 50 percent of Middle Eastern men are married by their late twenties, compared with more than 60 percent throughout the 1990s.[56]

In developed countries with aging populations, youth are often economically marginalized as a result of inflexible labor markets and cultural issues (for example, Spain and Greece). In least developed countries with very young age structures, youth are entirely politically marginalized, jobs are hard to come by for everyone, and adulthood sets in fast. Does the economic marginalization in the former set of countries make conflict just as likely as the omnipresent marginalization of poverty and/or autocracy in the latter group? Opportunity comes into play here. When youth are marginalized or excluded from opportunities in democracies, they should have some recourse through the regular political process, and thus we would be more likely to see low-intensity conflict or protest. In countries where youth are also politically excluded, however, we might see more violent conflict. These hypotheses would be interesting for future research.

To some extent, youth everywhere face common issues just because of their stage in the life course, but young people in countries with youthful age structures have some unique challenges. Because their countries are often extremely poor and weakly governed, even their ability to meet basic needs, like water, food, and housing, is in question. Education and health usually suffer, as well. Less than 30 percent of youth attend secondary school in sub-Saharan Africa.[57] Globally, there are about 300,000 child and youth combatants actively involved in armed conflicts.[58] About half the refugees, asylum seekers, and stateless persons, as well as returnees and IDPs of concern to the United Nations High Commission for Refugees (UNHCR), are children.[59]

The strains that large proportions of youth put on the education systems, job markets, and services provided by the state are part of the causal chain linking age structure and conflict. Governance problems, combined with the strains of a youthful age structure, have overwhelmed Pakistan's public schools. In some parts of the country, like Southern Punjab, *madrasas*, or Islamic schools, have stepped in to fill the gap. Most of these only prepare male students for religious positions or teaching. Some of these *madrasas* are affiliated with radical religious groups. These radical groups can easily take hold in the educational system, because needs aren't being met by the government.[60] According to *The New York Times*, Punjab police say that two-thirds of the suicide bombers who have struck in Southern Punjab had attended *madrasas*.[61] At the same time, in weak states, like Pakistan, demography alone is not the reason for the country's lack of development. Pakistan has little political capacity: Pakistanis in cities and tribal areas alike have limited access to basic services like clean water and sanitation. In Karachi, 30,000 people die each year from consuming unsafe water.[62] As long as the state fails to provide for citizens' basic needs, these citizens have the motivation to look to other groups, such as extremists, for help.

The issue of terrorism highlights the feedback cycle between security for the state and security for the individual. It is logical that large proportions of disadvantaged and disenfranchised youth would be more susceptible to terrorist recruitment. Indeed, in one study, Urdal finds that youth bulges tend to increase the risk of both terrorism and riots under conditions of educational and economic stress, although he warns us to be cautious when interpreting the data (because of possible flawed measurements).[63] Some states, then, may negatively perceive their young populations. As a result, the individual can be oppressed by the state in the name of national security. According to the UN, "[t]he most serious threat to the citizen's security in some Arab countries, in the context of fighting terrorism, is providing the state with pretexts to violate individual rights and freedoms without legal recourse."[64] And by that oppression, the individual becomes more alienated from the state, and therefore more susceptible to recruitment. States in the region, with the exception of maybe Iraq and Israel, tend to fear uprisings, coups, and riots as much as, or more than, terrorism. Naturally, youth can be mobilized for uprisings and riots, too, but fighting terrorism has taken on a particularly important place in national security policy in the post-September 11th security environment.

## Civil Violence

Population growth and poor economic conditions set the scene for civil conflict, the ultimate embodiment of regime insecurity. The role of youth in civil conflict is well documented; several of the countries experiencing civil conflict in recent years, such as Nigeria, East Timor, and Fiji, also have high proportions of young people age 15 to 24 years. Most research demonstrates that youth bulges increase the risk of outbreaks of minor conflicts, but not necessarily of major interstate wars. In a sense, demography is a structural condition that provides opportunity for a rebel group to wage war against a government because the very existence of a large youth cohort lowers recruitment costs for rebel armies.[65]

Rachel Brett and Irma Specht have found that child soldiers are "overwhelmingly from the poor and disadvantaged sectors of society, from the conflict zones themselves, and from those with disrupted or nonexistent families."[66] A survey of 300 demobilized child soldiers in the Democratic Republic of the Congo found links between poverty, demography, and conflict. Sixty-one percent of the children said that their families had no income, and more than half had at least six siblings.[67] Brett and Specht point out that many poor children do not become child soldiers, and so poverty is obviously not the only factor leading them to join these groups. Any combination of factors leads children to become soldiers, but there is usually some trigger for the decision to join, although it may be different in each case. Youth may know that joining such a group will bring a tough life, but usually feel that the gains outweigh the costs, particularly by providing a way to earn a living. At least when they are part of an organized armed group, they are more likely to know where their next meal is coming from and may be able to earn enough money to buy food for their families, as well. In poor countries, soldiers often have a higher standard of living than the civilian population.

The same links between demography, opportunity, and conflict are obvious in other regions as well. Afghanistan has an extremely young age structure, high unemployment, and is embroiled in civil conflict. The U.S. military has partnered with the Afghan government to create employment opportunities that would dissuade young men from joining the Taliban. A leader of the Abdulrahimzai tribe was quoted in *The New York Times* as saying, "Most of the Taliban in my area are young men who need jobs . . . We just need to make them busy. If we give them work, we can weaken the Taliban."[68]

Controlling the existence of conflict itself may be one of the most important ways to prevent youth from joining in violence. Brett and Specht point out an obvious, but often ignored, relationship: young people get involved in war first and foremost because there is war—meaning, that if we can control the breakout of conflict, then we can control children's involvement. War becomes the norm for them. Again, causality runs both ways; war forces schools to close, can break up families, and increases poverty—factors that can motivate involvement in conflict.[69] The context "creates feelings of insecurity, and an atmosphere in which violent behavior is considered legitimate and is linked to the ready availability of weapons." The displacement caused by war can also leave youth to fend for themselves or to take care of younger siblings.[70]

Thus motives, often driven by deprivation, are important in civil war as they are in low-intensity conflict. Youth who lack economic resources—jobs or money, or who are relatively poor compared with their expectations; or those who lack political resources (representation or other freedoms)—are seen as especially likely to engage in political violence or to join a rebel or terrorist group that engages in violence. Grievances are necessary, but not sufficient, to lead to collective violence. Opportunity, through the financial means to conduct the war, the soldiers to fight it, and the political opening provided by a weak state, must also be present.[71]

## DEMOCRACY

Thus far, this chapter has explored connections between youthful age structures and various types of civil conflict, ranging from nonviolent to organized violence. We know that countries with youthful age structures have a higher likelihood of experiencing civil conflict than countries with more mature age structures, but they also have a lower likelihood of being fully democratic. What do trends in fertility mean for the future of democracy and the future of conflict? Democracies, at least in theory, are more peaceful because of democratic norms, openness to trade, and checks and balances, among other things. According to liberal democratic peace theory, then, the more democracies there are in the world, the more peaceful the world should be, and the fewer countries with youthful age structures there are, the more democracies there should be. Following this reasoning, if fertility continues to decline and more countries complete the demographic transition, then, the world will likely be more peaceful.

Though measures of global democracy have recently leveled off, because of the correlation between age structure and regime type, this may be temporary. As their youthful demographic profiles mature, states in Latin America, North Africa, and Asia could all likely see the emergence of new and more stable liberal democracies before 2020. Iran, which has experienced rapid demographic change, has been one of the exceptions to the relationship between age structure and government type, as leaders have thus far been able to resist democratization despite Iran's completion of the demographic transition and more mature age structure.[72] What accounts for the difference and why might youthful age structures be less likely to have democratic forms of government? One argument is that governments with large youth populations need to use more authoritarian means to govern, because mobilized youth are often a risk to the regime. The government protects itself by cracking down on youth— limiting free speech, curtailing organizational rights, and suspending legal protections. According to this theory, then, democracy is stifled because of demography.[73] If this is true, then Iran's leadership is apparently doing a better job of controlling youth and preventing the transition to democracy that has seemed somewhat inevitable in countries with similar age structures.

A different theory, proposed by Richard Cincotta, is that countries with youthful age structures have less democratic governments because the young, and usually jobless, population supports authoritarians. Cincotta argues that theoretically, if we follow Thomas Hobbes, we should expect that support for authoritarian regimes should rise when the population is young and unstable, especially among "the commercial elite." The relationship between age structure and regime type, he argues, is a two-stage process. In stage 1, countries "are saddled with a social environment where the regime's legitimacy is strained and the political mobilization of young men is relatively easy." Politics are fractious and violent. Regimes try to "preserve their position by limiting dissent and maintaining order," which helps them gain the support of property owners and other elites.[74] This is not generally a stage conducive to democracy, unless youth lead a democratic revolt, but even then these democracies are fragile. A few success stories include Costa Rica, India, Jamaica, and South Africa. During the second stage, the proportion of youth relative to workers declines, which "relieves pressure on child health and educational services, stimulates savings, contributes to productivity, and facilitates increased human capital investment and, ultimately, wage growth."[75]

Although previous sections have described the pitfalls of political exclusion of youth, a premature transition to democracy is not necessarily more likely to result in a more peaceful society. Most Latin American countries have transitioned to some form of democracy while their age structures were still young. Cincotta says this "may partly explain why 60 percent of these states have flip-flopped between a liberal democracy and a less democratic regime at least once since the early 1970s, far more than any other region." A country with a young age structure has half a chance (literally, 50 percent) of being rated a liberal democracy after its young-adult proportion drops to about 0.40. Some of the countries projected to pass the half-a-chance benchmark before 2020 are Azerbaijan, Iran, Kazakhstan, Kyrgyzstan, Lebanon, Malaysia, Myanmar, Turkey, Morocco, Algeria, Tunisia, Libya, Egypt, Colombia, and Venezuela.[76]

Measures as simple as lowering the voting age even by a couple of years can bring political voice to a significant portion of the population when a country has a youthful age structure. In February 2010, the Lebanese Parliament rejected a proposal to decrease the voting age from 21 years to 18 years because the measure would mostly benefit Muslims, who make up higher proportions of youth.[77] Given that youth age 15 to 29 are about a quarter of Lebanon's population, this would bring a huge change to the electoral landscape of Lebanon and would be a major step in giving young people political voice. If youth were more politically engaged in countries with very young age structures, they might press more actively for democratic reform, which could create regime security since full democracies experience few civil wars.[78] At the same time, Cincotta's research shows that age structure could doom such movements to failure (or only short-lived success). Historically, democracies that emerge after a youth bulge goes away have a better chance of lasting. In Colombia, Ecuador, Fiji, India, Malaysia, Papua New Guinea, Peru, Sri Lanka, Turkey, and Venezuela, among others, democratic governance was introduced before the youth bulge declined, and democracy did not fully take hold. Does this mean that a more mature age structure is a necessary condition for fully democratic governance? The answer, which future research can address, matters for policy. This is a relatively new area of research, and more study should be done to determine the actual direction and relationship of causation. Figuring out the relationships between youth and democracy is important from a policy standpoint, given the many resources that are devoted worldwide to democracy promotion.

In nondemocratic countries, of course, youth have an extremely limited ability to participate in governance. However, exclusion is an issue in democracies, as well. In Japan, suffrage only extends to those age 20 and older, although there is a push to lower the voting age to 18. Why might this matter for structural security? According to the Democratic Party of Japan, which supports reform: "Having the right to vote means taking responsibility for one's words and actions as a member of society. By both granting voting rights and lowering the age of majority to 18, we hope that young people's self-awareness will also be enhanced."[79] Given that youth are already outnumbered in Japan and will continue to be so as the median age rises as a result of low fertility, bringing the youth into the political process has major implications for generational equity. Youth there already vote in very small proportions—far less than older cohorts—and have low labor force participation. It is possible that these issues are related. Without a voice in politics, Japanese youth cannot ensure that their needs are protected through the government.

## CONCLUSION

Youth face many problems around the world. Although their situations differ depending on the size of their cohorts and the country into which they were born, there are plenty of commonalities. In developing and developed countries alike, youth are often economically marginalized and passed over for employment in favor of someone with more experience. Many are victims of exploitation and child labor. In some countries, young women face major health problems, including pregnancy at very young ages and high fertility, both of which elevate risk of maternal mortality. Many young people are disenfranchised or marginalized from the political process. In some developing countries, youth are displaced and become refugees or are forced into a situation of violence as child soldiers. Youth not only engage directly in conflict, but youthful age structures tend to be in states with weak institutions and extreme poverty. Those governance and economic challenges can then make it difficult to put the conditions in place—namely, health and education—that would reduce fertility and allow the age structure to mature. Weak institutions and extreme poverty also provide the fodder for conflict. As Brainard, Chollet, and LeFleur say in their book *Too Poor for Peace:*

> Extreme poverty exhausts governing institutions, depletes resources, weakens leaders, and crushes hope—fueling a volatile mix of desperation and instability. Poor, fragile states can explode into violence or implode into collapse, imperiling their citizens, regional neighbors, and the wider world as livelihoods are crushed, investors flee, and ungoverned territories become a spawning ground for global threats like terrorism, trafficking, environmental devastation, and disease. Yet if poverty leads to insecurity, it is also true that the destabilizing effects of conflict and demographic and environmental challenges make it harder for leaders, institutions, and outsiders to promote human development.[80]

Several clear policy implications emerge from the review of connections between youth and conflict. The first is that the state should create positive opportunities for youth so that they will have less motivation to engage in violent behavior that threatens the regime. Reducing labor market rigidities is but one way to increase demand for employees. The state also needs to invest in the private sector and move away from reliance on the public sector for jobs. To do so, governments should work to create a regulatory climate conducive for investment and establish security within the borders to make any potential investment seem more attractive. Resource-rich states should diversify their economies to make use of the variety of skills their educated and noneducated youth will have, because in many countries it is highly educated or highly skilled youth who lack opportunities.

One recommendation is to shift perception of youth as a burden and try to see them as a force that can also contribute to security. As noted by Brainard et al.: "The challenge, then, in crafting an effective response to the 'youth bulge' is to resist the temptation to view young people solely as a threat—and instead approach them as a valuable resource to be protected and cultivated."[81] This approach gives latitude to promote policies that will empower youth and break the cycle of violence. Most important, this perspective puts the onus on governments to capitalize on their age structure, and not on the youth themselves, who lack such tools.

The clear, although complicated, relationship between youth and conflict leads to the obvious policy prescription of lower fertility. Although it takes time to see age structure change to a more mature population, eventually, a well-governed population with a greater balance among age groups will likely be more peaceful. Population policies must be driven by individual choices backed by political and financial commitments from the government and civil society. Education is one of the most powerful determinants of lower fertility; each year of a girl's education reduces fertility by 10 percent.[82] Making contraception available is also important, because 100 million women across developing countries have an unmet need for family planning.[83] Health is another key policy area; there is a high economic toll of lost productivity resulting from maternal mortality, much of which is caused by unintended and too frequent pregnancies.[84]

The Asian Tigers—Hong Kong, South Korea, Taiwan, and Singapore—provide an example of areas that were able to lower fertility and capitalize on young workers. Their population programs of the 1960s and '70s had widespread public acceptance, and the resulting early fertility declines allowed for higher per-child investments in education—an important condition for economic growth.[85] In Chapter 4, which discusses transitional age structures, we will see how investments in education and human capital and a shift away from agriculture helped East Asian states take advantage of the demographic dividend. China, which has also experienced economic success, chose to institute restrictive population policy to ensure an economically and politically manageable populace. China's policy, like many states', was coercive and limited individual choice over fertility; the same outcome can be accomplished through policies that empower women, as was the case in Iran.

Iran regulated fertility early on, and is therefore a demographic outlier among its neighbors. Iran had high fertility of about 6.5 children per woman during the 1980s, but government officials, concerned about the economic consequences of providing public service jobs for all of its young people, convinced clerics of the need for a family planning program.[86] Iran had one of the fastest demographic changes in history. In just one generation, the fertility of rural Iranian women went from an average of eight children to around two children. Today, Iran has one of the most successful family planning programs in the world. The infrastructure was built starting in the 1970s, when the government instituted a free national family planning program, delivered through a statewide network of primary health care facilities. Iran's program is comprehensive in that it meets both supply and demand needs; women have access to free counseling and services for all modern contraceptive methods, and more educational opportunities. Many women seek a university education—indeed, women outnumber men in Iranian universities. Longer time spent in education has raised the average age of marriage for women to 23 years, which itself helps delay the onset of childbearing.[87]

The UN is very optimistic that fertility will continue to decrease in places where it has been on the decline and will begin to fall in places where it is still high, especially Central Asia and sub-Saharan Africa. They anticipate that the world's median age will rise from 28.9 to 38.4 years by 2050. Under the medium variant, the UN projects that TFR in Afghanistan will fall from 6.6 in 2005 to 3.1 by 2050. For sub-Saharan Africa, the medium variant projects a decrease in fertility from around five children per woman in 2010 to 2.46 children by 2050. However, there are bold assumptions behind these projections, which are based on the past experience of all countries with declining fertility from 1950 to 2010.[88] While it is true that recent declines were more rapid than Western Europe's decline due to the diffusion of technology and knowledge, a global demographic transition will only occur by 2050 if fertility in high- and medium-fertility countries follows this pattern. Such a sharp decline in fertility does not happen automatically, and the development and security challenges of continued high fertility necessitate serious investment in education and health to decrease fertility. States should also promote the education and empowerment of women, and better health services to reduce infant mortality and improve family well-being.[89] So far, sub-Saharan Africa, in particular, is making only slow progress toward each of these goals. Despite its inclusion in the UN's Millennium Development Goals, sub-Saharan Africa receives little sustained attention by the international community and many states outside the region repeatedly fall short of their aid promises. The economic recession that began around 2008 has further slowed the flow of development funds.[90] Leadership is essential, but governments need not shoulder the responsibility on their own. Nongovernmental organizations and the private sector can play a role as well. The UN's projections show us what these states' age structures could look like with meaningful policy reform; whether governments, nongovernmental actors, and the private sector can step up to meet the challenges is questionable.

In the meantime, states with high fertility and youthful age structures need not view their youth solely as a burden or security risk. Rather, if they focus on policies that engage youth in areas where they are currently marginalized, they can mitigate the potential security risk of young populations and actually benefit from young peoples' contributions to society. To capitalize on a youthful age structure and prevent frustration that can lead to several forms of conflict, governments must create the structural conditions conducive to engaging youth. They must provide opportunities for political expression, an economy that will utilize young workers of all skill levels, higher education, and social freedoms. All of these are scarce in a country with a youth bulge; but, although no country has gone from a mature age structure to a youthful one, numerous countries in the world have gone from very youthful age structures to more mature ones. As a result, they are less likely to experience conflict and more likely to be democratic. It can be done. Youth do not typically have the tools or political access to institute such large-scale changes. Nongovernmental organizations can work to provide smaller-scale opportunities, but only the government can make large structural changes.

# 3

## Chapter

## Population Aging

A powerful force has the potential to unseat today's great powers by decimating their militaries, crippling their economies, and changing the landscape of their politics. This force is not a new weapons system, a new tactic, or a chemical or biological agent. It is something much slower and more mysterious: population aging. Some have argued that population aging will deliver on these threats with a vengeance.[1] Yet, most assessments of national security do not even consider aging as a major factor; instead, terrorism and nuclear proliferation dominate the agendas of graying states.[2] What are we to make of the security implications of this modern age structure? The news is mixed among the three realms of national security that we have been using to frame the discussion of demography. Military security will likely decrease for the world's most aged states, which are also the world's great powers, although not to the degree predicted by some. Aging will somewhat decrease the ability of these states to project political, economic, and military power, and thus will have implications for global security. However, there are avenues states can take to compensate for the effects of aging on economic growth and government spending. Population aging will also compromise structural security. Large proportions of dependents and few workers means that states will find it difficult to provide generous benefits to seniors, one of society's most vulnerable groups. Yet in the realm of regime security, there is good news. States with mature age structures have been some of the most peaceful and democratic in the world. As other states enter the fraternity, they, too, may experience a peace dividend. The following sections demonstrate the national security implications of population aging for the world's most aged states and consider those that are on the horizon.

Population has long been seen as an indicator of geopolitical strength. Leaders of both ancient empires and modern states have realized that, at a minimum, a healthy and robust population affects how others perceive them on the world stage, if not their actual ability to project power. Russian ex-president Vladimir Putin has expressed concern over his nation's perceived demographic weakness several times. In his May 2006 state of the nation address he called Russia's demographic issues the most acute problems facing the country, citing the fact that Russia is shrinking by around 700,000 persons per year.[3] He may have been right to worry. To some, Russia's low fertility and high mortality make the country appear weak. U.S. Secretary of Defense Robert Gates wrote in a January 2009 *Foreign Affairs* article that, "As someone who used to prepare estimates of Soviet military strength for several presidents, I can say that Russia's conventional military, although vastly improved since its nadir in the late 1990s, remains a shadow of its Soviet predecessor. And adverse demographic trends in Russia will likely keep those conventional forces in check."[4] Whether Russia can be written off because of its demographic issues—or whether Gates truly believes that it can—may not matter as much as the perception that it can. If there is a demographic Cold War, the United States seems to be winning.

In addition to perception, though, population aging does have measurable effects on military manpower and funding. To have a robust military, states need fresh crops of skilled soldiers, and the military must compete with other budgetary areas to secure funding. In an aging state, shifting proportions of workers and dependents means that there are fewer military-age youths to supply those troops, and there are a greater number of elderly dependents competing for a portion of the shrinking budgetary pie. In addition to the manpower and economic challenges, a final issue concerns changes in the political mood of aging states: What will be the political willingness to have a strong military when older cohorts demand health care and pensions? To what extent will societies willingly sacrifice dwindling numbers of youth for foreign causes, such as humanitarian missions?

## POPULATION AGING

Growing populations with youthful age structures have dominated the post–World War II population agenda. For most of the world, the past several decades were characterized by high fertility and, as many states saw improved health care and development, decreasing mortality. At the same time that advanced industrialized states were focusing their attention on helping less developed countries with family planning and aid programs to meet the needs of their burgeoning populations, the world's richest states were having the opposite problem: declining fertility that would eventually lead to population

**Figure 3.1** Population tree for Japan, 2005. (Population Action International)

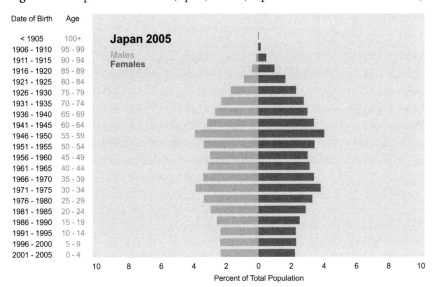

aging. Population aging, and a resulting mature age structure, occurs whenever fertility rates decline over a period of time. Fertility rate (most often total fertility rate, or TFR) refers to the number of children who will be born to a woman in her lifetime. As fewer young people are born into a society, the median age rises, and eventually the proportions of youth dramatically decline whereas the proportions of elderly dramatically increase. The number of births required to "replace" both the mother and father is two, but the replacement level is slightly higher than two (2.1), because some children will die before reaching reproductive age. For those societies with low childhood mortality, such as the ones on which this chapter focuses, the replacement value is probably between 2.0 and 2.1; for those with high mortality, the replacement level is probably just over 2.1. Theoretically, the size of a population with a fertility rate of 2.1 will stay static. Subsequently, one above that level will be young and growing, and one below will age and eventually shrink. Japan has had low fertility since the 1970s, and now boasts the largest proportion of elderly in the world (Fig 3.1). Most European states have mature age structures and because of their very low fertility, South Korea, China, and Singapore are aging and well on their way.

One of the consequences of a mature age structure is that the number of youth entering the workforce decreases over time, whereas the number of those exiting into retirement increases. These "top-heavy" proportions are what worry military planners, economists, and others. Many of the world's currently aging states also had low fertility before the post-World War II baby booms but their age structures were still relatively young. Although we are acquainted with the effects of high youth proportions, until recently the world had never seen age structures with such large numbers of elderly dependents. For the most part, security scholars still focus on projecting future effects of aging instead of studying how states have responded so far. A combination of the two approaches is most useful because even though population aging is entrenched in many states, the trend is still developing and intensifying. On the one hand, we do have the ability to study the past effects of population aging on security. Most developed countries have had low fertility for decades, and in 2008 there were 72 states and territories with a TFR less than 2.0.[5] On the other hand, because aging will intensify to levels never before seen, the accuracy of our extrapolations may be limited; we have to allow for a healthy margin of uncertainty.

In general, the states that have the most aged populations are also some of the world's most powerful and economically or politically strategic states, but there is wide variety regarding the degree to and rate at which states with mature age structures are aging. Japan and Germany have the world's highest proportions of those age 60 years and older, and, because of prolonged low fertility, cohorts of elderly dependents in these states, plus most states in Western Europe, will continue to grow while each cohort of youth gets progressively smaller. Eastern Europe, including Russia and its successor states, has fairly high proportions of older persons as well, although their shrinking populations are also the result of emigration, in the case of the former, and lower life expectancies in Russia's case. Any fertility level below replacement will eventually cause a population to age and shrink, but of greater concern is the emerging pattern of lowest-low fertility—rates just above one child per woman. Sometimes called the second demographic transition, this phenomenon reflects modern lifestyle preferences and changing norms regarding the value of children. Lowest-low fertility has firmly taken hold across East Asia.[6] South Korea only achieved replacement fertility after 1985, but because the country now has one of the lowest fertility levels in the world (1.2), their aging is accelerated. Singapore, too, has very low fertility, and by 2015, more than 20 percent of the population will be older than 60 years of age. China is just behind those two states in terms of its aging. As of now, China has a transitional age structure, but its window of opportunity is closing and, unless fertility increases, by 2015 their median age will be nearly 36 years and only 19 percent of the population will be between the ages of 0 and 14 years.[7]

The United States is one of the few advanced industrial democracies whose fertility has hovered at replacement level for a while, with a TFR of 2.0 in 2006. Table 3.1 provides a snapshot of some of the states with mature age structures, with China and India listed for comparison. The countries are ranked according to the proportion of those age 60 years and older as of 2005. If fertility rates

**Table 3.1** Percent of Population Age 60 Years or Older, Constant Fertility Variant

| Country | Years | | | Population Change 2005–2030 (thousands) |
|---|---|---|---|---|
| | 2005 | 2015 | 2030 | |
| Japan | 26.4 | 32.8 | 38.2 | −2,176 |
| Germany | 25.1 | 27.5 | 37.0 | −1,091 |
| United Kingdom | 21.2 | 23.8 | 27.3 | +1,497 |
| France | 20.8 | 24.7 | 30.2 | +1,156 |
| Canada | 17.8 | 22.4 | 29.3 | +1,425 |
| Russia | 17.1 | 19.6 | 25.7 | −3,616 |
| United States | 16.6 | 19.9 | 24.8 | +14,897 |
| South Korea | 13.3 | 18.5 | 31.6 | +171 |
| Singapore | 12.3 | 20.9 | 36.0 | +225 |
| China | 11.0 | 15.2 | 23.6 | +27,417 |
| India | 7.5 | 8.8 | 11.5 | +93,858 |

*Source:* United Nations Population Division. "World Population Prospects: The 2008 Revision Population Database." New York: United Nations, 2009, http://esa.un.org/UNPP/.

were to stay at current levels, the ranks change dramatically between 2005 and 2030. Using the UN's constant fertility variant is useful, because it allows us to see how an individual state's age structure will develop if fertility stays at 2005 to 2010 levels, with normal mortality and normal migration (mortality and migration projections for the constant fertility variant are the same as for the UN's low-, medium-, and high-fertility projections). One of the more striking developments during this time period is that China will move from a country with a transitional age structure in 2005 to an aged state by 2030, with nearly the same percentage of the population age 60 years and older as the United States. Among the great powers listed, China, Russia, and the United States are the only ones with proportions age 60 years and older that will remain less than 30 percent of the total population. India, which we can consider a rising power, is still far from aging, because even though fertility in some regions has dropped below replacement, it remains high in poorer states. The divide between the states that already have mature age structures and those that are on their way becomes clearer when we look at population growth rates. The populations of states that already have mature age structures are projected to shrink soon, if they are not already, whereas the younger states will continue to grow because of population momentum. China, for example, is projected to grow by 0.59 percent between 2010 and 2015, even as the number of elderly dependents increase and youth decline. South Korea will register its first net population loss between 2020 and 2025. Singapore is projected to avoid that fate for the time being because of their very high immigration rate.[8]

As I argued in the previous chapter on youthful age structures, demography can create conditions for security or insecurity, but states play a large role in mediating the effects of trends. The same is true for population aging, although much of the literature on aging and security seems to offer little hope for adaptation. Most assessments of aging claim that states have a choice between two responses. They can either make their militaries a priority and abdicate responsibility for the care of the elderly, or they can reallocate military spending toward social programs for retirees. The assertion that states are playing a zero-sum game between their militaries and their elderly is inaccurate. Population aging has measurable effects on states' politics, economies, and militaries, but policy—the way a state deals with its demography—can play an important role in tempering its effects. Developed aging countries are not likely to face complete national security crises because of aging, although they will need to continue to take an active role in mediating its effects.

## MILITARY SECURITY

The category of military security focuses attention on the ability of states to protect themselves from outside threats and to project power in the international system. At the heart of both inward protection and outward projection is power. Power politics establishes the hierarchy of states in the international system and power is the ultimate goal of politics, even if as a means to other ends. International relations scholars and practitioners have long considered population one of the most basic elements of national power. Even millennia ago, when technology was obviously more limited, armies relied on having numerous, well-trained soldiers backed by a healthy and large civilian population for victory in battle. There is some correlation between population and power. As Jean-Claude Chesnais has noted, Europe's population grew faster than population anywhere else from the 18th century until the 1930s, a time of European supremacy in terms of territorial expansion, political domination, and economic success.[9]

The belief that population equals power runs through both theory and practice. Numerous early international relations scholars, including Harold and Margaret Sprout and Hans Morgenthau, included population as a key element of power, but one of the most relevant theoretical lines is power transition theory.[10] Power transition theorists, like A. F. K. Organski, argue that power is shaped by a state's population size, productivity, and political capacity.[11] This dynamic theory tries to take into account how changes in these variables change state power and, when combined with preferences, affect the hierarchy of states in the international system.[12] In practice, the belief that population equals power has led a wide range of states to institute pronatalist policies specifically to increase their standing in the international system, including

Hitler, Mussolini, Stalin, and Ceausescu, and more recently Russia's Vladimir Putin and Iran's Mahmoud Ahmadinejad.

Yet, a large population does not guarantee great power status. Indeed, as the discussion on youthful age structures demonstrated, a large and growing population can be a burden on a state and can lead to regime and structural insecurity. International relations scholar Anne-Marie Slaughter has pointed out that "[i]n 2007, the ten countries with the highest per capita [gross domestic products] all had populations smaller than that of New York City, with one notable exception: the United States."[13] Still, there are links between military manpower and economic production—two key elements of power—as the following sections demonstrate. The divide in age structure among states in various stages of the demographic transition from high fertility and mortality to low fertility and mortality will also be important forces that shape the future distribution of power in the international system.

## Military Manpower

One of the most obvious implications of population aging is that it leads to fewer potential military recruits. At first glance, the numbers are alarming. For example, just as they have been establishing more independence with their national security forces, during the next couple decades, Germany and Japan will both see a major decline in the proportions of their populations that could be mobilized for military service. In Japan, the number of men and women age 20 to 34 will fall from 26,105,000 in 2005 to 18,091,000 by 2025—a decrease of 31 percent. During the same time period, Germany will have 1.5 million fewer potential recruits.[14] Though most projections of U.S. population assume it will continue to be youthful, there is no guarantee because a low median age relative to the other great powers relies on the continuation of two major demographic trends: high immigration and higher fertility of immigrant groups. Migration to the U.S. declined during the recession in the late 2000s and given that the United States historically uses policy to vary migration to meet economic and political goals, we cannot be sure how immigration will change during the next several decades.[15] Optimistic assessments of U.S. population growth are based in part on the results of the 2000 census. In most cases, the birthrates of immigrant groups eventually converge with those of the host country; demographers may be surprised after the next census if data show that immigrant birthrates have decreased and the U.S. population is not predicted to grow as quickly as previously thought. As a point of contrast, Pakistan and Afghanistan, two states that have dominated the global security agenda during the past decade, will have an overabundance of military-age youth.

Given these projections, aging states will have to rely on other sources of military power than large troop reserves. They have several options and, for various reasons, many states have already been moving in these directions. Although militaries once failed and succeeded based primarily on the number of men they could mobilize, successfully projecting power is enhanced by technological superiority, strong alliances, and military efficiency. The question is: Can achievements in these areas really compensate for the lack of recruits? States have limited ability to shape demographic trends directly, but the continued military supremacy of aging advanced industrial democracies is possible if states are willing to commit to serious reforms. Military measures to ensure technological superiority, alliances, and efficiency must be accompanied by economic reforms, and even serious changes will not prevent the rise of the next generation of competitors, like Brazil, India, and China. The wildcard is the right global political climate. For example, states with manpower shortages will need to avoid becoming involved in manpower-intensive conflicts, something that may be difficult depending on their collective security commitments.

The first consideration is technology. For the most part, technological superiority is a major military advantage. More sophisticated weapons systems can help a military root out and defeat an enemy, and can even deter potential assailants from acting in the first place. From the standpoint of population aging, technology can, to some degree, replace lost manpower. The United States is one country that has been turning to technology for jobs that are cost-efficient to automate. By the end of 2008, U.S. forces were projected to have as many as 12,000 robotic units on the ground in Afghanistan and Iraq, including the PackBot, a small robot that helps to defuse improvised explosive devices. In these conflicts, at least 22 different robot systems are operating on the ground. It seems that these robots can replace soldiers when cost-efficient. For example, the MARCBOT is a small, $5,000 robot that looks for enemies and searches under cars for hidden explosives.[16] When a soldier is killed doing the same work, not only is it a tragedy for the life lost, it is also costly for the military, because they can no longer reap the benefits of that soldier's expensive training.

Although robotic armies are firmly the stuff of science fiction, the ability to preserve a soldier's life by using such technology is still a promising trend in light of population aging. Militaries in aging states that are able to rely on robotic technology instead of soldiers may also save money. One of the biggest parts of any military budget is training, feeding, housing, and providing health care and pensions for soldiers. In 2006, the EU member states (with the exception of Denmark) spent about 55 percent of their military budgets on personnel.[17] Robots, as P. W. Singer points out in *The Wilson Quarterly*, require none of those things.[18]

Of course, robots cannot replace soldiers in all areas of combat. Although unmanned aerial vehicles, by definition, fly without a pilot in the cockpit, they still require a soldier to maneuver them remotely through their mission. Unmanned drone strikes have been successfully used throughout recent conflicts in the Middle East and Central Asia, including strikes in the remote tribal areas of Northern Pakistan. Yet the use of this technology comes with a price. Some experts argue that drone strikes are undermining the American mission by leaving a bad impression among the tribal communities, who have little respect for what they see as a dishonorable method of killing. Instead, the leaders have far more respect for action taken by soldiers. Seth Jones, of the defense analysis firm RAND, argues that drones not only fail to address the core problem in Pakistan—militancy among local residents—but continued strikes may lead to more trouble and instability.[19]

A larger issue is that technology can do little to carry out the counter-insurgency strategy that the Pentagon has been pursuing in Iraq. Counter-insurgency operations require soldiers with local knowledge, leadership and language skills, and a commitment to building institutions to operate on the ground.[20] In addition, struggles in the region have clearly shown that technology does not guarantee victory—or at least easy victory. As the 2010 U.S. Quadrennial Defense Review pointed out, the full spectrum of potential conflict will run from proliferation of weapons of mass destruction to instability caused by climate change and rapid urbanization of littoral regions. The capabilities required to meet these challenges will need to be varied as well.[21]

Alliances are a second source of military power that can help states compensate for declining manpower. As part of strong alliances, states have strength in numbers, even if they are individually weakened by aging. The EU is a clear example of aging states intentionally working in concert to increase their diplomatic, political, and economic strength and influence. Although not without disagreement, during the past several decades, member states of the EU have been growing closer, ceding autonomy in areas traditionally reserved for the state—such as labor and border control—and developing common policies. Part of the reason may be their increasing awareness of population aging; the trend is mentioned in documents concerning nearly every area of policy. The area of security policy is no different. For some of Europe's military powers—in particular, Germany, Italy, and Poland—strengthening EU defense can help compensate for a population that is already (or on the cusp of, in Italy's case) shrinking because of extended periods of very low fertility. According to Germany's Federal Ministry of Defence, one of the major goals of German security policy is to strengthen the EU's security capabilities.[22] The Minister of Defence of the Czech Republic, who held the EU presidency in 2009, echoes the German Ministry of Defence and explains the importance of EU defense:

By including a defence dimension to the process of Europe's uni-fication . . . we realized that our efforts might, one day, make the EU a key military as well as political and economic player on the world stage. It is my belief that the [European Defence Agency] has an indispensable role to play in helping Europe to build the defence capabilities necessary to make the EU more independent, more vigilant and better able to address not only "soft" but also "hard" security threats to European interests.[23]

In contrast to its Western neighbors, Turkey still boasts a growing population and had a TFR of between 2.3 and 2.4 for 1995 to 2005.[24] Folding Turkey into the EU is highly contested; however, if population makes an important contribution to power, then Turkey's accession would give the EU a much-needed boost in power in the future. Turkey can potentially help bolster the population of the EU, which strengthens that organization's ability to meet its goals. In particular, the overall populations of many post-Soviet states are already shrinking, or are projected to shrink very soon, and if they wish to counter Russian influence, strengthening their ties with Western European counterparts through the EU is a good way to compensate for population loss. Gains in technology and efficiency reduce reliance on manpower, but formal alliances are also important for projecting solidarity and strength. Even as Japan and Europe age, they can build new alliances, strengthen existing ones, and therefore protect mutual interests. Threats of extremism coming from Afghanistan have led to widespread recognition that advanced industrialized states have mutual interest in successfully quelling those threats. As a result, a wide range of states and alliances have been active in conflict there. For example, the European Defence Agency has helped meet NATO operational requirements in Afghanistan. On the other hand, lack of widespread and sustained commitment to U.S. operations in Iraq demonstrates that alliances are not always characterized by unity of purpose. Disagreements among members regarding the best way to use pooled resources arise frequently.

There is theoretical precedent for considering strong alliances as actors in the international system. Many power transition theorists, from Organski to contemporary scholars such as Woosang Kim, encourage us not only to measure the population and power of states, but also to measure those of political units.[25] Table 3.2 shows some of the most populous states in 2010 and 2030, and how aging states can increase their standing by strengthening their alliances as political units.

In addition to the EU, NATO can potentially increase the influence of aging states. Some argue that the advancing age of NATO members means the organization may become increasingly irrelevant, but the opposite could just as likely happen.[26] Although the Cold War is over, NATO member states still hope to counter Russian influence, but they also have a broader desire to express solidarity in the face of other threats, such as extremism and nuclear proliferation in Iran and North Korea. Perhaps the organization could see a renewal, as evidenced by France's recommitment to NATO in 2009.

**Table 3.2** Most Populous States and Political Units in 2010 and 2030, Constant Fertility Variant*

| 2010 | | 2030 | |
|---|---|---|---|
| **Country** | *n* | **Country** | *n* |
| China | 1.4 billion | India | 1.6 billion |
| India | 1.2 billion | China | 1.5 billion |
| NATO[†] | 909 million | NATO[†] | 988 million |
| European Union[†] | 498 million | European Union[†] and Turkey | 604 million |
| United States | 318 million | European Union[†] | 513 million |
| Indonesia | 232 million | United States | 377 million |
| Brazil | 195 million | Pakistan | 295 million |

* The constant fertility variant demonstrates that even if fertility stays the same, institutions still matter for outcomes.
[†] As of April 1, 2009.

*Source:* United Nations Population Division. "World Population Prospects: The 2008 Revision Population Database." New York: United Nations, 2009, http://esa.un.org/UNPP/.

Likewise, Russia could use the Shanghai Cooperation Organization to strengthen its ability to counter Western democratic influences in its former republics and gain support for its foreign policy goals. The Shanghai Cooperation Organization is a collective security organization founded by China, Kazakhstan, Kyrgyzstan, Russia, Tajikistan, and Uzbekistan that tries to promote political, economic, and scientific cooperation, and maintain and ensure peace and stability in the region.[27] Having some of its former republics as part of the same collective security organization is one way for Russia to maintain some influence over their policies and dissuade democratization efforts; joining forces with China—another powerful state—is a way to present a united front on some issues and band together as a nonwestern forum for negotiation.[28] There have been many points of contention among the organization's members, including over Russian military action in Georgia in 2008, but if Russia can foster accord, the alliance could be a platform to ensure that Russia's interests are represented on the world stage, even as its population ages and shrinks.

For all of their benefits, alliances have several disadvantages compared with states when it comes to projecting force and deterring enemies. As the examples of the EU, NATO, and the Shanghai Cooperation Organization all show, internal disagreements can weaken and fragment the alliance; unity of purpose is less of an issue with single states. Alliances can entangle states in conflicts from which they otherwise would wish to stay away, and there is no guarantee that allies will come to aid in the face of serious threats. When they work well, though, they can help relatively weaker states find a platform for their interests and can help stronger states consolidate their power.

The third area in which states can compensate for population aging is military efficiency. Increases in military efficiency can reduce reliance on military manpower and relieve pressure on budgets. Aging EU member states have been working to combine their military resources and reduce redundancy to improve efficiency. As Dimitrios Moutsiakis, writing for the European Defence Agency, argues: "Pooling of airlift assets would enhance their availability and generate economies of scale (on personnel, infrastructure and material), increased military efficiency and a more effective use of the limited capabilities in the airlift area."[29] Demography is not the only trend driving greater cooperation. The global financial crisis of the late 2000s strained defense budgets and increased the need to reduce redundancy, collaborate on research and development, and increase efficiency.

Technology, alliances, and efficiency can help states compensate for a lower number of potential military recruits, but there are some other demographic trends that may reduce military security for aging states. The first area concerns the quality of potential recruits in European states, Japan, and the United States. Not only will these states lack enough people, but they will also be increasingly comprised of only-children. Some scholars suggest that societies of only-children will be less willing to send their children off to war, and the population's willingness to fight will decrease, weakening the state's ability to project military power. In one of the most frequently cited articles on this subject, Edward Luttwak, in 1994, argued in *Foreign Affairs*:

> No advanced low-birth-rate countries can play the role of a classic great power anymore, not the United States or Russia, not Britain, France or, least of all, Germany or Japan. They may still possess the physical attributes of military strength or the economic base to develop such strength even on a great scale, but their societies are so allergic to casualties that they are effectively debellicized, or nearly so.[30]

There are several weaknesses in his assertion. First, we should not assume that modern societies are casualty averse because somehow the life of an only child is more valuable to parents than that of a child who has other siblings. As Kummel and Leonhard point out, "a violent death has always been in need of justification." Throughout time the attitudes toward a soldier's death and toward war have shifted. They point out that in 18th-century Prussia "the educated bourgeoisie was opposed to the royal wars . . . and . . . a rather fatalistic attitude towards death prevailed." As of July 2004 there were about 7,000 German soldiers involved in international military missions.[31] Other states with mature age structures regularly mobilize troops for a variety of missions.

Second, we could expect that with the right enemy and the right conflict, societies of only-children would still mobilize for their country in war. Patriotism and "the other" are powerful concepts. Technology may also mean that societies will not be casualty averse and will be more willing to use a military response when appropriate. Many aging European states have committed troops to fight terrorism and conduct humanitarian missions. The German military plans to continue to use troops to prevent international conflicts and to conduct crisis management, including the fight against international terrorism.[32] Finally, a low birthrate does not mean that the society is comprised solely of only-children. In these societies, a TFR of 1.3 means that some couples are choosing to have only one child, but many are choosing to have none and others to have several. However, the role of only-children in casualty aversion is an area ripe for further research. As the demographic transition proceeds in countries like China and India, if the hypothesis about only-children is correct, perhaps the risk that these states will go to war will also decrease.

There may also be advantages to having an army with increasing proportions of only-children. Writing about the People's Liberation Army (PLA) in China, Xiaobing Li says: "Regarding the only-child soldiers, [one] study shows that . . . there is little significant difference in the personality, training records, and service achievement of only-child and non-only-child soldiers, especially those from rural areas. In technological training, only-child soldiers seem to outperform non-only-child soldiers in verbal tests, communication skills, and computer skills."[33] And because nearly all the great powers are aging, the playing field is level. Although members of the U.S. national security community, especially, are worried about China's rise, China faces similar demographic challenges as Europe and Japan. The percentage of only-children in the PLA went from around 21 percent of the force in 1996 to more than 42 percent of the force in 1998, and was estimated to be more than 50 percent by 2006. Li also cites estimates that only-children will make up half of the PLA officer corps between 2010 and 2020.[34]

Increasing numbers of only-children are not the only change in the composition of potential recruits; migration is changing the landscape as well. The ethnic composition of U.S. youth implies that a much higher percentage of the military in the decades to come will be Hispanic, given not only their numbers, but their penchant for military service. A study of Hispanics in the U.S. Marine Corps found that Hispanic recruits were more likely than recruits of other races or ethnicities to complete boot camp and the first term of service—even after controlling for other differences.[35] This seems to be isolated to U.S. immigration, as Muslim migration to Europe has so far had very little effect on Europe's forces. Although minority ethnic groups numbered about six percent of overall UK society in 2001, their representation in the armed services was only about one percent.[36] It is too early to determine whether European armies will begin to rely on immigrants to fill their ranks, but the xenophobia in many states is likely to prevent this from occurring anytime soon. For the United States, although migration brings benefits for the U.S. military, overall domestic trends in all ethnic groups reduce the total number of qualified recruits. Soaring obesity rates, mental or medical conditions, and juvenile crime in today's 17- to 24-year-olds mean that 70 percent are ineligible for service.[37]

## Military Funding

Personnel requirements are only one of the challenges of an older age structure. An even more fundamental challenge to military security is the ability and willingness of aging states to fund their defense. How will the military compete with other budgetary priorities in aging countries, particularly in regard to pension and health care promises? Without adequate funding, states can neither train and equip soldiers nor compensate for a lack of soldiers through technology. Part of the answer to this question of whether states will have the ability to fund their defense is found in the effects of population aging on economic health overall. Basic economics tells us that a state's gross domestic product (GDP) need only grow as fast as the population to preserve the status quo. Not only will the military have to compete with entitlements and health care for a slice of the state's budget as large older cohorts retire and seek their benefits, but they may have to compete for a shrinking pie as the economies of aging states contract.

The size of the total population is not the primary concern in aging states; which segments of the population are growing matters more. In aging states, growth in elderly dependents is accompanied by a reduction in the proportion of workers. Pay-as-you-go pension schemes are effectively crippled in these cases because there are not enough workers paying into the system to support those who have retired and are drawing from it. Although an abundance of child dependents has its own strains, elderly dependents are relatively more expensive than child dependents because of pensions and health care, the latter of which has grown increasingly expensive. Health spending has been sharply increasing in the United States, Japan, and Germany, among other states, and health care costs as a percentage of total GDP expenditures have increased for all the countries with mature age structures.[38] Aging can also hurt economic growth if it reduces savings that provide capital for investment. Retirees may try to dispose of their assets and gradually use up their savings as they grow older.[39] Yet, a state rarely considers its economic health in isolation; states also worry whether their economies are growing as fast as their peers'. In a comparative context, then, aging threatens a state's ability to project economic power or fund its military because a shrinking labor force and growing proportions of elderly dependents threaten to retard GDP growth at the same time that more youthful rising powers like China, Brazil, and India continue to experience record growth.

The problems for aging states are grave, yet governments' efforts to address these issues have been weak. As the 2010 financial crisis in Greece—a rapidly aging state—illustrates, many members of the OECD are basically going bankrupt because reforms have been too slow. Because GDP growth is driven not only by growth in the working-age population, but also by technology, efficiency, and capital, aging states will need to pursue meaningful reform to take advantage of currently available labor, opportunities to increase efficiency, and ability to attract investment. The following discussion highlights the potential role of policy in mediating the effects of an aging population as a way to demonstrate the serious steps aging states will need to take to secure their militaries in the face of demographic change.

The pool of potential workers, just like the pool of military recruits, is projected to shrink for all industrialized states between 2005 and 2025. Japan, Germany, France, the United Kingdom, the United States, and even China, to name but a few, will all have decreasing proportions of their working-age populations.[40] Yet nearly all of the world's most aged states have large, underutilized segments of their working populations—in particular, youth, women, and older workers age 50 to 64. If states can bring those underutilized segments into the workforce, they may be able to compensate for a portion of the workforce lost as a result of population aging. Female labor force participation lags across the OECD, but if OECD countries brought their female labor force participation rates up to the current average labor force participation for both males and females, they could likely see their total GDP increase somewhat. In South Korea, Greece, and Japan, especially, female labor force participation is significantly lower than male participation. Policies that try to reconcile work and family life may help close the gender gap. There may also be a role for education and training in contributing to GDP growth.[41]

Population aging will force difficult policy choices. Policies that offer generous benefits toward the elderly cannot continue indefinitely, but states that allow for older cohorts to have a say in policy making may be slowest with reform. Many OECD states, such as Germany, Italy, and Japan, are instituting higher retirement ages, reforming pay-as-you-go pension systems, and scrapping early retirement at the same time that their electorates are older than they have ever been before. However, progress across the aging OECD is uneven and some reforms are only to be phased in over decades, so they may not be ambitious enough to make a difference.

Besides increasing labor force participation, aging states can also work to remain attractive for capital and investment. Because aging states are generally also stable and democratic, with well-educated populations, and sound physical and legal infrastructures, they are relatively attractive for foreign capital and investment when compared with a more youthful, yet less-developed state without those positive attributes. Aging states need to emphasize their comparative advantage in providing an atmosphere for slow, steady growth, even if they lack the kind of risk and reward of emerging markets. Efficiency can also make a meaningful contribution to GDP growth. Although the size of working-age cohorts will decrease over time in aging states, new generations of workers could still be as productive as their parents. The need for productivity could itself drive innovation. Japan's strides in robotic technology are one example of population aging driving innovation. The engineers of Paro, the robotic seal, won an award from the Japanese government in 2006 for their innovative use of robotics for therapy in nursing homes.[42] Technology like Paro can help compensate for a potential lack of workers to care for the large elderly cohorts.

Although aging means that the average age of a state's population will increase, and the proportions of young and old will shift, it does not mean that everyone in the society is old. To supplement natural increase, developed aging states can try to keep their position as centers of innovation by attracting skilled migrants from developing countries. The migration of skilled workers highlights how interests may conflict, because although immigration benefits receiving states, emigration is often to the detriment of the sending states when their well-educated and highly skilled workers leave. Developed states theoretically have superior education opportunities and transparent governance, whereas some developing states have weak institutions, poor governance, and lack property rights or legal protections for innovation. Applicants from four aging states—Japan, the United States, Germany, and South Korea—received 73 percent of total patent grants worldwide in 2006 according to the World Intellectual Property Organization. Yet, China is positioning itself as the next center of innovation, and its patent filings and grants have grown tremendously during the past several years.[43] Whether China takes the lead will depend on several factors, including what Anne-Marie Slaughter calls China's lack of a "culture of innovation" resulting from the excessive presence of the government in private and business spheres.[44]

Whether states have the ability to fund their militaries is an economic concern; whether states have the will to fund their militaries is a political concern. We must consider how complex the drivers of defense spending are. In theory, the citizens of democracies have some say in whether and when their militaries are used. If aging societies are more casualty averse—as a result of higher proportions of elderly, increasing numbers of only-children, or some other reason—then there may be little support for defense spending. In practice, though, we know that the ability of citizens to shape national defense is limited, even in a democracy. If faced with a sufficiently high threat level, even aging states would likely reallocate spending away from social programs or other areas and toward defense. Alternatively, they might run up a high debt to ensure they can counter the threat. Despite geographic limitations, states are still able to project power by adapting and focusing on their strengths; the same could be true with demography. External threats are a powerful driver of defense spending, even when a state lacks the ability to fund its defense. For example, the United States ran up the federal debt to mobilize for World War II.[45] More recently, the global economic recession of the late 2000s had little effect on defense spending, except, arguably, to increase it as states spent more to boost demand. Worldwide, military spending grew by 49 percent from 2000 to 2009, and increased by 5.9 percent in 2009 alone. Aging Germany and Italy spent $46 and $36 billion, respectively, on defense in 2009.[46]

In forecasting, we must consider some of the major past and present drivers of defense spending, which are competition among the great powers, regional security threats, and terrorism. Although relations are mostly tepid among the great powers, there are still territorial disputes between India and China, Japan and Russia, and Japan and China. The particular personalities of each state, and fear of being eclipsed by another great power (often the United States) is another factor. Regional challenges often drive spending, as in the case of Japan's defense program, which is in part a response to China's growing global power and uncertainty over its ambitions, including its intentions toward Taiwan.[47] Finally, as the security situation changes globally, there will always be new threats to reinvigorate defense spending. Some of these, like terrorism, will continue to have a shelf life for at least a few more years; others, likely to occur between now and 2030, we cannot predict.

Japan is one aging power that illustrates the complex drivers of defense spending. Despite holding the title of oldest state on the planet, or perhaps because of the title, Japan has been adjusting its military forces in response to a changing geopolitical environment. Most of Japan's low military spending during the first part of the decade was the result of the austerity of then-Prime Minister Junichiro Koizumi, who cut military spending and focused on economic growth instead. Under new leadership, Japan sought its first increase in military spending in four years in August 2005. Although demographically strained, geopolitical concerns and the restructuring of U.S. forces are driving Japan's increasingly independent security role. Japan spent almost $52 billion on defense in 2009.[48] The presence of several powerful states and several unstable ones in Japan's region is one key driver of Japan's defense spending. The antisatellite weapons test that China conducted in January 2007 was a particularly striking incident. North Korean nuclear ambitions and instability on

**Figure 3.2**  Population tree for the United States, 2005. (Population Action
                International)

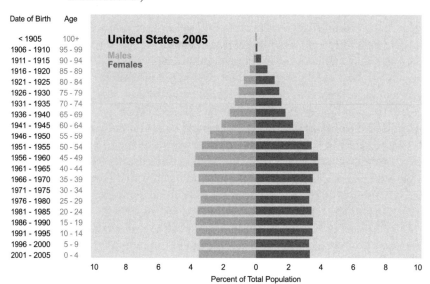

the Korean peninsula are other factors that encourage Japan's defense spending. In part because of the North Korean threat, the 2005 defense budget proposal included "a new three-billion-yen package for joint development with
the United States of a sea-based system to intercept ballistic missiles."[49] Even
the resurgence of Russia and considerations of terrorism have played a role.
One influential development is that, in agreement with Japan, the United States
plans to relocate a significant number of troops from Japan to Guam. Although
the United States will still guarantee security for its close ally, this move has
prompted Japan to upgrade its defense agency to a full Ministry of Defense.

   Although the United States is not projected to age as rapidly or as greatly
as Europe and Japan, it will still face increasing proportions of elderly. As the
U.S. baby boomers retire, the health care and social security promised to them
will create great budgetary strains. At the same time, the United States finds
itself embroiled in two wars, and with potentially expensive security guaran-
tees to South Korea and NATO. A new agreement with South Korea extends
the guarantee of U.S. military security until 2015 in the event of conflict with
North Korea.[50] How long the United States can continue to operate as a hege-
mon under the strain of population aging is questionable. As Figure 3.2 shows,
the bulge of baby boomers is concentrated around the ages of 40 to 55 in 2005.
These cohorts will soon be retiring, and the cohorts that follow will be much
smaller, meaning that the amount of tax revenue these younger cohorts pay

into the system will be less than the baby boomers, who will at that time draw from the system instead of paying into it.

## CONCLUSION

Population aging presents a unique puzzle for political demographers because it is an unprecedented trend. This chapter analyzed the likely effects of population aging on national security by focusing on a few examples from the states with the most mature age structures. A few themes emerge from the analysis. Military funding is perhaps the biggest challenge of aging, as increasing proportions of elderly dependents drain financial resources that could be used for defense spending. Aging also brings the opportunity for peace as more states are perhaps unable or unwilling to risk casualties of war. Aging also suggests that states adopt strategies that compensate for individual weakness through alliances. One of the implications of population aging for national security is that states with mature age structures may want to consider strengthening partnerships with states that have younger age structures. These states, if governed well, are likely to become increasingly democratic and experience economic growth that can make them better partners in global security. The implications of these traditional age structures will be explored in detail in the following chapter. In the Western Hemisphere, the demographic profiles of states in Latin America will increase their likelihood of becoming capable partners to the United States and Canada. At the same time, the United States should not abandon its long-standing relationships with European allies. Certainly, European states, as much as we often treat them as quite similar, will have differing degrees of population aging and a variety of approaches to dealing with aging. Likewise, younger South Asian states can be partners in regional security for Japan. India's policing of the Gulf of Aden is one example of a state with a transitional age structure working to secure the global commons. As for capabilities, aging suggests that technology and efficiency will be increasingly important. The connections between aging and security in the world's great powers illustrate that demography is shaping the ability of Western European states and Japan, especially, to project power.

The primary area of national security affected by aging is military security, but there are some implications for regime and structural security, as well. According to a study done by Population Action International, states with 15 to 26 percent of the population age 60 and older had only a six percent risk of civil conflict between 1970 and 1999, and were 83 percent likely to have fully democratic governance during the same time period.[51] As worldwide trends toward lower fertility continue, the number of states with mature age structures will grow, and if the relationships among age structure, democracy, and absence of conflict continue to hold, the world may be a more peaceful place.

Whether the relationship between age structure and democracy will hold for China as we move toward the middle of the century is uncertain.

As for structural security, however, aging challenges the ability of the state to provide for the population because of the strain it puts on economic growth and national budgets. The first issue concerns seniors themselves. Large proportions of dependents and few workers means that, for the most part, states will be unable to provide generous benefits to seniors, who are one of society's most vulnerable groups. The section on military security showed that states are unlikely to forego defense to continue to provide generous benefits to seniors. Different political institutional arrangements in aging states would mediate differently the interests of seniors, so there will be some variation. However, on the whole, as long as military threats persist, states will continue to seek the ability to defend themselves. What this means for individual elderly is that the kind of generous benefits that first brought seniors out of poverty when social security was introduced may be at risk. Individuals will bear more of a responsibility for their own well-being, and those who have not had the means to save will likely suffer the greatest. Similar issues arise for the aged in less developed states. Although there has been some concern in the media about the rapidity of aging in developing states, the implication is really limited to the welfare of seniors. Many developing states lack widespread social security coverage for seniors, so aging mostly harms individuals and not the budget of the state itself. China is one example of a rapidly aging state with sparse coverage for seniors.

The final issue is the ability of aging states to help foster structural security abroad. As I asked in the introduction: To what extent will societies willingly sacrifice dwindling numbers of youth for foreign causes, such as humanitarian missions? The primary demographic problem leading to conflict and failed states in developing countries is a youthful age structure, not an old one. Problems with population growth and resources, and an abundance of youth contribute to making the world in general more tumultuous and violent than peaceful. As Jeffrey Sachs notes, "virtually every case of U.S. military intervention abroad since 1960 has taken place in a developing country that had previously experienced a case of state failure."[52] Afghanistan is one of the youngest countries on the planet, with 45 percent of its population younger than age 15.[53] As they age, the industrialized great powers may not be able to respond to these conflicts to the extent they have done in the past, meaning that they will have a limited ability to intervene in conflicts in younger states or even help with post-conflict reconstruction.

# 4

Chapter

# Transitional Age Structures

In 1944, Dudley Kirk predicted that China's overpopulation and extreme poverty "will prove a great barrier to the economic progress of the country and hence to its rise as a world power."[1] As the chapter on youthful age structures showed, Kirk likely would have been right, had China not used a heavy hand to lower fertility and slow population growth. China turned what was a burdensome age structure into one that catapulted their economic growth and, in tandem, their global power and influence. Now, many consider China nearly on par with the United States as a center of power.

Population extremes—like booming or shrinking populations, very young age structures or very old ones—have multiple connections to insecurity, because the youngest countries are often plagued by ethnic conflict and civil strife, whereas the oldest face the challenge of funding and staffing a military. Indeed, the two extremes of the global demographic divide seem to paint far more challenges for national security than they do opportunities. However, the extremes leave out a large swath of countries in the middle, where the majority of world population resides.[2] The broad definition of security used in this book points our attention not only to ways that population can create insecurity, through strains on resources or clashes of identity, but also to ways that population can be a force for increasing security. Transitional age structures provide a demographic environment conducive for increasing national economic and military power, and thus can help establish competent partners for increasing regional security. Countries with transitional age structures also have higher chances of peaceful democratic governance and of being able to provide for their populations in terms of health and education. Having greater economic resources is one way to increase security; states are able to spend more on defense and, if resources are distributed evenly, may become more stable as citizens pursue economic opportunities instead of violence against each other or the state. The United States and other world powers have not historically paid much attention to the potential of countries in the window of opportunity and are missing the chance to draw on these states, which can become global partners in addressing transnational issues like crime and terrorism, and can help boost the economies of developed states through stable and fruitful trading relationships. Economic resources have become the new currency of power in the postmillennial security environment, and transitional countries are best positioned to increase their economic resources.

The decades in which a state has a transitional age structure are often referred to as the "demographic bonus" or the "window of opportunity." Theoretically, during this time the state receives more in productivity from workers than it pays out to dependents. East Asian states are the most cited examples of success at capitalizing on their demographic bonuses. Yet, many Latin American countries going through the transition have not experienced the same levels of growth that East Asian countries did. A large part of the disparity comes from the necessary role of policy in making sure that states take full advantage of their demographic dividends. The window of opportunity is just that—an opportunity, not a guarantee. Because fertility has decreased in every major region of the world, more countries will enter the window of opportunity, and it is thus very important to understand the challenges and opportunities of this age structure for national security.[3] One of the biggest opportunities is the ability to plan for aging and establish sustainable pension and health care systems, since countries with transitional age structures and below replacement fertility will eventually have mature age structures. At the same time, in some countries unless progress is made along the demographic transition, no window will present itself and these states will have an even harder time developing. For example, if Kenya follows the UN's high-fertility projections, no demographic window will occur there.[4]

## WHAT IS THE DIVIDEND?

In 1972, A. F. K. Organski, Bruce Bueno de Mesquita, and Alan Lamborn offered the idea of the "effective population" as a way to conceptualize the contribution population makes to national power. Somewhat harshly, they note: "The majority of the people in any nation do not make any significant contribution to the nation's power, either through economic production, political participation, the payment of taxes, or military service."[5] Instead of focusing on population size, they disaggregate the population variable and argue that we should consider "the portion of the population that makes a contribution to the furthering of national goals."[6] Their description is applicable to the demographic bonus that comes from a transitional age structure. The bonus, in essence, describes the portion of the population that is economically productive, participates in politics, pays taxes, and serves in the military. Organski et al. note that there are often vast differences in economic productivity among individuals, but this is also true among states. Therefore, we also have to ask: How effectively does the system aggregate the efforts of the individuals who make up the 'effective population?'[7] To some degree, this question describes political capacity and the government's ability to mobilize the population. Even relatively underdeveloped countries can be very good at this. China's 1951 invasion of Korea and the efforts of the Viet Cong are two examples. For the most part, though, the more foresight and capacity the state has to set up institutions and an environment conducive to taking full advantage of the dividend, including roles for civil society and the private sector, the greater the dividend. Mexico, although its age structure has been favorable, has not reaped the same level of economic and political dividends that states like Brazil or even Argentina have. Instead, Mexico continues to have problems with corruption and organized crime, which have caused instability at home and have spilled over to create a security problem for its neighbor to the north, the United States.

A transitional age structure is a temporary stage that occurs as a country progresses along the demographic transition from high to low fertility and mortality.[8] A transitional structure, which has declining proportions of youth, growing proportions of those entering or in prime working age, and low proportions of elderly dependents, occurs after a youthful age structure, characterized by high fertility, and before a mature age structure, which results when fertility has been low for a long time.[9] Regionally, transitional age structures predominate in Latin America and the Caribbean, but are also found in parts of the Middle East, like Iran and Kuwait, and in Asia, including China and India. The window of opportunity that affords these states a bonus of workers and a lower onus of dependents is fleeting. Brazil, whose journey along the demographic transition is typical, illustrates how fleeting the window is. In 1970, Brazil still had a youthful age structure, with 42.4 percent of the population younger than age 15 and less than six percent older than the age of 60. By 2010, the bulk of the population (64.4 percent) was between the ages of 15 years and 59 years, whereas the proportion younger than 15 had dropped to less than 26 percent. By 2030, though, the working-age population will still be large, and the proportion 60 years and older will have increased to 18 percent.[10] States must invest in health and education to take full advantage of the window and to position themselves to weather the challenges that will come as they age rapidly.

The demographic transition can be a sign that states are doing something right. When states try to play a role in facilitating the demographic transition by supporting family planning and health programs, they are in essence making a statement that they believe slower population growth and an older age structure will benefit the state's development. Not all states choose such benign tactics. Some states adopt coercive policies to speed up the demographic transition and get to the window of opportunity sooner. China is a particularly notable example. The average Chinese woman in 1950 had more than six children in her lifetime, about five in 1970, but only four by 1975. Famine and stalled progress toward economic development eventually convinced China's leaders to institute the one-child policy so China could emulate the economic success of Europe and the United States and hopefully increase its power. Chinese fertility reached replacement level during 1990 to 1995.[11] The policy mostly has continued, and the continuation of that policy is the embodiment of the leadership's choice to let China's age structure mature, rather than revert to a large and growing population. Coercive policies are not necessary to usher the demographic transition, and states that try to lower fertility through empowering women, universalizing education, and building a health care infrastructure are actually better positioned for their demographic bonus than states that rely on coercion. Though their policies have been coercive, China has also made an effort to encourage equality and strengthen education, policies that have helped them reap their demographic dividend.

There are many reasons why demographic transition is beneficial to the state. Specifically, the demographic dividend refers to increases in the growth rate of income per capita that results when the productive population grows at a faster rate than the total population.[12] On the individual or household level, fertility decline theoretically reduces the energy and resources needed for child rearing and permits these to be reallocated to other activities more productive for the state.[13] Female labor force participation, in particular, should increase as fertility decreases. Fertility declines also permit the state to make higher per-child investments in education, which help fuel economic growth, as was the case in many parts of Asia after early fertility declines in the 1960s and '70s.[14] Individual output, which is the most widely used indicator of economic performance, tends to increase when the population of working-age individuals is relatively large. When the population has high proportions of both young and elderly dependents, however, that measure is lower, because those of working age tend to produce and save in line with what they consume.[15] Like some East Asian states, Ireland also positioned itself to take advantage of its demographic dividend by putting the right policies in place. Starting in the 1950s, when fertility was still more than three children per woman, the government encouraged a more open economy, including foreign direct investment and export promotion, and also instituted free secondary education starting during the mid 1960s. As a result, the growth rate of income per capita jumped from 3.5 percent a year between 1960 and 1990 to 5.8 percent during the 1990s, earning the country the title of "Irish Tiger."[16]

A transitional age structure is certainly not sufficient for economic growth, and there are scholars who believe other population characteristics are more important. Economist Esther Boserup argues that population density is far more important than growth in particular segments of the population as a tool for modernization or technological progress. She says preindustrial Europe was not actually a labor surplus economy. In Europe, "when the [population] density needed for urbanization was reached and transport facilities improved, the way was opened for all the urban-linked, advanced technologies and intellectual achievements which had accumulated in other parts of the world."[17] In the chapter on urbanization, we will see how density can foster innovation and improve quality of life, as Boserup suggests. But, evidence from East Asia, Latin America, and India supports the argument that the demographic bonus of workers can be an economic—and national security—boon for states.

## CONNECTIONS TO SUCCESS

Europe, as the first region to go through the demographic transition and then become a leading economic power, is clearly one success story. Their demographic changes made a huge impact on their society, particularly in terms of increasing the population's standard of living. But Europe's utility as a modern model is limited for two reasons. First, of course, the context within which international political, economic, and military relations takes place has dramatically changed, particularly because of globalization. Second, most European states experienced very gradual fertility and mortality declines, the latter as a result of accumulation of medical knowledge about how to control infectious diseases.[18] Today, countries go through the demographic transition much faster with the help of organized and often global family planning initiatives and modern contraception. Table 4.1 lists the countries that went from having young age structures in 1970, with 60 to 67 percent of their populations age 0 to 29 years, to only 45 to 60 percent by 2005.

There is a more recent success story of the demographic bonus that may serve as a better model for states in and entering the window of opportunity: the East Asian economic miracle. The economies of these states collapsed during the late 1990s, due to government policies regarding currency, but the demographic story takes place before that time. Between 1965 and 1990, when East Asia's working-age population grew nearly 10 times faster than its dependent population, the resulting changes in life expectancy, age structure, and population density had a significant impact on the region's economic growth rates. Demographic effects can explain one-third to one-half of East Asia's "miraculous" economic growth.[19] Three key factors seemed to be associated with Asia's high economic growth: (1) the size of the working-age population relative to total population, (2) the productivity of labor in all sectors of the

**Table 4.1** Countries Going from Young Age Structures in 1970 to Transitional Age
Structures by 2005

| | | |
|---|---|---|
| Albania | Armenia | Azerbaijan |
| Brazil | Chile | China |
| Colombia | Costa Rica | Ecuador |
| Guyana | India | Indonesia |
| Israel | Jamaica | Kazakhstan |
| North Korea | Kuwait | Lebanon |
| Malaysia | Mauritius | Mexico |
| Myanmar | Panama | Qatar |
| Sri Lanka | St. Lucia | St. Vincent and Grenadines |
| Suriname | Thailand | Trinidad and Tobago |
| Tunisia | Turkey | United Arab Emirates |
| Venezuela | Vietnam | |

*Source:* Elizabeth Leahy, Robert Engelman, Carolyn Gibb Vogel, Sarah Haddock, and Tod Preston. *The Shape of Things to Come: Why Age Structure Matters to a Safer, More Equitable World.* Washington, DC: Population Action International, 2007, pp. 87–91.

economy, and (3) the way labor was allocated among the low-productivity agriculture sector and the high-productivity industry and service sectors.[20]

Age structure by itself did not guarantee East Asia's growth; rather, the actions by the states to take advantage of their transitional age structures, like greater educational investment, and the shifts in behavior of the people, like increased savings, made the difference. In Taiwan, South Korea, and even Thailand and Indonesia, the governments invested in literacy and health care even before population growth began to decline, and therefore these states were better positioned to take advantage of their demographic windows of opportunity. In Indonesia, for example, the literacy rate for youth age 15 to 24 years went from 85 to 96 percent between 1980 and 1990, and for all adults older than 15 went from 63 to 82 percent. Unlike these East Asian states, however, India's health and education indicators lag. Although literacy for all adults older than 15 years of age has increased from 41 to 63 percent between 1980 and 2006, this is still low. Health lags as well; average life expectancy is around 64 years.[21] India has certainly done well economically, but lack of investment in these areas will likely limit India's ability to take full advantage of their window of opportunity. Bangladesh is another example of a state that has failed to take advantage of declines in fertility and mortality, because the population is mostly rural, and education and living standards are low.[22] When countries are not fully able to employ their bonus working-age population, it can be a burden rather than an asset, as we saw in the chapter on youthful age structures.

To understand how countries take advantage of their demographic bonus and why this is an opportunity for national security, we can examine the cases of Japan, China, Thailand, and Indonesia. Japan's economic growth during the second half of the 20th century is remarkable. Gross national product (GNP) per capita was only $153 in 1950, lower than both Mexico and the Philippines. By 1968, Japan's GNP had become the second largest in the free world, and by 1990, was comparable with the United States and Germany. Japan had a rapid accumulation of physical capital in the 1950s, followed by universal medical care in 1961.[23] What has this meant for Japan from a security standpoint? The early economic growth of Japan and its integration into the world economy helped establish a peaceful and democratic Japan that, not too much earlier, had been one of the most aggressive states in the international system. Additionally, Japan's economic power has given the state leverage in international bargaining and a greater voice in international affairs, an essential part of national security. China, which transitioned to low fertility later than Japan, has also benefited from the window of opportunity, but the national security implications of China's transition are a bit different.

The speed with which China's demographic transition has taken place is remarkable. In only 30 years, the proportion of people age 60 years and older in Shanghai's population increased from 9 to 18 percent; in France, a similar transition took place over 140 years and in Sweden over 85 years.[24] The emphasis on gender equality during socialism has left a positive legacy in China whereby employment is fuller than in other developing (and even developed) states; in 2004, women were 45 percent of China's workforce. Higher female labor force participation is one of the reasons China has been able to take advantage of its demographic bonus. One estimate is that from 1982 to 2000, age structure accelerated China's economic growth by 2.3 percent per year, and contributed to more than one-quarter of China's economic growth.[25] The literacy rate for China went from 94 to 99 percent between 1990 and 2000.[26]

China's economic growth has been the engine of its rising military power, a clear national security implication of China's age structure. As the country's security has increased, this has led to a feeling of decreased national security for China's rivals. Although with many transition countries the dividends of greater regional and structural security can spill over into their ability to foster stability in surrounding states or states with whom they have relationships, China has shown little inclination that it desires such a role. Indeed, China's increasing involvement in unstable, resource-rich countries around the globe has not been accompanied by pressure on those leaders for better governance. For example, although they are highly involved in resource extraction on the continent, China shows little inclination to help stabilize

Africa. China's business ventures throughout Africa and Latin America—and their economic rewards—have continued to bring China a greater voice in international politics.

China's global reach and the consequent increase in power have quickly become something the next generation of global powers seeks to emulate. Poorer states are now benefiting from other emerging economies.[27] Brazil's contribution to foreign assistance, including goods and services, commercial loans, and direct assistance, is estimated to be as high as $4 billion a year, an amount similar to contributions of Sweden and Canada, who are known for their largesse.[28] Along with the other fast-growing BRIC economies (Russia, India, and China), Brazil is taking a larger role in global politics, as its aid efforts show, and is even campaigning for a permanent seat on the UN Security Council. All four of these states are behaving like great powers in several ways, such as increasing security cooperation with states in other regions and delivering foreign aid, among other efforts. Although European states, the United States, and Japan may find some of these behaviors threatening, because they increase the influence of non-Western states, increased capacity to contribute to global security operations and greater prospects for peace and development at home mean that these states' success also lifts some of the burden on the world's biggest powers. The economic growth and increased political power of the BRICs is no coincidence from a demographic perspective. Russia aside, which has unique demographic issues discussed elsewhere and a unique energy-based economy, the populations of the BRICs have transitional age structures, providing favorable conditions for economic growth, peace, and democratization.

China's demographic situation is not a totally positive one for increasing security, however, particularly when we look at China at the subnational level, rather than the age structure of the population of 1.3 billion as a whole. Fertility is generally lower in the East than in the West, and minority ethnic populations have the highest fertility. China's rural, Western areas have fewer employment opportunities and are missing the demographic window. In the East, argue Xizhe Peng and Yuan Cheng, the shortage of working-age youth is a major constraint to further economic development and is prematurely closing the window of opportunity there.[29] Shanghai, in particular, has an age structure similar to many of the world's wealthiest countries, as fertility there declined about 10 years sooner than in many other provinces during the 1960s. They estimate that Shanghai's TFR may be as low as 0.8. In 2000, already about 18 percent of the population was age 60 years and older. The mismatch between economic opportunities and age structure is encouraging migration of working-age men and women out of Western areas to China's coastal cities. China's migrants are pulled eastward by the fast-growing cities, their numerous economic opportunities, and higher standard of living, in many cases. For the Chinese leadership,

**Figure 4.1** Population tree for Indonesia, 2005. (Population Action International)

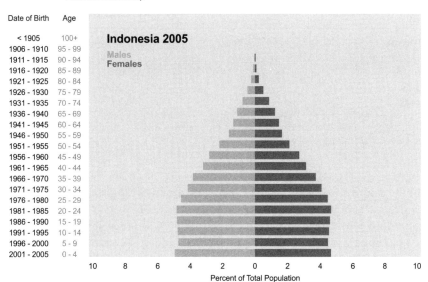

this does not seem to be a problem, because their plan is clearly to strengthen Eastern coastal cities. On the one hand, internal migration could "prolong the time span for harvesting the demographic bonus in the urban areas while providing opportunities for the poor rural areas to be able to harvest the demographic bonus, thus resulting in a win–win situation."[30] On the other hand, the uneven economic growth within China could create fissures within the country and undermine regime stability.

A brief look at Thailand and Indonesia show some of the future prospects for economic growth, democracy, and political capacity in Asia. Southeast Asia has recently begun to benefit from the demographic dividend, and South Central Asia is likely to follow, as Figure 4.1 shows.

Benefits may not only be economic, however; they may also be aligned with governance. Richard Cincotta has argued, as mentioned in the chapter on youthful age structures, that the recent leveling off in measures of global democracy is temporary and will increase again as youthful demographic profiles mature. Latin America, North Africa, and Asia are all likely to see the emergence of new and more stable liberal democracies before 2020.[31] At the country level, an increased number of stable liberal democracies is a positive development for security; there will be more stable trading partners and less of a need for peacekeeping or diplomatic intervention. Within states, at the subnational level, we may be able to look to demographic trends among

**Table 4.2** Indonesian Ethnic Groups and the Demographic Transition

| Ethnic Group | Projected Start of Demographic Transition |
|---|---|
| Javanese | 1990 |
| Madurese | 1990 |
| Sundanese | 2010 |
| Malay | 2025 |
| Batak | 2025 |

*Source:* Ananta, Aris. "Demand for Democracy in Indonesia: A Demographic Perspective." *Asian Population Studies* 2, no. 1 (2006): 1–2.

ethnic groups to determine the likelihood of democratic transition or consolidation. Population economist Aris Ananta argues that there is a correlation between the growing importance of individual values during the second demographic transition to very low fertility and an increase in demand for democracy at the state level and at home. Examining the case of Indonesia, Anata notes the following:

> It may not be coincidental that the democratic transition in Indonesia occurred in 1999, after the fall of Soeharto in 1998. The Javanese, the largest ethnic group, and Madurese, the fifth largest ethnic group, in Indonesia had already begun to experience the second demographic transition, starting from the year 1990. Altogether, they formed 45 per cent of the total Indonesian population and played a significant role in Indonesian politics—including Soeharto's fall.[32]

The subnational ethnic groups in Indonesia are at different places along the demographic transition (Table 4.2). If all were transitioning to very low fertility at the same time, then Ananta's proposition would mean that Indonesia might be permanently leaving behind some of the violence that has plagued it in the past. Because fertility is uneven, if the correlation with democratic values holds, these groups may increasingly come into conflict as their attitudes and desires for governance change.

Thailand's demographic window of opportunity is open between about 1990 to about 2030.[33] Already, the country has had major growth in its working-age population. The proportion of population between 15 to 59 years was 56 percent in 1980, 62 percent in 1990, and 66 percent in 2000, resulting from fertility declining from 6.4 in 1960 to 1965 to 1.8 in 2000 to 2005.[34] As its window opened, Thailand's GDP growth per capita increased from 3 percent in 1985 to 10 percent in 1990 and stayed above 5 percent until the financial crisis

**Figure 4.2** Population tree for Thailand, 2005. (Population Action International)

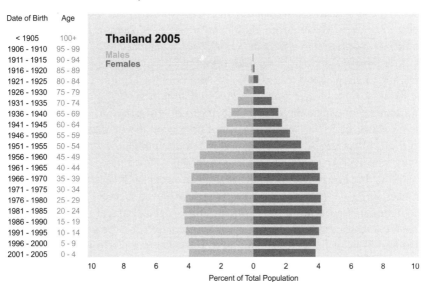

of East Asia during the late 1990s.[35] As the country's window starts to close, like many of its peers, Thailand needs to work now to set up institutions that will support the population as it ages, while still allowing for economic growth and military security (Fig. 4.2). Some of the policy conditions for a more productive workforce include open economic markets, flexible labor markets, quality health care and education, and investment and saving incentives. Already, Thailand has started importing low-skilled labor from neighboring countries to compensate for the declining labor force at entry-level ages. As Wongboonsin, et al suggest, Thailand should move away from low-skill, labor-intensive industries, because they will have too much competition from others with more favorable demographic profiles.[36]

## LATIN AMERICA

Perhaps the best way to show how important it is to take advantage of the window of opportunity to increase national security is to examine states that have missed the boat, or are in danger of doing so as their window closes. Many Latin American countries have not made necessary investments in human capital. Nor have they had the political capacity to rid themselves of corruption and violence. Together, these factors hinder them from taking full advantage of the window of opportunity. Although East Asia exhibited a GDP per-capita annual growth rate of 6.8 percent between 1975 and 1995—the time that many countries were experiencing the demographic bonus—during that same time Latin America's growth rate was only 0.7 percent.[37] Ronald Lee and Andrew Mason argue that, in Latin America, demographic dividends could have contributed economic growth of 1.7 percent a year.[38] Policy, or lack of it, is largely responsible for the disparity. In particular, as Latin America began its demographic transition, on the whole the region relied on domestic demand instead of export promotion. Corrupt governments and a series of financial disasters discouraged savings and investment.[39] The degree to which states in Latin America have taken advantage of their demographic bonuses differs greatly, however. A closer look at Mexico, which has missed many opportunities with its window, and Chile, which has done a much better job taking advantage of its demographic bonus, will illustrate how policy choices and other factors can play a role in economic success and in establishing national security for a state with a transitional age structure. In particular, a stable and successful Latin America is important for the national security of other states in the Western Hemisphere. Stemming the transnational drug trade and illegal migration, and establishing Latin American states as capable defense partners is a way for the United States, in particular, to increase its own national security. Outside of the Western Hemisphere, Latin America provides resources and markets for China and India. Some Latin American states have even played a role in development initiatives in Africa. On the whole, for the region, economic prospects are improving, but the benefit might have been even greater if necessary reforms had not been delayed. Both Mexico and Chile still have the opportunity to take advantage of their demographic profiles but the following discussion shows how decisions they've already made are having consequences for their security.

Mexico is an important case to understand, because, as demographer Jacques Vallin says, "very few intermediate countries will do better or earlier than Mexico."[40] Between 1954 and 1974, Mexico's population increased by more than three percent a year. Mortality dropped sharply, in part because of expanded education opportunities, sanitation infrastructure, and health care. Mexico's total fertility rate decreased from 6.5 children per woman in 1975 to 2.2 by 2010.[41] Emigration, though it can be beneficial as a release valve for unemployment and provide remittances, can also prevent a country from working to make use of its human capital and develop industries that will employ these laborers at home. In Mexico's case, emigration, particularly to the United States, is reducing the population by 0.4 percent per year.[42] In the future, Mexico's economically active population is projected to increase from 42 million in 2000, to 51 million in 2010, and to 64 million by 2030. This could be a very positive development for Mexico, but also means that between 2000 and 2015, Mexico would need to create at least 800,000 jobs a year.[43]

On June 12, 2010, the Bloomberg news agency reported a story with a shocking headline: "Mexico Has 85 Organized-Crime Deaths, Bloodiest Day of Calderon Presidency." The deaths included 19 execution-style killings in Chihuahua and 20 shootings in Tamaulipas, a Gulf of Mexico state that borders Texas.[44] Since President Felipe Calderon took office in December 2006, Mexico has been plagued by regime insecurity, particularly with efforts to stem the drug trade, in addition to illegal trafficking of persons and weapons. One newspaper reports that more than 19,000 people were killed in drug-related crime between Calderon's ascension and March 2010.[45] That month, four people were found beheaded and another nine were killed in the resort area of Acapulco, a popular destination for international tourists. Five of the victims were police officers who were battling with the drug gangs.[46] The U.S. State Department regularly issues travel advisories to Mexico because of the violence and kidnapping there. The presence of crime inhibits Mexico from taking full advantage of its demographic bonus, because it prevents revenue from tourism that could be reinvested in the economy and, without tourists, jobs in tourism are threatened as well. Mexico's lack of authority over its domestic affairs has also spilled into a national security issue for the United States, as these drugs, people, and guns cross the border and contribute to crime in the United States. It is thus in the best interest of both Mexico and the United States that Mexico take advantage of its demographic window of opportunity to build its governance capacity and get the country on the right economic track.

Another consequence of Mexico's failure to provide economic opportunities is the illegal migration to other parts of North America, particularly the United States. Not all migrants who pass from Mexico to the United States are Mexican—they come from many parts of Latin America—but the fact that they are able to carry out their illegal entry to the United States from Mexico is itself evidence of Mexico's regime insecurity (and of course, the United State's, which is unable to stop the flow). In 2008, 88 percent of the 792,000 migrants apprehended crossing from Mexico to the United States were Mexican nationals, and most of the remainder were from other parts of Latin America. The UN estimates that the income for the smugglers who help these migrants cross is about $7 billion a year, although the market has been declining since 2005 as the recession in the United States reduces opportunities for migrants.[47] What happens with Mexico, and indeed with any of the countries in the window of opportunity, may rest on how fertility trends develop during the next several years. Thus, we can look to Mexico to understand the relationship between fertility decline and window of opportunity. If the UN's low fertility projection of 1.4 comes true, Mexico's demographic dividend could be much greater, because the working-age population could reach about 65 percent. According to Vallin, such a high proportion has never been obtained in developed countries.[48] Yet there are problems with encouraging such low fertility, because it would speed population aging even more.

Mexico has already missed some opportunities to create the jobs and human capital it takes to successfully position the country for a future mature age structure. Chile, on the other hand, provides a model for how a state with a transitional age structure can put the right institutions in place to prepare for aging and set the conditions for regime and structural security. Their more sustainable pension system means that they may be positioned as a good future partner and anchor of regional stability, even if their transition to a mature age structure is rapid. A stable South America is important for other states of the hemisphere because of potential mutually beneficial economic gain through trade. Chile achieved a literacy rate of 98.6 percent in 2008, up from 91 percent in 1982. Life expectancy is 79 years and gross national income per capita in 2008 was $9,870. More than 95 percent of children complete primary school.[49] Infant mortality, the number of infant deaths per 1,000 live births, has gone from 120 in 1950 to 1955 to seven in 2005 to 2010.[50] Even before their window of opportunity, Chile had the foresight to introduce one of the first privately managed pension systems in 1981 under Augusto Pinochet, replacing the public pay-as-you-go pensions system. The "Chilean model" has since spread to Argentina (1994), Bolivia (1997), Colombia (1993), Costa Rica (1995), the Dominican Republic (2003), El Salvador (1998), Mexico (1997), Panama (2008), Peru (1993), and Uruguay (1996).[51] This actually puts the region ahead of the United States and Europe's government-run pay-as-you-go systems, as far as sustainability is concerned.

Chile's system of fully funded individual retirement accounts actually has helped the country take advantage of its demographic window of opportunity. Since its inception in 1981, the program has required workers to deposit 10 percent of their earnings into personal accounts managed by private pension funds, up to $2,427.[52] According to Eduardo Gallardo of *The New York Times:* "The mandate created a huge pool of capital that spurred a new wave of investment. Pension funds accumulated $111.4 billion by the end of 2007—70 percent of gross domestic product—and helped to drive growth in what became known as Chile's 'miracle' economy."[53] Since 1981, Chile has had an average of 62 percent of the population between the ages of 15 years and 59 years. The more people who are working, the more assets there are for investment in the pension funds.[54]

Chile's system is not without issues. Competition has decreased throughout the years, costs have increased, and coverage is not comprehensive; however, overall structural security is improved. Because Chile has been doing so well economically, it has been able to expand the program to those seniors who worked in the informal economy—about 1.2 million of them—and therefore would not have paid into the private system. These seniors are the most likely to suffer from poverty in old age. In March 2008, a law was enacted that expanded benefits to include a larger portion of the population, while also promoting gender equity, and encouraging greater competition within the pension fund industry.[55] At a time when more advanced industrial states are struggling to meet promises to seniors, in July 2008, nearly 600,000 poor Chilean seniors were scheduled to begin receiving $125 a month, followed by $158 a month in 2009—payouts well above the country's monthly urban poverty line of $95. Nearly two-thirds of elderly urban poor are projected to benefit from the payout by 2012.[56]

Part of the reason Chile has been so successful at capitalizing on its window of opportunity is the governance of the country. Chile is rated by Transparency International as the least corrupt country in South America and the 23rd least corrupt in the world.[57] Although Chile is by no means as rich as the most developed countries, as Transparency International points out: "Poverty does not necessarily need to entrap a country in a downward spiral of bad governance and economic deprivation. . . . Countries such as Bhutan, Botswana, Cape Verde, Chile, Jordan, Uruguay and some Caribbean islands continue to exhibit relatively low levels of perceived corruption despite being relatively low-income."[58] To continue along its positive path, Chile should raise retirement for women from age 60 to at least 65 (the age for men), given that women typically have a longer life expectancy. A woman born between 2005 and 2010 could expect to live, on average, to almost 82 years, whereas a male born during the same period only has a life expectancy of 75.5 years.[59] The pension system itself has reflected gender imbalances. "Since women generally live longer than men, but retire at a younger age and have lower account balances, women's pensions have been between 30 percent to 40 percent less than men's."[60]

On the whole, Latin America's favorable age structure could position the countries in the region to be stable partners to the more developed countries in the Western Hemisphere, particularly the United States and Canada, and could make them attractive trading and security partners for states in other regions, such as China. There are still a few factors that hinder the continued growth of this region, however. Recently, cocaine use has been increasing in the Southern Cone, as trafficking has spread southward on the South American continent and has recently become concentrated there. Today, South America is the third largest consumer market for cocaine. The problem is most intense in Argentina, where 2.6 percent of the adult population was estimated to use cocaine in 2006, up from 1.9 percent in 1999. Transnational aspects are important here, because the UN assesses that the consumption increase in the Southern region is linked to production increases in Bolivia and Peru.[61] Bolivia is still a youthful state, and Peru is young relative to Argentina and Chile, both of which are further along the demographic transition.

At the same time, the economic growth of the region is continuing. Brazil is leading the region's recovery after the downturn of 2009, and Brazil's economy grew at nine percent in the first quarter of 2010 from the same period last year. Brazil's central bank projects that growth in 2010 could reach 7.3 percent, which would be the country's fastest expansion in 24 years. Even Mexico's economy grew 4.3 percent in the first quarter of 2010. The economic success of Latin America in recent years "largely reflects a deepening engagement with Asia, where China and other countries are also growing fast." In 2009, China surpassed the United States as Brazil's top trading partner; China is also the second largest trading partner to Venezuela and Colombia.[62] Trade relations could spill over into national security issues for the United States, because Colombia has become a major ally for the United States in the region. Although commodities have played a large role in the economic success of the region, this has not been a bad thing for several of the countries. As an article from *The New York Times* reports: "Chile, for instance, saved revenues from copper exports when commodities prices climbed, allowing it to enact a stimulus plan last year and rebound from the February earthquake."[63]

## INDIA, BRAZIL, AND SOUTH AFRICA

The partnership of India, Brazil, and South Africa (IBSA) is a good case study of the opportunities transitional countries can have for increased cooperation among themselves, and their ability to band together as capable partners in global security and development efforts. These three states together formed an official partnership, the IBSA Dialogue Forum, in 2004 at the urging of South Africa, which saw cooperation among the three states as a way to increase the voice of Southern countries at the margins of the G-8. Since that time, IBSA has worked to raise the profile of issues and concerns of countries from the Global South—and of the three members in particular—within such forums as the UN, the UN Security Council, and the World Trade Organization. As Francis Kornegay of the Institute for Global Dialogue says: "The African Agenda [to promote the interests of Africa] also reflects the broader global mega-trend toward regional and sub-regional cooperation and integration as a process in what might be termed the regionalization of multipolarity."[64] Certainly, India, Brazil, and South Africa have much in common, as powerful emerging economies and as countries undergoing or completing the demographic transition. Brazil's fertility has already dropped below replacement level and was 1.9 in 2005 to 2010. India and South Africa are a bit behind, at 2.8 and 2.6, respectively, for the same time period.[65] The three states together have almost 1.5 billion people and a GDP of more than $3 trillion.[66]

Not only does the IBSA partnership elevate the interests of these states internationally, but this partnership has benefits to developed states, especially those interested in global stability, as well. If India, Brazil, and South Africa are stable and flourishing themselves, they can work to foster regional stability in their three respective regions. Each of these states is located in a region that has been the origin of transnational threats: South Africa with HIV/AIDS, Brazil with the drug trade, and India with extremism to the East and nuclear proliferation on the subcontinent. Regional stability is, of course, in these three states' best interest. A stable neighborhood creates conditions beneficial for economic growth and trade, and investment in the region. Additionally, there will be fewer problems with refugees or conflict that spills over the border.[67] Alleviating poverty in other, poorer countries of the Global South is one of the major goals of the group. For this purpose, they established the IBSA facility fund in 2004 as the vehicle through which they can finance poverty reduction programs in the Global South.[68] Thus far they have funded projects in Haiti, Guinea-Bissau, Timor-Leste, Burundi, Laos, and Cape Verde.[69] Of course, such efforts increase the soft power of these states not only individually, but of the partnership itself. South Africa could potentially work to support stabilization efforts in Sudan, India in Afghanistan and Pakistan, and Brazil with the South American drug trade.[70] Thus far, these respective efforts have not been the focus of the IBSA states, but would be in their best interests, because these achievements would go far towards stabilizing their regions.

One of the unique strengths of IBSA is that its three partners are all coastal states. This gives them the unique ability to contribute to naval security. Individually, they are each active in patrolling their respective regions of the globe. They have also joined forces for the trilateral maritime exercise, exercise IBSAMAR I, which took place in Southern African waters in early 2008. The second iteration is planned for the same area for late 2010. The Indian Navy already makes a significant commitment to patrolling for pirates in the Gulf of Aden, between Yemen and Somalia.[71] Brazil's 2008 National Defense Strategy outlined a plan for increasing their naval capabilities, as well. They want to develop the ability to monitor and control Brazilian airspace, territory, and jurisdictional waters. The adoption of land, sea, air, and space monitoring technologies could be used to support efforts in other regions, even natural disaster response. They explicitly say that they intend these capabilities not just for national defense, but also "[t]o expand the country's capacity to meet international commitments in terms of search and rescue. A priority task to the Country is the improvement of the existing means and training of the staff involved in search and rescue activities in the national territory, within the Brazilian jurisdictional waters, and in the areas Brazil is accountable for, as a result of international commitments."[72] Brazil would like to play a greater role in peacekeeping operations, whether under the UN or in support of regional multilateral organizations, because they believe "the strengthening of the collective security system is beneficial to world peace and to the national defense."[73] South Africa, too, has participated in international naval exercises with a number of militaries. South Africa has deployed defense capabilities in support of African Union and UN missions. In particular, the South African National Defense Forces have supported peace operations, and some postconflict reconstruction, in the Democratic Republic of the Congo, Burundi, Côte d'Ivoire, and Sudan.[74]

As with any partnership, there are still some hindrances to cooperation among the IBSA states. As Paolo Sotero, Director of the Brazil Institute at the Woodrow Wilson International Center for Scholars, notes, differences between Brazil and India regarding agricultural trade have played a part in the slow negotiations of the World Trade Organization's Doha Round.[75] As the weakest of the three states, South Africa probably needs the partnership more than the other states; whether this will also lead to an imbalance in influence within the partnership remains to be seen. To the extent that the partnership is successful, the growing power of India may be perceived as a particular military security risk to both Pakistan and China, two nuclear powers. There is currently little security cooperation with in the Indian subcontinent. If India pulls away from efforts to cooperate in the region and instead pours its energies into outward orientation, the lack of cooperation could continue to hinder efforts to stem threats from nonstate actors in the region and make the region more sensitive to diplomatic issues.[76] There are external ramifications as well. For example, the 2008 Mumbai bombings disrupted progress in India–Pakistan peace efforts. Demographically speaking, the unevenness of the demographic transition in India is an impediment to India's ability to take advantage of the demographic bonus. South Africa's struggles with HIV/AIDS are a similar challenge to further development. Brazil, despite its age structure, has problems with governance, particularly illicit drugs. Despite these challenges, the fact that during the late 1990s "Brazil's economy was struggling . . ., South Africa was emerging after apartheid, and India was preoccupied with regional nuclear threats," shows that these states have the capacity to overcome their challenges.[77] If global powers give up some power and delegate responsibility to these states, it is a double-edged sword; their burdens are lightened, but they concede negotiating power to IBSA.

## DEMOGRAPHIC CONVERGENCE

As these cases clearly show, the window of opportunity is an important time for states to develop the capacity and institutions they need for a smooth transition to a mature age structure. For many, though, the speed with which they are moving along the demographic transition to a mature age structure is an impediment to reaping any benefit. It is widely accepted that the demographic transition—when states change from having patterns of high fertility and high mortality to low rates of fertility and mortality—contributes to economic health and well-being. However, is there a minimum threshold for an infrastructure before this transition occurs for a state to reap the benefits? Conversely, what happens when the demographic transition occurs before an infrastructure is in place? Could a state actually be worse off? If these states start to age before they develop, they may lack the economic infrastructure to deal with the problems associated with population aging. Dr. Gro Harlem Bruntland, former Director General of the World Health Organization, famously said: "We must be fully aware that whilst developed countries became rich before they became old, developing countries will become old before they become rich."[78] The term "demographic convergence" expresses the phenomenon by which developing states begin to emulate developed states demographically. Although demographic transition has been thoroughly studied with regard to the West, questions still remain about how the demographic transition will affect developed states. Aging in the Global North is different than aging in the South, where development and aging are simultaneous challenges.

Although no developing state yet has a mature age structure, in just a few decades many of the states in the window of opportunity will. Using any of the UN fertility variants, Mexico will have about 15 percent of its population older than 60 years of age in 2025.[79] Whether they will have fully developed before then may determine how well they weather the aging challenge. There are a few reasons why demographic convergence is a problem that merits attention from a national security point of view. For the most part, the implications are structural, meaning that the biggest concern is the ability for an aging developing state to provide for its population. Insofar as they are concerned with humanitarian efforts, westerners should be attentive to any dynamic that threatens to undermine development, as a contracting workforce and growing proportions of elderly dependents could if the workforce is primarily low skilled and industry is labor intensive. There are also gender implications, because, worldwide, women typically have lower mortality rates than men; their longer life expectancies leave them a vulnerable segment of the population, because much of women's work is unpaid, and the death of the family wage earner (the husband) may leave some women without income or health care.

Because there are some developing states that do not have institutions set up—public or private  to care for elderly after they exit the workforce, the experience of aging in a country that is still developing can be quite different from aging in a developed country. Albert Hermalin et al. attempt to forecast what the educational attainment and family size characteristics of future elderly in 13 developing states will look like between the first decade of the millennium and 2045. Because these states are getting old before getting rich, "they may face a more limited range of societal responses to a situation where the future elderly have smaller kin networks while ongoing social trends, such as increased education and migration, have disrupted their traditional sources of support."[80] Future elderly in developing countries will have smaller kin support networks, but probably less coverage in old age coming from the state. Coresidence rates of elderly with children or grandchildren are much higher in developing countries than in industrialized countries. In the former, UN figures from the decade of the 1990s showed that the majority of those at older ages were residing with one or more children. Those who are never married are more vulnerable, because they do not have their spouse as a source of caregiving and support. In some countries, more than 10 percent of the women older than 65 are estimated to be never married by 2025; in South Africa, this number will reach about 20 percent.[81] Percentages for males are similar, although we should note that females tend to be more vulnerable both because of their longer life expectancy (they therefore need support longer past working age) and because of their lower labor force participation rates. As family sizes shrink, individual elderly will be less able to rely on their families for support, as they have traditionally done.

China, in particular, will face the simultaneous challenge of population aging and development in just a few decades. The aging of China could have national security implications for several reasons. One issue is that the world is becoming increasingly economically integrated, so there are economic implications for developed states if China's economy slows due to aging. Yet, when China does become an aging state, their experience with aging is likely to be very different from that of Europe and Japan, the latter of which have had long histories with economic growth and industrialization and, for Europe, an ingrained commitment to social welfare.

A brief comparison of China and Japan demonstrates how China's situation is unlike that of the industrialized great powers. The Japanese and Chinese "social contracts" are very dissimilar in obligations to the elderly. Unlike Japan, relatively few workers in China actually get a pension, either from the private or public sector. State-owned enterprises usually provide some sort of meager pension, but public-sector employment is no longer pervasive enough for this to translate into a real welfare system. Private companies do not necessarily provide any significant benefit for retirement. Individuals in China are not reliant on the state for their welfare. The Chinese government's share of the health burden is extraordinarily low compared with that of Japan. In 2003, the Chinese government paid only 36 percent of the total health bill, leaving 64 percent to private plans and families. Because very few families have private plans, we can conclude that households are picking up most of this burden. Indeed, 88 percent of the private expenditures are out-of-pocket. Although 64 percent of China's health expenditure is private, only 19 percent is private in Japan. This translates to a much higher household burden in China.[82]

Pension programs cannot be fueled by workers in pay-as-you-go systems; these systems are present in most industrialized states, and hence there are worries about the sustainability of these systems. In China, the government has relatively few social entitlement promises to its population—coverage of only 25 percent.[83] The lack of social entitlements is actually a bigger problem in China than overly generous promises. China currently has a very weak social welfare system, pensions are meager, and coverage is sparse. The state is not likely to move toward a universal pension system if it continues to place economic growth as one of its highest priorities. For the leadership, there is little perceived benefit to the Chinese economy from paying out significant benefits to the elderly, who are seen to be the least productive segment of society.

Although for Europe the worry is how to fund defense as elderly entitlements grow,[84] China will not face the same dilemma for several decades, because its working-age population has yet to peak. In addition, the Chinese leadership will likely not view the issue of whether to continue economic growth plans and defense or take care of seniors as a major moral dilemma. The Chinese government has so far demonstrated its willingness to reprioritize the environmental health of the nation, the physical health of its citizens, and democratic freedoms to meet economic, military, and geopolitical goals. More important from a budgetary standpoint, although absolute numbers of elderly will increase, absolute numbers of workers will also increase; China will stay relatively young compared with the other great powers in the next couple of decades. We cannot be sure of the degree to which China will capitalize on its favorable age structure during the next half century, and how its economy and military will change as a result. Thus, there is limited utility to comparing contemporary Europe and Japan with future China.

Aging will indeed become a major demographic issue for China, but not the only one. Urbanization is likely to be much more important. If aging creates an unstable China, there are a few possible scenarios that would have negative implications for the United States. The first is if the Chinese regime looks upon its graying future and feels that it must act while its power is ascendant to achieve international objectives that require military force, such as unification with Taiwan. The second is if China becomes embroiled in conflict with any of its other neighbors, especially India, which could face similar instabilities from its population trends (including differential growth of various ethnic and religious groups). Third, if the Chinese government reasserts power over its domestic population and becomes even more authoritarian, the economy could suffer. Future treatment of the elderly is very likely to become a controversial political issue in an industrializing and urbanizing China. The Chinese people are still vulnerable to the state, and will likely be marginalized as the state chooses national goals over humanitarian ones. What happens in

China may well be a harbinger of things to come in the less industrialized world. India will face some similar challenges when its population ages, but has more immediate demographic trends—in particular, continued population growth—that should be at the forefront of analyses of power.

## CONCLUSION

The window of opportunity afforded by transitional age structures is just that: an excellent opportunity to increase military, regime, and structural security. Not only do states with transitional age structures have these opportunities, but other states can take advantage of transitional countries' likely growing economies, peaceful and democratic governance, and social stability. The United States, for example, should pursue partnerships with Latin American countries to help support their missions, and regional trade could continue to be mutually beneficial. It is important for these states to develop sustainable pension and health care systems. These states must invest in future generations through education and employment opportunities, and simultaneously prepare to take care of older generations.

There are several strategic states in the midst of the transition that the international security community could work to foster stability in and build partnership capacity, as Table 4.3 shows.

There are also several key states that world leaders should invest time and attention toward helping along the demographic transition and positioning to take advantage of a future window of opportunity. Pakistan, in particular, would be valuable as a stable and competent partner in the South/Central Asian region. Yet, the country is making little progress on key indicators. Fertility is still high, an average of four children per woman, although it was 6.5 20 years ago. If fertility continues to decrease along the lines of the UN's medium projection, Pakistan could enter the window of opportunity in another 20 years.[85] Even so, the population will grow from 185 million in 2010 to 266 million in 2030 and 335 million by 2050. If fertility is not reduced, and instead stays constant, Pakistan's population in 2030 will be 29 million higher and could reach 460 million in 2050. Given that literacy is only 54 percent, there needs to be a lot of progress for the country to reap the benefits of an older age structure.[86]

Although demographic convergence—when developing states begin to emulate developed states demographically—is occurring, aging in developing countries is a problem of the future, not the present. States with transitional age structures need to position themselves to take full advantage of their window of opportunity by making the necessary economic reforms, rooting out corruption to encourage savings and investment, and establishing strong education and health care infrastructures. Developed countries should not focus

**Table 4.3** Key States Progressing through the Demographic Transition

| State and Year | 0 to 14 Years | 15 to 59 Years | 60 Years and Older |
|---|---|---|---|
| Brazil | | | |
| 1970 | 42.4 | 51.9 | 5.7 |
| 2010 | 25.5 | 64.4 | 10.2 |
| 2030 | 20.1 | 61.9 | 18.0 |
| Indonesia | | | |
| 1970 | 42.4 | 52.4 | 5.2 |
| 2010 | 26.7 | 64.4 | 8.9 |
| 2030 | 22.6 | 62.0 | 15.3 |
| Iran | | | |
| 1970 | 44.6 | 49.7 | 5.8 |
| 2010 | 23.8 | 69 | 7.1 |
| 2030 | 19.6 | 66.8 | 13.6 |
| Mexico | | | |
| 1970 | 46.6 | 47.9 | 5.5 |
| 2010 | 27.9 | 62.7 | 9.4 |
| 2030 | 22.6 | 60.5 | 16.9 |

*Source:* "World Population Prospects: The 2008 Revision Population Database." New York: United Nations, 2009.

too much on the aging of developing states, because this would lead them to underestimate the economic and military potential of states like Brazil, India, and China. When countries currently in the window age, their experiences are likely to be different from those in Europe and Japan. Many states in Latin America are already ahead of Europe and the United States in implementing privately funded pension systems that are more sustainable and take some of the burden off the state. Trade-offs between spending on social welfare and on defense may not occur in some developing states, because the government has fewer social welfare obligations to the population. However, if it is up to the citizens to cover themselves and they are unable to do so, there could be social unrest as citizens demand more from their governments. Though we usually think of student movements when we think of protest, older people certainly also protest. During a trip to Poland during the summer of 2009, I witnessed this first hand as retirees protested for housing reform in the Krakow city center. Examples from China, the United States with Tea Party activists, and protests in Bangkok in March 2010 also show that elderly people are willing to protest.

Some states in the window of opportunity are actually better positioned to age than states that are already aging. Many Latin American states implemented private pension systems, at the recommendation of the World Bank, in the 1990s; Europe is actually trying to catch up. Chile, which had the first privately funded pension system, has been the leader, having embarked on this system during the 1980s. Developing states, especially those of middle income that may be in the window of opportunity, will experience many different demographic trends between now and 2050. A focus on future experiences with aging can cause us to lose sight of current trends, including growth and urbanization.

# 5
Chapter

# Migration and Internally Displaced Persons

At the beginning of 2007, around 2,000 Iraqis fled the country each day and during that summer 802,860 people were displaced within the country in a one-month time frame.[1] The speed and scale of Iraq's internal and external migration threw together people of different nationalities, religions, and ideologies, creating the potential, though not necessarily the spark, for conflict. Migration has a unique relationship to national security. Fertility and mortality, two drivers of demographic change, can dramatically alter a country's growth rates and age structure, and present numerous challenges and opportunities for security. Migration, the movement of people across international borders, is the third pillar of demographic change but is the only population driver that can change the composition of a state or a community within months, weeks, or even days. Fertility and mortality look glacial in comparison.

Speed is not the only reason to focus on migration, though. Migration is not just about the movement of people; it is about the movement of their interests, values, politics, religion, and customs. Mass migration can alter a country's religious, ethnic, gender, age, political, and cultural landscape within a much shorter time than birth and death cycles. For the most part, migration, whether for political, economic, or family reasons, can benefit migrants by giving them a better life; it can benefit receiving states by providing specialized skills or labor; and it can benefit sending countries by providing a release valve for a crowded labor market and high unemployment or by providing remittances. In some cases, though, migration can create major national security challenges. Just as with youthful age structures, there is a reciprocal relationship between migration and conflict. In many parts of the world, especially the Middle East and Africa, migration itself is often conflict driven, as the Iraq example shows. At the same time, refugees also carry their domestic political skirmishes across borders and their presence can, in some cases, catalyze or exacerbate conflict. Within countries there are similar issues with internally displaced persons (IDPs). Refugees and IDPs are outside the economic sending and receiving patterns that frequently drive migration. By definition, they are displaced by emergency situations, which pose a very different kind of security problem. A receiving state may face regime or structural issues with the influx of new participants in the governance process. If the individuals are displaced internally, they can create additional pressures on a community that is already stressed. Likewise refugees who are internationally displaced, can strain the labor markets, educational systems, and even physical infrastructure, like water resources, of their receiving community. The plight of refugees and IDPs makes it difficult to find any positive attributes to this aspect of migration, except perhaps the safety of migrants themselves.

Migration affects developed and less developed countries differently, and security implications vary widely for both. In the aging developed countries, migrants often face xenophobia and even racism, as those "receiving" countries struggle with questions over identity, nationalism, and economic equality. In Germany, for example, Turkish migrants are poorly integrated into society and are often ostracized. However, for aging states, migration also brings the opportunity to shore up the working-age population. Where the "native" population experiences low fertility and increasing numbers of elderly dependents, migrants can help the working-age population grow, and their often higher fertility rates slow the process of aging. Part of the reason the United States and Canada have relatively less of an aging problem compared with Europe or Japan is the high levels of migration to those North American states. Migration into advanced industrial democracies affects military security in a positive way by providing more people of working age who can contribute to the economy and serve in the military. The United States, in particular, has seen both economic and military benefits of migrants, who have a relatively high propensity for military service.

Yet, for receiving countries, migration can also create regime insecurity when questions of identity turn into political challenges and even conflict. These identity clashes securitize migration, and stopping migration can take on symbolic status since, as scholar William Durch phrases the xenophobic sentiment, "if the state cannot defend its borders against ragged civilian hordes, what can it defend against?"[2] Much of the world's migration takes place among less developed countries, and these questions of identity and conflict are salient there as well. About 40 percent of international migrants move from one less developed country to another.[3]

When less developed countries are the "senders" of migrants, they face their own challenges with brain drain to more developed economies and, as a result, they may suffer from a weak professional class of doctors, administrators, and teachers, creating structural insecurity as the state's capacity to meet the needs of the population is challenged. Remittances may mitigate the near-term economic impacts, because these expatriates can provide a substantial proportion of a sending country's revenue. With the right governance to capitalize on these income flows, sending countries can use remittances to develop at home. In this sense, emigration can actually create structural security by increasing the capacity of the state.

Of all the demographic trends, migration is hardest to predict. Population flows wax and wane depending on global and local economies, political developments, and, as has been increasingly recognized, on changes in environmental conditions. The variety of causes means that the security implications of migration are broad. There are some obvious links to conflict—refugees and IDPs—and more subtle connections between the changes in national identity that migrants can bring, and political and social resistance to those changes. Although this chapter will work to establish clear connections between migration and the three realms of national security, Fiona Adamson, an expert on migration and security, reminds us that states' responses are essential in determining the outcome. She says: "Here, again, the intervening variable between migration and national security is policy: if states have the capacity to design and implement effective policies that 'harness the power of migration,' international migration flows can enhance, rather than detract from or compromise, state power."[4] Policies like protection of minority rights and inclusive educational institutions may help.

The following sections focus on a few issues regarding migration, particularly how migrants directly engage in conflict and how their very presence creates insecurity. The first section explores how international refugee flows and internal displacement, although often driven by conflict, can themselves create or exacerbate conflict through refugee militarization or clashes of interest and identity brought about by large-scale migration. The next section focuses on the insecurity perceived and experienced by developed states that receive migrants, mostly in search of economic opportunities. The final section discusses how emigration creates economic opportunities for sending states, but can also drain human capital that could provide the foundation for development and increasing structural security. Finally, the chapter concludes by discussing the emerging literature on migration and climate change, and some challenges for policy with securitizing migration.

## REFUGEES AND INTERNALLY DISPLACED PERSONS

Between July 14 and 18, 1994, the largest and quickest mass exodus in history took place as approximately 850,000 people, primarily Hutus, fled Rwanda into Eastern Zaire. Most were not actually fleeing the genocide, which had basically ended around the middle of 1994, but were forcibly marched by the recently ousted government before the Tutsi Rwandan Patriotic Front could take over and possibly seek retribution for genocide.[5] When we think of the relationship between refugees and conflict, we generally think about cases like Rwanda's—the ways that conflict causes insecurity for individuals and therefore creates refugees. Thanks to a cessation of numerous conflicts in Africa and Central America, there was a general drop in the number of refugees in developing regions between 1990 and 2005, from 16.5 million to around 10.8 million.[6] However, since then the situation has again grown worse for many other areas. In 2008, the United Nations High Commission for Refugees (UNHCR) and the United Nations Relief and Works Agency (UNRWA) estimated that Arab countries host approximately 7.5 million refugees, 47 percent of the 16 million global refugees registered under those bodies for 2008.[7] The largest number are Palestinians and Iraqis, mostly relocated to Jordan, Syria, and Palestine. Jordan's 1994 census showed 44 percent of the population was Palestinian refugees and displaced persons.[8] The jump in refugees since 2005 in these places has been dramatic. In 2008, Jordan's total population of refugees, asylum seekers, and stateless persons (what the UN calls "persons of concern") went from 17,544 in 2005 to 501,110 in January 2010. In Syria, the number increased from 328,006 to 1,055,810 during the same time period.[9] IDPs, those who are displaced but who have not crossed an international border, add millions more to ranks of those forced to move. The Internal Displacement Monitoring Centre, operating out of Geneva, Switzerland, estimated that there were 26 million IDPs around the world at the end of 2008. Of these, the UNHCR helped about 14.4 million in 22 countries, including Sudan, Colombia, and Iraq, who host the three largest IDP populations.[10] The number of IDPs worldwide has steadily increased from 17,400,000 in 1997 to 27,100,000 in 2009.[11]

Refugees and IDPs are a special class of migrants, because by definition they are intimately connected with conflict. As the preceding statistics show, conflict clearly creates insecurity for individuals, leading to refugees and IDPs, but refugees and IDPs can themselves create insecurity in the military, regime, and structural realms; these instances are the focus of this section. Refugees create military insecurity when they become militarized and used as tools in ongoing conflicts. Fleeing one's home country does not guarantee an improvement in living conditions. Often, refugees will seek asylum in neighboring countries, which may also be in the midst of conflict.[12] This was the case for Rwanda, whose neighbors were also in the midst of conflict, even as there were large influxes of people, exacerbating tensions in Africa during the 1990s.[13] IDPs may create conditions for regime insecurity when they are seen as encroaching on the territory of others, such as indigenous groups.

The first area to explore is refugee militarization. Certainly, the majority of refugees are victims of their circumstances, but some refugees engage in political violence and are manipulated by warring groups, including states. About 15 percent of refugee crises involve refugee militarization. During the 1990s, this happened in Sudan, Liberia, West Bank/Gaza, Afghanistan, Rwanda, Bosnia, East Timor, and Burundi.[14] Stephen John Stedman and Fred Tanner refer to this subset of refugees as "refugee warriors," defined as "disaffected individuals, who—with the assistance of overseas diasporas, host governments, and interested states—equip themselves for battle to retrieve an idealized, mythical lost community." They say that this phenomenon "has turned refugees into resources that can help prolong civil wars and threaten the security of surrounding regions. Any army that loses a civil war on its own turf need not admit defeat as long as it can regroup in exile, make claims on refugees, and use international assistance to recover."[15] Aristide Zolberg et al. define refugee warriors as "highly conscious refugee communities with a political leadership structure and armed sections engaged in warfare for a political objective, be it to recapture the homeland, change the regime, or secure a separate state."[16] These refugee warriors generally operate across international borders to disrupt governance in their homeland. Refugee warriors can be created by a host of circumstances, even involving the world's most powerful states. As Stedman and Tanner say: "During the [C]old [W]ar the manipulation of refugees and the refugee regime became part of the struggle between the superpowers . . . the United States aided the manipulation of Afghan refugee camps in Pakistan in the 1980s in order to create a potent armed force capable of defeating the Soviet army occupying Afghanistan."[17] Refugee militarization is relevant to national security for at least two reasons: it can cause conflict to spill over borders; and militarization allows combatants to regroup in exile, using aid and remittances to fund conflict.

The first implication to consider is the way that refugee militarization facilitates the spread of conflict. Warrior refugees may engage in several types of violence, including cross-border attacks between the sending state and the refugees. For example, from their refuge in Uganda, Rwandan Tutsi refugees launched an invasion of Rwanda that sparked a civil war and genocide.[18] According to Daniel Byman and Kenneth Pollack, the fall of the Zairean ruler Mobutu Sese Seko and the subsequent civil war in the Democratic Republic of the Congo (formerly Zaire), which claimed roughly four million lives, can be traced directly to the arrival of Rwandan refugees in 1994.[19] In the Middle East, the cross-border attacks between Palestinians and Israelis played a role in provoking the 1956 and 1967 Arab–Israeli wars. Within states, attacks between the receiving/host state and refugees are another common type of violence. There may also be ethnic or factional violence between the refugees. For example, there was conflict in Burundian Hutu camps in Tanzania, which threatened that state's security, and conflict between the Palestinian Liberation Organization and other rival organizations in Lebanon during the 1980s and '90s.[20]

In Jordan and Lebanon, the refugees turned their anger against their host states, sparking civil wars in 1970 and 1971, and 1975 and 1990, respectively. The civil instability caused by some refugees is a direct regime security implication. As Daniel Byman and Keith Pollack say: "The 'Palestinian question'—and the paltry Arab-state reaction to it—has also contributed to coups by militant Arab nationalists in Egypt, Iraq, and Syria."[21]

The second connection to national security is the way that refugee camps may allow combatants to regroup in exile and use aid and remittances to fund their efforts. A special class of refugees are those that face long-term persecution, with little to no hope of returning to their homeland. These refugees may form a de facto "state in exile." Highly organized, these refugees become more prone to violence over time, if leaders are able to unite the refugees in political and military action.[22] Often, the leadership may use international aid to fund their activities. One of the most well-known examples is Palestinians forming the Palestinian Liberation Organization. Their modern refugee problem began when 750,000 Palestinians fled their homes after the 1947–1948 war in British-mandated Palestine. These families and individuals sought refuge in hastily built camps in the West Bank, Gaza, Lebanon, Syria, Jordan, and Egypt, provided by a number of relief agencies. In December 1949, the UNRWA was established specifically to manage these refugee camps and to provide education, health, relief, and social services, and income generation assistance through programs like microcredit and vocational training.[23] Unfortunately, "[j]ust as political entrepreneurs can mobilize resources and political support for a conflict within diasporas in Western industrial states, refugee populations can also provide a base for political mobilization activities in conflicts."[24] Some political entrepreneurs use humanitarian relief as a resource of war. In Rwanda, humanitarian aid and the refugee camp structure actually facilitated the conflict. The organizers of the genocide were able to blend into the camps in Zaire and draw on the humanitarian aid to meet their needs so they could focus on conducting attacks across the border in Rwanda.[25] Given the small percentage of refugees who are militarized, halting aid would mostly harm those who are merely victims. Ending the conflicts that created camps in the first place is the obvious, though most challenging, solution.

In addition to aid, refugee militarization is often supported through diaspora funding, where dispersed populations are funding the cause back home. Writing for the World Bank, Paul Collier found that diaspora funding helped provide resources for violent conflicts during the 1990s. Indeed, "countries experiencing violent conflict that had significant diaspora populations abroad were six times likelier to experience a recurrence of conflict than states without such populations."[26] It is possible that diaspora funding could prolong conflicts when those with the will to fight are removed from the consequences of the fight.

In addition to refugees, which are designated by the crossing of international borders, internally displaced persons can also change the composition of a subnational population, and this also has implications for stability. James Fearon and David Laitin have identified what they term "sons of the soil" conflicts between groups that consider themselves "indigenous" and incoming domestic migrants from other ethnic regions. Though their theory is not based on the issue of IDPs, it is relevant to this situation as well. Migration changes the balance of power in a region and leads to competition over scarce resources such as land and jobs.[27] Conflict in Iraq has created huge numbers of IDPs (see Table 5.1). As a result of the scale, in 2007, individual governorates within Iraq began to restrict IDP entry because of concerns that IDPs were creating conflict locally or were collaborating with insurgents, and because of the strain that the increasing numbers were placing on resources. Even as the security situation improves, many IDPs are unable to return home because of the expense. Many have been unable to file a request to transfer their food ration cards, which also provide fuel.[28]

In addition to creating international and civil conflict, the presence of refugees and IDPs can also exacerbate structural and regime insecurity in other ways. One way is through lack of protection for migrants themselves, or their own structural insecurity. In September 2007, there were a total of 4.5 million internally and externally displaced Iraqis, and most were in Syria (1.2–1.4 million) and Jordan (450,000–500,000).[29] Although the outside world would consider Iraqis displaced into neighboring countries as refugees, in their host countries, like Jordan and Syria, they have not been labeled as such, in part for fear that doing so will announce the permanency of their plight and discourage the possibility of return. It is because Palestinians were given citizenship rights in Jordan that Iraqis are not granted citizenship; Jordan fears that, like the Palestinians, the Iraqis might not resettle in Iraq, but may instead remain in Jordan. Lack of official designation hurts the Iraqis, because it may limit their ability to register for official status and receive assistance and protection.[30] Syria, Jordan, and Lebanon are actually not signatories to the 1951 UN Convention on the Status of Refugees, and so, in general, refugees there have limited and frequently shifting legal protection; most refugees are lucky to receive tourist visas. Many Iraqis fear that an entire generation of Iraqi children may end up without formal schooling, although the Jordanian government is allowing Iraqis access to public education and the Syrians have begun to allow more children access. Lack of jobs and second-class status also mean that the majority of Iraqis cannot find employment.[31]

The economic strains and social discord between refugees and citizens of the host state can create regime insecurity. Resentment between local populations and migrants is a particular problem when resources are scarce and competition over them increases. To avoid competition with their citizens, Jordan and Lebanon prohibit most Iraqis, except some highly skilled professionals,

**Table 5.1** Number of Internally Displaced Persons (IDPs), Selected Countries (2007)

| Country | No. of IDPs | Reason |
|---|---|---|
| Afghanistan | 132,246 | Mostly Pashtuns and Kuchis displaced in South and West because of drought and instability |
| Angola | 61,700 | Twenty-seven-year civil war ending in 2002; four million IDPs already have returned |
| Azerbaijan | 580,000–690,000 | Conflict with Armenia over Nagorno–Karbakh |
| Bangladesh | 65,000 | Land conflict, religious persecution |
| Bosnia and Herzegovina | 131,600 | Bosnian Croats, Serbs, and Bosniaks displaced in 1992–1995 war |
| Burma | 503,000 | Government offensives against ethnic insurgent groups near Eastern borders |
| Burundi | 100,000 | Armed conflict between government and rebels |
| Central African Republic | 197,000 | Ongoing unrest following 2003 coup |
| Chad | 178,918 | N/A* |
| China | 90,000 | N/A* |
| Colombia | 1,800,000–3,500,000 | Conflict between government and illegal armed groups and drug traffickers |
| Congo, Democratic Republic of the | 1,400,000 | Fighting between government forces and rebels since mid 1990s |
| Congo, Republic of the | 48,000 | Multiple civil wars since 1992 |
| Côte d'Ivoire | 709,000 | 2002 coup |
| Cyprus | 210,000 | Turkish and Greek Cypriots, many displaced for more than 30 years |
| Ethiopia | 200,000 | Border war with Eritrea from 1998 to 2000, ethnic clashes in Gambela, and ongoing Ethiopian military counterinsurgency in Somali region |
| Georgia | 220,000–240,000 | Displaced from Akbhazia and South Ossetia |
| India | 600,000 | About half are Kashmiri Pandits from Jammu and Kashmir |

**Table 5.1** (*Continued*)

| Country | No. of IDPs | Reason |
|---|---|---|
| Indonesia | 200,000–350,000 | Government offensives against rebels in Aceh |
| Iraq | 2,400,000 | Ongoing U.S.-led war and ethnosectarian violence |
| Israel | 150,000–420,000 | Arab villagers displaced from homes in Northern Israel |
| Jordan | 160,000 | 1967 Arab–Israeli War |
| Kenya | 250,000–400,000 | 2007 Postelection violence; Kenya African National Union (KANU) attacks on opposition tribal groups in 1990s |
| Liberia | 13,000 | Civil war from 1990 to 2004; IDP resettlement began in November 2004 |
| Montenegro | 16,192 | Ethnic conflict in 1999 and riots in 2004 |
| Nepal | 50,000–70,000 | Remaining from 10-year Maoist insurgency that officially ended in 2006 |
| Peru | 60,000–150,000 | Civil war from 1980 to 2000; most IDPs are indigenous peasants in Andean and Amazonian regions |
| Philippines | 300,000 | Fighting between government troops and Moro Islamic Liberation Front (MILF) and Abu Sayyaf groups |
| Russia | 18,000–160,000 | Displaced from Chechnya and North Ossetia |
| Senegal | 22,400 | Approximately 65% of the IDP population returned in 2005, but new displacement is occurring as a result of clashes between government troops and separatists in the Casamance region |
| Somalia | 1,100,000 | Civil war since 1988, clan-based competition for resources |
| Sri Lanka | 460,000 | Both Tamils and non-Tamils displaced because of long-term civil war between the government and the separatist Liberation Tigers of Tamil Eelam |
| Sudan | 5,300,000–6,200,000 | Civil war from 1983 to 2005; ongoing conflict in Darfur region |

(*Continued*)

**Table 5.1** (*Continued*)

| Country | No. of IDPs | Reason |
|---|---|---|
| Syria | 305,000 | Most displaced from Golan Heights during the 1967 Arab–Israeli War |
| Turkey | 1,000,000–1,200,000 | Fighting from 1984 to 1999 between Kurdistan Workers' Party (PKK) and Turkish military; most IDPs in Southeastern provinces |
| Uganda | 1,270,000 | 350,000 IDPs returned in 2006 after ongoing peace talks between the Lord's Resistance Army and the government of Uganda |
| Zimbabwe | 569,685 | Mugabe-led political violence, human rights violations, land reform, and economic collapse |

*The CIA does not list a reason for these conflicts.

*Source:* Central Intelligence Agency. *CIA World Factbook,* accessed June 19, 2010, http://www.cia.gov.

from working.[32] Still, the presence of refugees can affect the local economy. For example, Jordan has had major cost of living increases due to the influx of people. The consumer price index has been on the rise, and housing costs increased by 300 percent between roughly 2004 and 2008, as more people has meant increased demand for housing.[33] The perception that refugees are straining the economy may be as important as their actual strains. Citizens in both Jordan and Syria blame Iraqi refugees for the rising prices of real estate, rent, and food; overcrowded schools and health facilities; and shortages of electricity and water.[34] The Syrian government estimates that it costs them $1 billion a year to host Iraqi refugees, and the country is already plagued by high unemployment and a weak economy.[35] Yet, with some exceptions, the migration of Iraqi refugees into Syria and Jordan has not resulted in the eruption of sectarian violence many expected to occur. Part of the reason may be that the refugees do not have the means to rebel, because they spend much of their time worrying about basic needs. Another reason may be that the flow of refugees is dynamic. Unlike Palestinian refugees to Syria and Jordan, Iraqi refugees are not permanently settling on the same scale. The refugees who have been living in places like Syria are returning to Iraq, not because the country is necessarily safer now, but because they are having legal and financial difficulties in Syria.[36]

Discussing the militarization of refugees creates the same dilemma we face with other population trends in this book: How do we explore and acknowledge the security implications of refugee populations without making the refugees themselves the enemy? We can, to some extent, separate refugees as victims from refugees as perpetrators or tools of war (although refugees as tools of war are often victims). But, the fact that any refugees are militarized creates another dilemma. As Stedman and Tanner phrase it: How can agents "provide for the comfort and safety of refugees without furthering the political and military goals of those who control access to them and hence prolonging the war and their suffering?"[37] Refugees can make positive contributions to the societies that accept them, but the small percentage that are militarized and the large numbers that overwhelm their receiving states and areas can end up decreasing security for their host states. Part of the problem is the duration of conflict. Life in a refugee camp can be a different experience for those adults who suddenly find themselves displaced, versus children who grow up knowing no other home. For youth in refugee camps resulting from protracted conflicts, they have been entirely raised in camps and thus often prefer to stay there than go "home." As one third-generation female living in Syria said, "I feel I belong to Yarmouk camp, even if I am asked in the future to choose between staying here in Yarmouk camp or returning to Loubieh (Palestine) I would prefer to stay here. I went to primary and preparatory UNRWA schools here and met all my friends here."[38] As these generations grow up in refugee camps under such stressful conditions, a permanent solution to their plight and long-term prospects for peace are both jeopardized. Stedman and Tanner argue that there have been few sustained efforts to stop refugee manipulation. They also criticize the world powers and the UN Security Council for treating refugee manipulation as a humanitarian problem, instead of as a security problem.

Another part of the problem is the capacity to deal with the refugee situation in general. Many times, neither international institutions nor state and local governments are prepared to deal with the massive scale of refugees and internal displacement. As William Durch says: "The West designed the current UN refugee convention for individuals, not masses, and for transit across the Iron Curtain, not the Caribbean or the Adriatic."[39] As the world's population has rapidly grown, particularly in areas already plagued with conflict and instability, the sheer number of people who are at risk of being displaced has risen as well. The ability of states to control their borders and prevent refugees from entering is a key variable of state capacity, but many states want to help refugees. Receiving states need both the capability to secure their borders and to demilitarize refugees, but they also have to have the desire to prevent violence. As Lischer says: "The spread of civil war is likely in situations where a capable state allies with militant refugees or where an incapable receiving state cannot control militarism. Conversely, a highly capable receiving state with no sympathy for the refugees' militant aims can forestall the spread of civil war."[40] The receiving state actually bears the primary responsibility for ensuring the safety of the refugees and preventing militarization, according to international law.[41] This seems to be an important point, because it puts the burden on the receiving state, which may already be weak, like in the case of most African nations.


## REGIME SECURITY AND IDENTITY

> . . . encircled by seven billion people, only seven hundred million of them white, hardly a third of them in our little Europe, and those no longer in bloom but quite old. They face a vanguard of four hundred million North Africans and Muslims, fifty percent of them less than twenty years old, those on the opposite shores of the Mediterranean arriving ahead of the rest of the world! Can one imagine for a second, in the name of whatever ostrich-like blindness, that such a disequilibrium can endure?
>
> —Raspail (2007, xv)

In 1973, French author Jean Raspail published an apocalyptic parable describing a human tide of poor, hungry, and desperate migrants invading the shores of France and ending bucolic European life. Although the story takes place over a three-day period on the Southern French coast, Raspail once predicted that "in actuality, the unraveling will not take place in three days but, almost certainly, after many convulsions, during the first decades of the third millennium."[42] Raspail's views reflect the fears that often surround migration. When people move, so do their politics, their culture, and their religion. When these values clash, or are perceived to clash, with the values of the society they move into, these differences create regime insecurity. Certainly, migration into the Global North has always been controversial, but lately the security community has become increasingly concerned about internal instability arising over the debates about national identity stirred by migration. Reactions to migration in the Global North—whether Russian fears of a Chinese invasion of the Far East, or German fears of a Turkish invasion—are often more about perception than they are about absolute numbers of migrants. In fact, *overreaction* to migration can itself be a security risk, if it prompts action. As Jack Goldstone says, "[E]conomic migration often leads to substantial benefits for both migrants and the destination country. What appears to matter for conflict are those cases wherein migration leads to clashes of national identity."[43] Emphasizing the importance of perception and the academic community's complicity in creating that perception, Aristide Zolberg harshly criticizes a set of contemporary authors for perpetuating racist attitudes against the current wave of immigrants. Zolberg argues that the 20th century was not the "age of migration" as the well-known book by Castles and Miller would have us believe.[44] Rather, "the proportion of foreign-born remained at the same level between

1965 and 2000, approximately 2.3 percent, indicating that international migration grew at about the same rate as world population."[45] Whether real or perceived, migration often sparks heated discussions and sometimes violence as competition for resources increases and cultures conflict.

Between 1990 and 2005, developed countries took in 33 million out of 36 million migrants. In 2005, 28 countries accounted for 75 percent of all international migrants worldwide; the United States, Russia, and Germany were the three biggest host countries.[46] This section focuses on the regime security implications of migration into Europe, a region with large migration flows that has experienced political clashes over identity. Developed countries often play both ends against the middle when it comes to migration. They welcome highly skilled migrants or laborers that will do work in difficult industries, yet they are less welcoming of migrants' cultural, religious, or political views. It is no accident that international migration patterns tend to involve the mixing of people who are culturally distinct, because international development is uneven.[47] Therefore, one obvious implication is that if developed countries do not want immigrants from the Global South, they should work to boost the development of sending regions. But is stopping immigration to preserve identity in the best interest of the North? Regime and military security goals may be incompatible, because migration contributes economically and militarily, increasing state power, at the same time that clashes over identity create social and political fissures that can turn violent. At some level, economic and social goals may be at odds. The North quite possibly cannot have their cake and eat it too.

European states have a reputation of being culturally proud and frequently nationalistic, and, like many states, also have a long history as both sender and receiver of migrants. In the past, European states have often opened to migration when faced with severe labor shortages. Indeed, the Black Death was once a great impetus for migration. In an effort to entice laborers to stay, the city of Siena, Italy, hard-hit by the plague, extended citizenship to foreigners and their families who came to Siena and stayed at least five years in the aftermath of the plague.[48] Today's Italians are starkly divided on immigration. Given that theirs is one of the world's most aged countries, some Italians argue that migration is necessary to keep the workforce robust enough to support retirees. Others are unwilling to accept migration as the solution. For example, Italy's Northern League political party often runs on an anti-immigrant platform.[49] Italy provides a good example of the tensions and contradictions surrounding migration in Europe today. Although many Italians know that migration is necessary to make up for labor shortages in one of the world's oldest countries, the introduction and growth of new cultures, languages, and ideas create a backlash that disrupts social cohesion.

In Europe, the main connections between migration and national security are in the realms of military and regime security. Migration affects military

security because it is possible that controversies and tensions over migration could undermine the expansion and/or cohesion of both NATO and the
EU—two key collective security organizations. According to Jeffrey Simon,
writing for the U.S. National Defense University, the different ethnic backgrounds of migrants into the United States (Hispanic, Asian) and Europe (Arab,
Southeast Asian) will pull the two sides in different directions.[50] Depending on
the degree to which the domestic institutions of each empower immigrant
groups and turn politicians' interests toward their concerns, Simon's predic-
tion could come true. However, in the United State's case, despite large proportions of migrants from Central and South America, there is little evidence
that the United States is shifting attention southward. Though there was a
call to pay more attention to Brazil in the most recent Quadrennial Defense
Review published by the U.S. Department of Defense, the United States does
not seem to have shifted its overall strategy.[51] For Europe, the implications
may be slightly different. There is the possibility that European policy makers
will begin to focus more on internal stability than outward projection of force,
because the military is strained as a result of population aging and domestic
diversity is meeting with resistance. The extent to which focus shifts internally
may determine Europe's commitment to NATO.

Migration is becoming increasingly important as a means of mitigating
population aging and labor shortages, yet internal instability between immigrants and native born over representation, resources, and the questions of
identity that grow out of diversity could affect the future of the European
Union as well. A brief description of the immigration and citizenship statistics
and laws for Europe will help explain why. When people are able to acquire
status as EU nationals, they benefit from the liberal laws for internal freedom
of movement. EU nationals are allowed to travel to another EU member state
and "live, study, or work on an equal basis with native-born residents." Only
public-sector jobs can be restricted to residents born in the country.[52] During
2006, the countries of the EU-27 granted approximately 735,000 new citizenships. France, Germany, and the United Kingdom granted the most—about 60
percent of the total from 2002 to 2006. Most of the new citizens were previous
citizens of European countries outside the EU and of African countries. In
2006, 27 percent of new citizens were former citizens of an African country and
22 percent were from Asia. Turkey and Morocco were the main countries of
previous citizenship, making up 17 percent of total citizenship grants. Citizens
of Iraq, Ecuador, Serbia and Montenegro, and Algeria were also numerous. On
average, between 2004 and 2006, about 725,000 persons have been granted
citizenships annually, for a total of almost 2.2 million citizenships.[53] Although
there has been talk of Turkey joining the EU for a long time, fear over clashes
of identity—particularly between secular Europeans and Muslim Turks—is a
major stumbling block. Of course, there are many other hindrances, such as

concerns that Turkey's economy is too underdeveloped and will bring the EU down, but frequently those fears are couched in or turn into conversations about identity.

Even when religion is absent from the debate, other differences rise to the fore. About 3.4 million Turks live in Western Europe, and two-thirds are in Germany. They have high unemployment rates and often do not speak German. According to one report by the Berlin Institute for Population and Development: "While ethnic Turks born in Germany tend twice as often as direct immigrants to have earned an Abitur—the school diploma needed to attend an institution of higher learning in Germany—this seemingly promising result is 50 percent lower than the average figure reported for native Germans." Unlike other groups, people with a Turkish background are not integrating into the larger German society. Ninety-three percent select a partner with the same background.[54] This lack of integration is relevant to security because, as one publication from the Population Reference Bureau noted: "Fears that Turkish-speaking ghettos could become a source of Islamic fundamentalism complicate Turkey's bid to join the EU."[55]

An additional issue is that Turkey is a popular transit point for asylum seekers on their way to Europe, a role that makes Turkey's potential accession into the EU even more controversial. Under the Schengen agreement, when asylum seekers arrive in Turkey they would officially be in the EU. Having Turkey in the EU, then, removes a step in the migration process. Two institutional factors are designed to prevent a large tide of migrants: There is a gap of several years between acceding to the EU and to Schengen, and there is a "third country rule," whereby the third country has the right to return migrants to the point of entry. Nevertheless, the perception among some Europeans that expanding the EU to include Turkey will change the very identity of what it means to be European is a major stumbling block. Originally, Italy and Austria were held back from fully participating in the Schengen system (for about one year), because their borders were so porous.[56]

Outside of its potential effects on NATO and the EU, migration creates multiple other national security issues. In international relations, countries gain leverage through both hard power—or coercive means—and soft power—the attractiveness of their culture, system, or policies to others. Europe's treatment of some migrants threatens to undermine its reputation as a bastion of humanitarianism and therefore take away from its soft power. For example, Lampedusa, Italy, is a site of serious contention over migration, because it is a major point of entry for asylum seekers from North Africa. In January 2009, the UNHCR drew attention to the humanitarian situation of having 2,000 boat people, including asylum seekers, housed in a temporary reception center on Lampedusa that was designed to hold only 850 people. Many migrants arriving in Lampedusa are from Somalia and Eritrea. "According to preliminary figures for 2008, about 75 percent of those who arrived in Italy by sea last year applied for asylum, and around 50 percent of those who applied were granted refugee status or protection on other humanitarian grounds."[57] It is possible that refusing to grant asylum or being perceived as hostile to asylum seekers could reduce Europe's soft power and create resentment among sending countries that could actually increase European insecurity and increase vulnerability to outside threats and terrorism.

When considering regime insecurity, including both violent and non-violent civil conflict, it is important to emphasize that it is not necessarily minorities themselves that constitute a security risk. Rather, it is often reaction against their very presence that turns violent or foments unrest. Jocasta Matos, one of the organizers of a Parisian exhibit celebrating the 40th anniversary of Martin Luther King, Jr.'s, assassination, and a minority living in France, says: "It is tough here for all minorities. They don't beat us, but they insult us. They show disdain for us. This is perhaps even worse than being beaten, this sense of not being welcome, not accepted." In France, most estimates place the minority population at 6 to 10 percent, but it is illegal to gather data on race and ethnicity; this shroud has often fueled fears of a "takeover."[58] Some leaders try to capitalize on xenophobia. For example, during its 1995 presidential campaign, France's National Front proposed removing up to 3 million non-Europeans from the country to reduce the number of Muslim residents.[59] The divide between native-born and immigrant fertility rates drives some of the perception of "takeover." "In Austria, for example, Muslim women had a total fertility rate (an estimate of lifetime births per woman) of 3.1 children per woman in 1981, well above the 1.7 average for the majority Roman Catholic women. By 2001, the rate for Catholics had fallen to 1.3, but the Muslim rate had fallen to 2.3—leaving a difference of just one child per woman between Muslims and non-Muslims."[60] A difference of one child is pretty dramatic at these lower birthrates, because 2.3 is above replacement and 1.3 is far below. Over time, these differences will affect the population makeup, leading the non-Muslim population to age and eventually shrink while the Muslim population—if fertility stays high—grows. For example, Anne Goujon et al. have projected that the Muslim population in Austria will have gone from 4 percent in 2001 to between 14 and 18 percent of Austria's total population by 2051, and because of higher fertility, could comprise up to 32 percent of the population under 15 years of age.[61] Any estimates of the total Muslim population in Europe are difficult to make, because most European states do not collect such data, so numbers must be viewed in light of these shortcomings. Still, demographer David Coleman has conjectured that by 2050, populations of foreign origin (all origins) are projected to comprise between 15 and 32 percent of the total population in several Western European countries.[62] Muslims are generally the majority of Europe's non-European population.[63]

However, some demographers have found evidence that contradicts these projections, and point out that fertility rates among native and foreign-born women eventually narrow or converge. Demographers Westoff and Frejka found that "[w]omen who report firm adherence to their religious beliefs and practices tend to have higher fertility than less religious women, whether Christian or Muslim. But religiousness does not always mean higher fertility . . . Islam does not prohibit family planning, so women can have small families and follow their Islamic faith. The dramatic decline in Iran's fertility provides a recent example of how strict Islamic practices can coexist with widespread use of family planning."[64] Even as some evidence points to convergence, fear of religious differences finds fuel whenever extremists strike. In some countries, the far Right has seen major growth in support. In Austria, for example, the anti-immigrant Austrian Freedom Party received 18 percent of the vote in the 2008 parliamentary elections.[65] Support for anti-immigrant platforms seems to wax and wane over time depending more on events, like violent acts, or perception that may be motivated by political entrepreneurs, than on actual numbers of immigrants. In many ways, this is similar to the "sons of the soil" debate discussed earlier in the context of refugees in the Middle East. In both Europe and North America, a similar tension is taking place. Dominant ethnic groups who founded nation states and consider them "theirs" are frightened of losing the link between their ethnic group and their homeland, which has been mythologized in collective memory.

What about the migrants themselves? What role do they play in creating insecurity? Just as with refugees, the majority of immigrants do not engage in violence, but some do, and why they do so is important to understand. Fear of cultural changes or demographic disappearance provides the motive for native population groups to discriminate against minorities; discrimination and inequality can provide a motive for minorities to engage in protest or violence. Together, these reactions can form a vicious chain of regime insecurity. As the example of Germany's Turks showed, there is real inequality between immigrants and native-born citizens. In France, the *banlieues* (housing projects in the suburbs) are the most visible signs of inequality, as they are home to people of immigrant background. In 2006, the *banlieues* exploded in riots when minority youth protested their economic exclusion from French life. In these areas, youth unemployment is around 40 percent and many youth drop out of high school, closing off future opportunities.[66] As long as this inequality persists, the chance of unrest and civil violence—key expressions of regime insecurity—exists.

One of the reasons the riots in the *banlieues* made international news was that the youth were of Muslim immigrant background, and Western states have been particularly attuned to violence involving people with such backgrounds after the 9/11, London, and Madrid terrorist acts committed by

Muslim extremists. The violence in the *banlieues* occurred because of economic exclusion, not religious extremism, but both are issues that tie immigration and security. European governments have tried various strategies to counter extremism in Europe, but one of the major challenges is that the Muslim population of Europe is deeply fragmented along ethnic, linguistic, political, and sectarian lines.[67] Because they are fragmented, this may reduce the likelihood they will converge around an alternate national identity or otherwise destabilize Europe. Representation is one strategy to reduce exclusion. The number of first-, second-, and third-generation immigrants is fairly significant, yet there are very few elected minority officials.[68] Lack of representation is particularly surprising, because minority populations are not evenly dispersed; some communities may be made up of as much as 40 percent minorities. 2006 estimates published by the Greater London Authority are that 32 percent of Londoners were born outside of the United Kingdom. The largest sending countries include India, Bangladesh, Ireland, Jamaica, Nigeria, Poland, Kenya, Sri Lanka, South Africa, and Ghana. Together, migrants from these 10 countries comprise 42 percent of London's migrant population.[69] One strategy to reduce exclusion and regime insecurity, then, may be to work within existing democratic institutions to increase representation of minorities.

## SECURITY AND LESS DEVELOPED STATES

On the other side of the coin are the positive and negative regime security implications of migration for sending countries. Migration benefits the global economy by efficiently distributing labor, and benefits sending states by providing opportunities for citizens to gain skills and receive education. Emigration can bring economic benefits that lead to increased regime and structural security in two ways. The first is the ability to encourage emigration as a pressure release during tight job markets. For countries that face crowded job markets because of large cohorts, emigration can help avoid some of the civil strife discussed in Chapter 2 with regard to youth. The second way emigration brings economic benefits and enhanced security is through remittances. Many workers send remittances home; these not only benefit individual families, they can also be used as a tool for development. The Philippines have been especially proactive in encouraging immigration and have seen major contributions from remittances. According to the Philippine government, the eight million Filipinos who live abroad remit $1 billion a month, which is equivalent to 10 percent of the country's GDP.[70] Nigerians abroad send more than $1 billion back home every year.[71]

There are limitations to using remittances as a tool for development. The first is how long remittances can be counted on. In countries with declining fertility, though there will be an initial bonus of workers while the country enters its window of opportunity, eventually that window will close and each cohort entering the job market will be smaller. As a result, crowding may be less of a problem, relieving pressure on citizens to go abroad for work. When states have weak economies and no industry of their own, remittances can provide the government with sources of revenue through taxes and can provide families in the receiving country with funds to start businesses, functioning as microcredit. However, when remittances go to families and individuals to meet basic daily needs, like food and shelter, then there is no real investment in the country coming out of the remittances and they serve as aid, not assistance for actual development. Remittances do not necessarily help the country to develop an economy or an industry that would create jobs at home if they are not available in the form of capital for investment. Additionally, remittances are not a reliable source of income because migration tends to decrease during economic downturns. Fewer jobs mean there is less of a pull for citizens to seek economic opportunities abroad and foreign governments may restrict migration to stem the saturation of particular sectors of the labor market. When a country depends substantially on remittances for income, but there are fewer migrants going abroad, the income flows slow. "Immigrants tend to be harder hit than native-born workers during an economic downturn. . . . because they are overrepresented in cyclically sensitive sectors, they have less secure contractual arrangements and they are subject to selective hiring and firing."[72] The recent global recession illustrated this, as northward migration to the United States slowed. Recession increased the vulnerability of migrants, who often lack safety nets and are the first ones fired as the economy contracts. Thus, it is important for countries entering the window of opportunity to channel remittances into development projects that meet long-term employment needs. That way, when the window of opportunity comes, these youth entering the labor market will have jobs at home.

There are also political benefits of emigration, particularly when emigration enhances the foreign policy agenda of sending states. Thanks to increased global communication and travel, emigrants can still engage in political activities in their home country from abroad. As Fiona Adamson explains, "Migration can enhance a state's ability to engage in diplomacy. . . . Small states in the international system can involve their diasporas in diplomacy by drawing on emigrants and their descendants within a target country, and by sponsoring lobbying and public relations activities."[73] Although this can be a form of insecurity for states hosting immigrants, it can be a way to enhance the power of sending countries. At the same time that Americans are surmising how immigration and integration will change Europe's political landscape, Europeans are debating the degree to which Latin American migration to the United States will change American domestic and foreign policy. Some political leaders have tried to capitalize on the ties immigration fosters between sending and receiving countries. For example: "In 2000, Mexican President Vicente Fox made improving conditions for Mexicans in the United States his top foreign policy priority.... Fox asked the U.S. government to approve broad immigration reform in 2001: the legalization of unauthorized Mexicans, a new and large-scale guest worker program, cooperation to reduce border violence, and an exemption for Mexico from the U.S. cap on the number of immigrant visas available for each country."[74] External pressure does not automatically translate to outcome, however, especially in light of opposing internal pressure groups.

Throughout history, diaspora populations have been politically involved in the affairs of their home country. To some degree, this trend may be increasing. As Yossi Shain argues, not too long ago "many countries felt threatened by citizens with allegiances to multiple countries . . . Today, more and more countries extend dual nationalities and even voting rights to their kin abroad in the hope of fostering homeland loyalties from afar and harnessing financial and political support from their organized diasporas."[75] Shain cites two recent examples of the roles migration and diaspora populations have played in sparking the conflicts that led to U.S. military involvement in Afghanistan and Iraq: Osama bin Laden and al Qaeda have continuously tried to recruit alienated migrants to commit terrorist acts and "In the Iraqi case, political exiles in the United States and England played a crucial role in discrediting Saddam in the international arena."[76]

On the other hand, there are several negative implications of emigration. Structural insecurity results when a state is unable to meet the needs of its population given the availability of resources and technology. Stresses from demographic change can result from structural insecurity, and they can also cause it. Population in the form of human capital can strengthen state capacity; on the flip side, emigration can be devastating to a sending country's reserves of human capital. The prospects of real development and progress are dimmed when the most educated or skilled citizens leave and take their skills to benefit another country, a phenomenon known as brain drain. Teachers, civil servants, skilled laborers, and doctors are all important resources for development. In their excellent book on migration, Devesh Kapur and John McHale say: "Of all the talent lost from developing countries, medical professionals are perhaps of the greatest concern—all the more so in the wake of the AIDS pandemic."[77] In Ghana, about half the physician graduates between 1985 and 1994 left the country within four and a half years, and three-quarters within nine and a half years.[78] Kapur and McHale claim that the "clear factor" pulling these doctors away is the salary gap between what they would earn in Ghana (somewhere between $200–$300 a month) and what they would earn in a more developed country. In many cases, the governments of less developed countries pay to educate health workers, only to see them leave and take those skills with them. As Celia Dugger of *The New York Times* says: "It is the poor subsidizing the rich."[79]

Lebanon provides another example of human capital flight. Almost 45 percent of Lebanese emigrants to member states of the OECD have more than thirteen years of schooling.[80] Highly skilled workers confront a mix of push and pull factors encouraging them to leave. In Lebanon, workers often have a desire to leave because of political instability and a high cost of living, if they can find a job at all. The mismatch between their education and the market needs in Lebanon leads to a tight labor market for skilled graduates. Some of the pull factors include high salaries in Arab oil-rich states, an established network of Lebanese abroad, which makes it easier to establish a new life and find work, and opportunities for graduate studies.[81] In the Gulf States, about 90 percent of private-sector jobs are filled by foreigners.[82] In general, population aging in Europe, Asia, and the United States is likely to increase demand for skilled immigrants from developing states.

Ideally, governments concerned about brain drain will try to entice their citizens to return. Since 1986, "countries of origin have become more active in encouraging the return of their citizens from abroad and in strengthening links with their expatriate communities so as to harness the potential contributions of those communities to propelling development."[83] Kapur and McHale argue that the prospect of emigration may give some skilled citizens more bargaining power for things like services, lower taxes, and better public-sector working conditions.[84] The Ecuadorian government launched a "Bienvenidos a Casa" (Welcome Home) program in August 2008, trying to encourage Ecuadorians living abroad to return home so that they can stimulate Ecuador's economy. Although the global recession closed many opportunities for migrants, only 384 families out of approximately 582,700 Ecuadorian immigrants—both legal and undocumented—returned to Ecuador from the United States between January and August 2009.[85] Clearly, the campaign was only mildly successful, and likely migrants felt that their long-term prospects were brighter in the United States. States suffering from brain drain face serious challenges to their ability to meet the needs of the population and with a reduced human capital pool, they will have a difficult time devising and carrying out development plans that would strengthen health care and medical services, increase the capacity to govern, and build an infrastructure for a productive economy—all aspects that might prevent brain drain in the first place.

## CONCLUSION AND FURTHER ISSUES

For the most part, when migration takes place it is to improve the lives of individuals, whether through opening economic opportunities or freeing individuals from persecution. In some cases, though, the mixing of values,

religions, and politics that migration brings can create multiple forms of insecurity for the state. In other cases, migration can create security for the state.
Sending countries can benefit from the remittances emigration brings and
from the release in pressure on the labor market. Sending states can also draw
on their diaspora populations to further political goals. Receiving countries
can benefit economically from the labor that migration provides, but migrants
can also increase receiving states' military security. Military security encompasses a state's ability to project power in the international system, and these
issues relate to military security as well. As Zolberg points out: "Powerful states
in the international system can project their influence abroad by manipulating immigration policy, by drawing on immigrant populations, and even by
mobilizing diasporas living within them for foreign policy ends. During the
Cold War, for example, the United States crafted a refugee policy that encouraged emigration and defection from the Soviet Union and Eastern Europe,
and, in the process, sought to 'inflict a psychological blow on communism.'"[86]
Migration can also create military security to the extent that it shores up the
military-age population or brings in individuals with specialized skills, as it
has in the United States.

Immigrants can "provid[e] technical and intelligence expertise (e.g., foreign language skills and analysis). An extreme example is the role that émigré
scientists played in developing the U.S. nuclear program in the 1930s. Albert
Einstein, Edward Teller, and others who fled National Socialism in Europe
put their scientific expertise to work in developing the first atomic bomb."[87]
Less than a year after 9/11, President George W. Bush signed an executive
order accelerating citizenship for noncitizens who had served in the military
since the 2001 World Trade Center attacks, instead of requiring three years
of service to become eligible to apply for U.S. citizenship. If they have permanent U.S. residency (a green card), noncitizens may serve in the military.[88]
Even more recently, the United States launched the Military Accessions Vital
to the National Interest Pilot Recruiting Program in early 2009 specifically to
accelerate citizenship for people with special language skills, or licensed health
care professionals who meet army standards. Rather than taking years, these
recruits could become citizens in as little as six months.[89] "In 2004 it was estimated that 40,000 noncitizens were enrolled in the U.S. military, or 4 percent of all enlistees."[90] The U.S. government is happy to trade citizenship for
military service because finding recruits has been challenging, and a strong
military is necessary to carry out U.S. foreign policy goals, particularly as the
country has been engaged in two wars.

Certainly, though military security has been enhanced, regime insecurity
results when identities clash. One policy response is to close borders, but this
creates its own issues. One of the implications of halting immigration highlights
connections between the North and South. As Europeans securitize migrants

and refugees, and close borders, this deepens insecurity for refugees still in the South awaiting resettlement. Closed borders also close opportunities for economic advancement. Migration could help extend the European welfare state in the face of aging, although demographer David Coleman estimates that in order for Europe to keep its current ratio of workers to dependents, migration would need to increase to an average of 25 million annually. The problem is that this rate would "treble Europe's population by 2050 from 754 million to 2.35 billion, and so on at an accelerating rate."[91] Such numbers would no doubt add further fuel to ethnic tensions over immigration in Europe, particularly if the numbers were unevenly spread throughout Europe.

Most of these issues with national security and migration are well documented but there are two trends in migration that deserve future research. The first is the increasing feminization of migration. According to the Population Reference Bureau, "Women now are increasingly likely to move for economic opportunity, rather than to join husbands or other family members as they did in the past." To what degree will the changing face of migration create new policy issues, particularly with women's security and human rights in both sending and destination countries?[92] The second emerging issue is migration prompted by climate change. For less developed countries, migration from climate change could lead to the same kinds of conflicts between migrants and residents in receiving areas that migration motivated by economic or political causes does, especially if there is already conflict in receiving areas and migrants end up joining sides.[93] Climate change will hit less developed states harder than developed ones, because it impedes even basic food and health security; the state cannot adapt as easily because it has less capacity in general. These states also have a hard time absorbing migrants because their labor markets and welfare services are likely strained already. In many of the areas most likely to be affected by climate change, clashes over identity are already a problem. South Asia provides one example, where, over time, Bangladeshis have intermittently moved to India because of storms, floods, and droughts.[94]

Migration illustrates the intricate relationships between intergovernmental organizations, like the UNHCR; state governments; and nongovernmental organizations, like Catholic Charities, who aid in resettling refugees, communities, and individuals. When migration is billed as a security issue, it falls within the realm of states, and there is only so much the UNHCR can do to resettle refugees and asylum seekers when states of the Global North cap the number of entrants to protect their own interests. The complexity of the issue is just one challenge with securitizing migration. Framing migration as a security issue can also reinforce the security problem because it encourages receiving countries to view migrants as "carriers of conflict" and security risks. The friction that results from this stigma could then become responsible for the outbreak of conflict. Thus, securitizing migration may be a self-fulfilling prophecy. Although always an issue with population, this tendency is much more prevalent with migration than any other population trend, because it is one of the only trends that draw distinctions between insiders and outsiders—identity lines that may already be tense.

# 6
## Chapter

# Urbanization and
# Urban Areas

During the days before the Lunar New Year, hundreds of millions of Chinese travel from China's cities, where they work, to their rural family homes. Termed *Chun yun*, or spring festival transport, this event is the world's largest annual human migration.[1] Such a rapid movement of so many people, albeit temporary, illustrates one facet of the modern phenomenon of urbanization, because the absence of transportation infrastructure would have made the trek impossible even a few decades ago. Although rural inhabitants have sought economic opportunities in cities for as long as cities have existed, the scale and scope of urban migration are far larger now than ever before. There are more cities, larger cities, and a greater variety of urban experiences available—some filled with opportunities to thrive and others marked by extreme poverty and overcrowding. Scale and scope are not the only changes. Another new phenomenon is the ability of these internal migrants to keep ties with their rural homes and to maneuver back and forth as travel and communication have improved. These changes connect to a host of national security issues, ranging from the vulnerability of urban areas as military targets, to regime insecurity caused by rural–urban fissures, to the spread of disease in urban slums. Although many equate urbanization with the growth of cities and transformation of economies, and see the phenomenon as a marker of progress, some urban growth is characterized by the growth in slums, spread of disease, and contestation over governance. However, cities provide many opportunities to increase security as well, through increasing economic power and concentrating the population in areas where they can better access education and health care.

## WHAT IS URBAN?

The plight of some of America's cities, such as Memphis and Detroit, is well known. These cities have seen an emptying of their downtown cores and a buildup of their suburban areas. In comparison with a metropolis like Chicago or even Miami, the phrase "urban living" hardly seems to describe both situations. This distinction is only a small representation of the diversity behind the word "urban." The UN's announcement in 2008 that more than half the world's population now lives in urban areas had been widely anticipated and discussed in scholarly publications for at least a decade before the milestone was actually achieved. Such a level of urbanization, some argue, represents a global tipping point of progress in economic and social life. However, the devil is in the details. As Carl Haub of the Population Reference Bureau points out, "urban" does not equate with "city." Thanks to the media's portrayal of the 50 percent urban milestone, argues Haub, "The distinct impression was created that a majority of people lived in very large cities."[2] That is not necessarily true, as each country in the world provides its own definition of urban. Though "urban" is usually defined as those living in towns or cities of 2,000 people or more, there is variety. Japan defines the urban threshold as 5,000 or more; the United States, as 2,500 or more.[3] China defines the urban threshold as cities designated by the State Council and other places with a population density of 1,500 or more per square kilometer. Mexico's definition of urban is localities of 2,500 or more.[4] Haub points out that in most countries, urban is more accurately thought of as nonagricultural, at least from the point of view of industrialized countries. Although Latin America and the Caribbean have high levels of urbanization (about 78 percent), in Africa and Asia 6 out of 10 people still live in rural areas. Just three countries accounted for 35 percent of the world's urban population in 2007: China, India, and the United States.[5] In contrast to the urban economic success of West Africa, East African countries are projected to experience their urban transition by the middle of the century. Burundi, Ethiopia, Rwanda, and Uganda are the least urbanized. Reasons include low industrialization, overdependence on subsistence agriculture, poor land policies, lack of urban development strategies, legacies of colonial policies that discouraged rural-to-urban migration, and lack of political will to urbanize.[6]

It is important to be aware of the variety of urban experiences to understand the security implications of urbanization. The diversity of the urban experience matters, particularly when we consider connections between poverty and violence or urban areas and susceptibility to natural disaster. Not all urbanization connotes progress toward economic development. As Haub says: "The classification 'urban' does not automatically mean that the population has become literate or lost its traditional rural values and social customs. In developed countries, the rural population, on the other hand, often has the same access to amenities and services as urban areas."[7] Most future growth in urbanization will take place in less developed countries, mainly because the populations of those states are growing whereas urban areas of developed countries, especially those in Europe, are already well developed and the population growth of those states is slowing. Given the differences in political capacity between developed and developing countries, the implications of urbanization in each will be vastly different. Subnational data on population characteristics are often hard to come by. Future efforts to collect data at the subnational level will help to clarify the connections between a host of population trends and national security implications.

In spite of all the variety, there are many cities and urban agglomerations in the world that reflect the common understanding of "urban." Megacities, those cities with populations more than 10 million, used to be a rarity. Now, there is a word for cities with populations more than 20 million: "metacities." Today, there are four metacities; by 2025, there will be nine (Table 6.1).

Cities can be major assets to their country, their region, and the global economy. Though urbanization does not necessarily imply economic development, economic development is fairly impossible without urbanization. As the UN notes, "no country has ever achieved sustained economic growth or rapid social development without urbanizing."[8] The more economically successful regions in a country are generally urban. Examples include the National Capital Region in the Philippines, the Mekong River Delta in VietNam, Maputo and the Southern Region of Mozambique, and Tangier–Tetouan in Northern Morocco.[9] Cities are economic entities in their own right. In high-income countries, cities generate 85 percent of the GNP; in low-income countries, they generate about 55 percent.[10] Cities that share geographic proximity often become linked and naturally form their own economic units, which the UN calls "megaregions." China's Hong Kong–Shenzen–Guangzhou megaregion has a population of 120 million; Brazil's Sao Paulo–Rio de Janeiro megaregion is home to more than 43 million people. The world's megaregions account for 66 percent of the world's economic activity and are the breeding ground for 85 percent of all technological and scientific innovation.[11] Urban corridors, which are distinguished from megaregions in that they are intentionally shaped through transportation networks, are another important urban configuration. Africa's greater Ibadan–Lagos–Accra urban corridor, which spans 600 kilometers across four countries, is "the engine of West Africa's economy."[12] Finally, urban areas are essential to the world economy. Tokyo alone accounts for almost two percent of global GDP.[13] Cities have this power because "[h]igh urban densities reduce transaction costs, make public spending on infrastructure and services more economically viable, and facilitate generation and diffusion of knowledge, all of which are important for growth."[14]

**Table 6.1** World's 20 Largest Cities

| | 2010 | | 2025 | |
|---|---|---|---|---|
| **No.** | **City** | **Population (millions)** | **City** | **Population (millions)** |
| 1 | Tokyo, Japan | 36.7 | Tokyo, Japan | 37.1 |
| 2 | Delhi, India | 22.2 | Delhi, India | 28.6 |
| 3 | Sao Paulo, Brazil | 20.3 | Mumbai, India | 25.8 |
| 4 | Mumbai, India | 20.0 | Sao Paulo, Brazil | 21.7 |
| 5 | Mexico City, Mexico | 19.5 | Dhaka, Bangladesh | 20.9 |
| 6 | New York–Newark, US | 19.4 | Mexico City, Mexico | 20.7 |
| 7 | Shanghai, China | 16.6 | New York–Newark, US | 20.6 |
| 8 | Calcutta, India | 15.6 | Calcutta, India | 20.1 |
| 9 | Dhaka, Bangladesh | 14.7 | Shanghai, China | 20.0 |
| 10 | Karachi, Pakistan | 13.1 | Karachi, Pakistan | 18.73 |
| 11 | Buenos Aires, Argentina | 13.1 | Lagos, Nigeria | 15.8 |
| 12 | Los Angeles–Long Beach–Santa Ana, US | 12.8 | Kinshasa, Democratic Republic of the Congo | 15.0 |
| 13 | Beijing, China | 12.4 | Beijing, China | 15.0 |
| 14 | Rio de Janeiro, Brazil | 12.0 | Manila, Philippines | 14.9 |
| 15 | Manila, Philippines | 11.6 | Buenos Aires, Argentina | 13.7 |
| 16 | Osaka-Kobe, Japan | 11.3 | Los Angeles–Long Beach–Santa Ana, US | 13.7 |
| 17 | Cairo, Egypt | 11.0 | Cairo, Egypt | 13.5 |
| 18 | Lagos, Nigeria | 10.6 | Rio de Janeiro, Brazil | 12.7 |
| 19 | Moscow, Russia | 10.6 | Istanbul, Turkey | 12.1 |
| 20 | Istanbul, Turkey | 10.5 | Osaka-Kobe, Japan | 11.4 |

*Source:* Population, Division Department of Economic and Social Affairs. "The 30 Largest Urban Agglomerations Ranked by Population Size at Each Point in Time, 1950–2025." New York: United Nations, 2010.

Large cities are important to consider because they are often politically and economically symbolic, but more than half the world's urban population lives in cities of less than 500,000 people. Much of the growth in urban areas is taking place in small- to medium-size cities that are often unequipped to deal with these changes. As the UN notes: "Smaller cities are expected to absorb half of urban population growth between 2005 and 2015, yet their capacity to manage this process with services and policies is weak."[15] Poor people in smaller cities under 100,000 inhabitants are often no better off than poor rural people because like rural citizens they lack clean water, waste disposal, and other services.[16] Gaborone, the capital of Botswana, is one such rapidly growing city facing huge challenges to accommodate its population. The city has grown from 17,700 people in 1971 to more than 186,000, and is expected to reach 500,000 by the year 2020. Botswana has some revenues from diamond mining, but money has not been enough to prevent high poverty, HIV/AIDS, and a growing informal economic sector. The city's growth is outpacing any planning efforts and is now plagued by low-density urban sprawl and high unemployment. Although land policies were put in place to help secure housing for large shares of the population while preventing speculation, the poorest of Gaborone still end up living in informal settlements where housing is unplanned, lacks water or sewage, and is difficult to reach.[17]

Globally, more people are moving away from rural areas into urban areas. Why is this happening? The UN divides causes into political factors, like instability, civil war, and repression; and economic, environmental, and social factors. Much like interstate migration, these combine to create push and pull factors that entice people to move. Some push factors include declining productivity of cropland and a reorientation of the state economy to export, rather than subsistence farming. Pull factors include better job opportunities and higher incomes in urban areas, and greater opportunities for education and health care.[18]

Urbanization is not just about the movement of people; it is also about the difference in experience of living in a dense city versus rural area. Hence, this chapter looks at both movement itself and the significance and variety of urban areas as population centers. Indeed, not all urban growth is because of in-migration. As Ellen Brennen points out in a paper for the Wilson Center, "net migration from rural to urban areas accounts for less than half of the population growth of cities. Around 60 percent of urban growth is due to the excess of urban fertility over urban mortality."[19] In some areas with weak institutions and state capacity, high population growth from both movement and natural increase outpaces the government's ability to support the population, resulting in slums that fall far short of the ideal of modern city living. Slums generally refer to the sprawling informal settlements in urban areas of developing countries, which are mired in poverty and have deficient organized infrastructures, such as sanitation or transportation. The UN Human Settlements Program defines a slum as "a multidimensional concept involving aspects of poor housing, overcrowding, lack of services and insecure tenure."[20] That urban demographic changes will mostly take place in less developed countries means that there will be an increasing urbanization of poverty, because many, if not most, of these states lack the ability to provide for a burgeoning urban populace. The term "slum" first appeared during the 1820s in London to describe "the poorest quality housing and the most unsanitary conditions; a refuge for marginal activities including crime, 'vice' and drug abuse; and a likely source for many epidemics that ravaged urban areas—a place apart from all that was decent and wholesome."[21] The idea that urban areas could be a refuge for unsavory—or, more importantly, illegal—activities is obviously not new, but continues to be one of the major connections between insecurity and urbanization. Individual insecurity and poor quality of life are perpetual problems in slums and a modern worry is that slums will become ungoverned areas and safe havens from which illicit actors can plot and hide. A former student of mine once referred to slums as the final glorious by-product of globalization, meaning that urban areas are the vehicle through which industry fuels the global economy, and also evidence that the benefits of economic growth are uneven. But, as the UN argues, it is not population alone, nor globalization, that causes a problem: "Slums must be seen as the result of a failure of housing policies, laws and delivery systems, as well as of national and urban policies."[22]

The following sections will describe how both the movement of people from rural to urban areas and the nature of urban areas themselves are connected to the three areas of national security. In most instances, urbanization contributes positively to state and individual security, but can increase vulnerability for both parties in areas with weak governance.

## MILITARY SECURITY

The military security implications of urbanization fall into three areas. The first is the ability of urban areas, as centers of power and economic activity, to contribute to a state's national power. Among the world's most powerful states, none are predominantly rural, although depending on how one views India's power status, it could be the exception at 29 percent urban.[23] Perhaps even more striking, if we were to think of the most powerful *areas* of the world, cities—not just states—would top our list. New York City, Tokyo, Shanghai, Beijing, Delhi, Mumbai, and Seoul, to name a few, are the drivers of their respective states' growth and progress. The second area of military security flips this lens, and instead of focusing on how urban areas contribute to state power, explains how urban areas can make a state vulnerable. As centers of activity, cities are prime targets for military and terrorist attacks. Finally, cities themselves—as they hold growing importance—become the locus of major conflict; soldiers must be prepared to conduct operations in urban terrain, which brings a unique set of challenges.

### Economic and Political Power

Urbanization, when it is a marker of progress, can make a positive contribution to a state's economic power and thus help increase its standing in the international system. As Raymond J. Struyk and Stephen Giddings argue, "Urban economic growth can . . . facilitate country-wide development by way of remittances, new markets, and increased human capital. Greater productivity means higher family incomes and therefore greater demand for products from the countryside—in short, a larger national economic pie."[24] Two of the "Asian Tigers," the highly developed urban areas of Hong Kong and Singapore, played a large role in the economic growth that took place in East Asia during the boom of the 1990s.[25] According to economist Esther Boserup, population density, not growth or a youthful population, is an essential tool for modernization and technological success.[26] Indeed, many believe that cities create the right environment for innovation. In the United States, China, and the Scandinavian countries, college graduates are increasingly concentrating in cities for economic reasons. Author of the best-selling book *Who's Your City?*, Richard Florida, writes:

> The proximity of talented, highly educated people has a powerful effect on innovation and economic growth. . . . Places that bring together diverse talent accelerate the local rate of economic evolution. When large numbers of entrepreneurs, financiers, engineers, designers, and other smart, creative people are constantly bumping into one another inside and outside of work, business ideas are formed, sharpened, executed, and—if successful—expanded. As the number of smart people increases and the connections among them grow more dense, the faster it all goes.[27]

If true, urbanization should be good news for aging countries; to some degree they can compensate for one demographic hurdle by investing in strong cities.

## Vulnerable Cities

The same thing that makes cities so attractive from an economic point of view—that they concentrate people, commerce, and power—also makes them attractive from a military point of view, as targets. As Roch Legault says in the *Canadian Military Journal*, "large cities are now key military objectives, even in third world countries, because that is where one finds the major centres of population, wealth, transportation, mass media and warehousing of goods."[28] This book's primary concern is *national* security, meaning security of the state, and given that cities are often the primary locus of a state's political and economic activities they are particularly important to secure. By definition, cities may be vulnerable to all sorts of shocks. Rather than being self-sufficient hubs, cities must import food to support their populations, and generally export the waste they produce. Their complex infrastructure can be easily disrupted. The August 2003 Toronto blackout is one example. Writing of this incident, Thomas Homer-Dixon describes how the "simultaneous failure of portable phones, automatic tellers, debit card machines, electronic hotelroom (*sic*) doors, electric garage doors, and almost all clocks," plus traffic signals, subways, e-mail, and news, brought to light how interconnected and complex the city infrastructure was and how devastating a breakdown of that complex system could be.[29]

All cities are vulnerable, but large cities are particularly attractive targets because they have global significance. Although megacities are home to only a small percentage of the world's urban population, these areas are still important to consider in a national security framework, because they are the site of so much of the world's economic activity. The past couple of decades have shown how popular megacities and other large cities of geostrategic importance have been as targets for terrorists. New York City on September 11, 2001, is only one example, but that devastation had global repercussions as the city "lost an estimated $110 billion in infrastructure, buildings, jobs and other assets in the wake of the World Trade Center attacks. . . . Global gross domestic product . . . dipped by 0.8% and some 10 million more people joined the ranks of the world's poor."[30] Threatening or attacking a large city can make a particularly large impact, shutting down commerce and normal social activity as citizens and governments become too afraid to continue business as usual. Ten gunmen from Karachi, Pakistan, held Mumbai, India, in November 2008, terrorizing residents with a four-day killing spree. The incident not only paralyzed the city, it caused a breakdown in the already fragile India–Pakistan relationship. Many Western diplomats feared that India would retaliate with air strikes and the subcontinent would erupt into war.[31] Rather than military attacks, a diplomatic war ensued, and India halted all talks with Pakistan in the wake of the attack. The high profile of the attacks in the megacity of Mumbai certainly highlights the strategic importance of these large cities. The July 7, 2005, London subway bombings and March 2010 bombings in Moscow are other examples of high-profile attacks on large cities. Given that terrorism is an urban phenomenon, it makes sense that concerns over terrorism are increasing as states become more urbanized.

Seoul, South Korea, highlights the potential vulnerability of megacities as military targets. Seoul is about 30 miles from the demilitarized zone, and the Seoul National Capital Area (Seoul and its surrounding satellite cities, which are mostly located in Gyeonggi Province) is home to half of Korea's population. As the capital, Seoul is home to most of South Korea's political activity, but it holds economic importance as well. Seoul is responsible for about half of South Korea's wealth.[32] The city is home to 12 of the 14 largest South Korean companies, including Samsung Electronics, LG, and Hyundai Motor.[33] Seoul's proximity to the demilitarized zone is a major vulnerability for South Korea, and, because of other problems, with social unrest stemming from rural income disparities, and unbalanced growth in the rest of the country, there have been efforts since at least the 1970s to reduce the growth of Seoul and to diversify the location of economic and political activities.[34]

## Effects on the Military

There is no doubt that warfare will continue to be varied, but the rising concentration of population in urban areas means that these areas could increasingly become the locus of violence and warfare. Writing in 2000, Roch Legault pointed out that "of the last 250 missions of the U.S. Marine Corps, 237 . . . involved urban combat operations."[35] He argues that operations in the Somali capital of Mogadishu in October 1993 were a wakeup call for Western armies about urban warfare because of the failures of U.S. Special Operations units. Street fighting in Mogadishu's Bakara marketplace was a particularly disturbing challenge. Military operations on urban terrain, such as Mogadishu, bring particular challenges; they can be especially costly to human lives, because urban areas make it difficult to separate civilians from combatants. Urban warfare could affect cities in Africa, which are projected to be the site of future urban growth, but also already face challenges with ethnic and other types of civil conflict. Potential increase in urban conflict in general also means that international peacekeeping forces may be called upon to respond to a variety of future urban challenges.

At the same time that fighting in Iraq has illustrated the challenges of urban warfare, for example through the use of car bombs and improvised explosive devices in crowded markets, engagement in the rugged and remote areas of Afghanistan shows that militaries must continue to prepare for conflict outside of urban areas as well. RAND researchers Jennifer Taw and Bruce Hoffman argue that "governments will have to develop a hybrid strategy that prepares them to fight a broad-based insurgency across rural and urban environments."[36] Urban operations require "a unique combination of the doctrine, training, and equipment appropriate for military operations on urban terrain (MOUT), counterterrorism, and traditional counterinsurgency operations."[37] The 2010 U.S. Quadrennial Defense Review says the United States will need to be able to succeed in "large-scale counterinsurgency (COIN), stability, and counterterrorism (CT) operations in environments ranging from densely populated urban areas and mega-cities, to remote mountains, deserts, jungles, and littoral regions."[38]

Urban challenges may increasingly blur police and military functions as areas of responsibility overlap. At the least, increasing urbanization may require better coordination between the police and military. In some places this could be a challenge, particularly many Latin American cities, where private security forces outnumber police. These forces are unregulated and decentralized, making any coordination attempts a major issue. In 1994, authorities in Mexico City tried to deal with the burgeoning number of private police firms by creating a Private Security Services Registration Department, which registered a total of 2,122 private security firms within the federal district its first year. According to officials, many more failed to register, and these remained beyond government scrutiny. Private security continues to be a model throughout Latin America. In Mexico City, there were approximately 22,500 private security guards employed in 2002. Lack of accountability is a problem; private police operate outside the authority of the state, and their presence may also reduce public police accountability.[39] Lack of regulation and decentralization would also be a challenge in the face of a natural disaster. Governance can lessen the stress on the military by preventing problems from occurring in the first place.

## REGIME SECURITY

Urbanization can be a particularly serious problem for regime security, as this section describes. Almost all countries face problems with urban crime and violence. As urbanization concentrates people, it can bring opportunities to commit crimes and motivations to do so when people from different backgrounds come into ever closer contact. In many developing countries, economic development is accompanied by increasing concentration of economic activities in cities, pulling rural inhabitants to migrate into these population centers in search of opportunities. There is evidence from countries like China that governments sometimes pour their resources into urban areas to the neglect of rural areas. Resulting inequality and resentment can create serious fissures that undermine the regime's authority and legitimacy. Finally, regime security is greatly threatened by the creation of safe havens for rebels and extremists in cities. In fact, safe havens, often born out of what some call "ungoverned areas," are the very embodiment of regime insecurity, because by definition they represent the existence of competing sources of authority within a state.

### Rural–Urban Divide

Regime security describes the ability of the government to function and to protect itself and its people from domestic disorder. Yet, governments themselves can, and often do, act in ways that potentially fracture their states. As states work on development, they usually pour resources into urban areas, trying to attract investment and establish various industries. They support universities and develop housing and cultural centers in urban areas. As a consequence, they may neglect rural areas. Additionally, as states try to compete globally, they may pay more attention to the global market than local interests.

The middle and upper classes—as the owners of capital—will often be the main recipients of government attention—to the detriment of the rural and poorer populations.[40]

China provides a prime example of inequality between urban and rural areas that has in large part resulted from intentional government policy. The engine of China's economic growth has been its cities, and in return, sky-high economic growth has mostly benefited the cities. National statistics on GDP can skew perception of China's progress toward becoming a fully industrialized country. In reality, there is a stark divide between rural and urban life. China has concentrated its economic development efforts on coastal provinces, to the neglect of the interior. Lack of opportunity in rural areas has lured around 200 million rural laborers and their dependents to migrate to cities, where opportunities are more plentiful.[41] In 2001, the GDP of coastal Shanghai—one of China's jewels—was almost five times the national average.[42] The GDP per capita of these cities continues to grow even larger, and so does inequality. The Gini coefficient, a measure of inequality, was 46.9 in 2004 for China as a whole, much higher than the United Kingdom or Germany, and surpassing the United States at 41 in the year 2000.[43] Chinese citizens have increasingly protested over many issues, including pensions and environmental injustice, but rural unrest has also been increasing as peasants start to resent the government's focus on urban areas to the neglect of rural ones.[44] Although many outside of China have the image of China as a bustling, growing site of development, some rural residents may not have seen any improvement in their daily lives since the time of Mao. Economic reforms in China have generally had an urban bias.[45] Farmers have always had fewer benefits than their urban counterparts. Even during the throes of communism, urban workers had generous pensions after their lifetime employment, whereas rural workers did not.[46]

As inequality has grown and protests have increased, there has been much speculation about what these rural–urban fissures mean for the Chinese government's ability to retain power and remain the sole legitimate authority. Some believe these fissures will lead to the downfall of the government, as rural inhabitants refuse to support a regime that ignores their needs. More likely, though, the central government will make a greater effort to redistribute wealth just enough to appease the rural population. Although there have been a few overtures to rural areas, the regime appears to feel unthreatened by the prospect of rural unrest. Policies reflect the changing population centers in China. On December 28, 2009, Premier Wen Jiabao announced a major reform to the household registration system that will guarantee equal rights for migrant workers as they resettle in urban centers, yet the focus is still on urbanites. Wen said: "Farmers-turned-workers who have been living in cities with a stable income are a priority. The government will create policies to encourage migrant workers to settle down in small and medium-sized towns and cities, as big cities have limited capacities."[47] In general, policies are still designed to accelerate urbanization.

The final connection between urbanization and regime security is ungoverned areas and safe havens where insurgents can find refuge. The U.S. Department of Defense has led a serious effort to understand the importance of safe havens and potential safe havens, which they call "ungoverned areas." In one report, Robert Lamb argues that preventing havens for illicit actors is a key aspect of counterinsurgency, counterterrorism, counternarcotics, stabilization, and peacekeeping efforts.[48] The changing nature of urbanization is also altering the urbanization of insurgency. Jennifer Taw and Bruce Hoffman of RAND have argued that urban insurgencies were traditionally the easiest kind to defeat, but much has changed so that it is now easier for insurgents to operate. They say: "The decreasing standard of living in the cities, the dispersion of security forces among increasing numbers of cities, and the development of impassable slums within cities have changed the three-way dynamic among the government, the population, and the insurgents."[49] The term "ungoverned areas" is a bit misleading, because there are very few places in the world that are actually ungoverned. Instead, the concern is over the way a place is governed. In a weak state, insurgents may exploit gaps and attempt to gain the allegiance of the people where the state has failed to secure it. Where the state is unable to provide needed services, other actors—such as nongovernmental organizations and tribal or local actors—will step in to fill in the gaps. Weakly governed states provide greater opportunities for freedom of action. Ungoverned areas and safe havens are not confined to urban areas, of course, but urban areas may allow illicit actors to "hide in plain sight." Thus, urban ungoverned areas have different challenges than rugged and remote hideouts. Yet, even in societies considered to have authority, there are still gaps that can be exploited. Lamb says that urban areas allow actors to be anonymous because of dense population and restrictive legal or social norms that protect rights like privacy and private property. "Many cities, even in Western liberal democracies, have entire housing projects, neighborhoods, or slums that are known to be controlled by drug traffickers or other illicit actors and are 'no go' areas for police."[50] In weakly governed or corrupt states, police themselves may not be the most reliable partners. Often there is an intimate relationship between the police and gangs.[51]

In the modern state system, one of the biggest challenges of preventing safe havens is the principle of sovereignty. An outside state may not be able to step in and secure an area because it would violate the weak state's sovereignty; yet, the catch is that the weak state is, by definition, too weak to prevent the safe haven from emerging. Urban slums seem a natural fit for safe havens, but cities in developed, Western countries can provide the same conditions. Three of the four terrorists responsible for the 2005 bombings in London were British nationals of Pakistani descent and lived in the neighborhood of

West Yorkshire.[52] Although urban areas on the whole provide many positive opportunities, the development of urban safe havens shows that urban areas do provide unique national security challenges.

## Urbanization and Increasing Security

Although on any given day there exists urban social unrest in some city around the world, the number of cities not experiencing conflict should give us hope that the urban experience is generally a positive one. As Henrik Urdal and Kristian Hoelscher point out in their study of youth and urban violence, "the growth in urban populations has been much greater than the growth in social disorder events."[53] An increasing urban youth population may be a positive reflection of legitimately better opportunities in cities, which youth are seeking. Globalization has mostly benefited and connected urban areas; likewise, investment and economic activities have been located in urban areas and people—including youth—have followed the jobs to the cities that investment creates.[54] Indeed, "under some conditions, the migration of young people from the countryside to cities could contribute to reduce overall youth exclusion, and should not necessarily be expected to increase levels of urban social disorder."[55] A problem occurs when job creation and economic growth are unable to keep pace with urban growth, thereby creating grievances, which can lead to violence and instability. Urban youth often face higher unemployment than the general population, as in Ethiopia, where urban youth unemployment is 38 percent and overall unemployment is eight percent.[56]

Despite the ability of cities to serve as release valves for the pressure of a young age structure, there is empirical and theoretical support for links between urbanization and conflict.[57] In a study of civil conflict during the 1990s, Richard Cincotta found that countries with a high rate of urban population growth were twice as likely as other states to experience an outbreak of conflict. There are a couple of reasons why this might be the case. First, just as dense urban centers make it easier to concentrate economic activity and can breed innovation, they also make it easier to organize political protest, resulting in regime insecurity.[58] The protests in Bangkok that started in March 2010 are one example. In Thailand during the 1970s, most ideological battles were fought in rural areas, because most of the population lived on farms. Now, urbanization there has created conditions where "radicals can recruit massive followings in cities such as Bangkok with millions of disaffected laborers who no longer have farms to return to."[59] Second, it is hard to separate youth bulge and urbanization, precisely because youth of working age tend to migrate to urban areas for economic opportunities. As a result, urban areas may have a disproportionate and crowded youth cohort, which, as the chapter on youth demonstrated, increases the risk of civil violence of many forms.[60]

On the other hand, there are several theoretical reasons why we should expect urban areas to have less regime insecurity in the form of protest. Gilbert argues that protest in less developed cities is actually rather infrequent. There are several reasons, including that the poor are too busy trying to earn a living to mobilize, that they face major crackdowns on protest if they live under authoritarian rule, or that they are placated under a political patronage system.[61] In addition, the poor may be less likely to protest because city life is still relatively better than rural life, so no matter how bad urban conditions are, urbanites may still feel relatively better off.

Despite much concern for the ills of urbanization, urban slum areas are not generally the site of conventional violent political conflicts between organized armed groups.[62] Thus, urbanization could mean good things for the future of conflict. However, because urbanization is just now taking place in developing states, our data on conflict and urbanization may be biased toward past experiences in places where governance capacity was higher. Just as mature age structures are unprecedented, and thus our ability to project the impacts of that age structure on national security is limited, new patterns of urbanization in developing states are also unprecedented; we cannot be sure if they will follow the same peaceful pattern of the past. Because of natural increase, "[i]t is estimated that as many as 60 per cent of all urban dwellers will be under the age of 18 by 2030. If urgent measures are not taken in terms of basic services, employment and housing, the youth bulge will grow up in poverty."[63]

## STRUCTURAL INSECURITY

The final area of national security is structural security. In this realm we see how urbanization can contribute to or take away from security, depending on the conditions. Concentrating people in urban areas can greatly improve the ability of the government to meet the needs of the people, because citizens can take advantage of sanitation and sewer, health care, and educational opportunities. Rural areas, especially when spread out or located in rough terrain, may have little to no hope of receiving such services. As mentioned, some even argue that the concentration of people in urban areas leads to the incubation of new ideas, because urban living breeds creativity. Yet for many countries, the growth of urban areas outpaces the state's ability to meet the needs of the population. Urban slums, rather than being the incubators of new ideas, become incubators for disease, conflict, and natural disasters. This section focuses on these latter issues.

### "Slumization": The Urbanization of Poverty

Ninety percent of slums are located in developing countries, primarily in the cities of Africa, Asia, and Latin America. In 2001, 78 percent of the urban population of least developed countries lived in slums.[64] Mumbai alone is home to one of the world's largest slum populations—more than five million slum dwellers. Sub-Saharan Africa has the highest slum growth rate of any region, at more than four-and-a-half percent per year; but, worldwide, the population of slum dwellers grows by 10 percent a year.[65] In North Africa, the number and proportion of slum dwellers have steadily declined—North Africa is the only subregion in the developing world to achieve this marker. The statistic is mostly driven by huge improvements in Morocco and Egypt, where in both cases strong political leadership, planning, and financing helped improve living conditions for millions.[66] Slums are the ultimate embodiment of structural insecurity. Individuals' basic needs for food, clean water, decent shelter, and protection from bodily harm go unmet in slums, and the very presence of slums reflects the state's inability to govern well. As Raymond Struyk and Stephen Giddings argue: "Slums result from a toxic combination of weak governance, underinvestment in basic infrastructure, poor planning to accommodate growth, unrealistically high standards for residential neighborhoods, infrastructure standards that are unaffordable for the poor, and insufficient public transportation that limits access to employment."[67] Some states purposely choose not to invest in slums and instead direct their financial resources and attention toward more developed areas of the city. Other times, neglect is not purposeful. Slum dwellers, like poor people everywhere, may just "fall through the cracks of urban planning; migrants are rejected or simply ignored in the vain hope of deterring further migration."[68] Contested governance is often a problem. In the slums of Port-au-Prince, Haiti, there have been situations when more than 30 different gangs have tried to control different parts of the city.[69] The education and health care infrastructure and benefits of the city proper often do not extend to slum areas. In Jakarta, Indonesia, overall literacy rates for women are 94 percent, but in slums and other poor areas they are as low as 50 to 63 percent.[70] In Mumbai, half of slum neighborhoods have no primary schools.[71]

Slums can exacerbate structural insecurity in several ways. First, the crowded and unsanitary conditions can mean that slums pose a risk for the spread of disease. The UN reports that there has been some progress in reducing the high death rates in cities, but that "the threat of urban pandemics remains real."[72] In general, cities often have lower mortality than rural areas, but in slums, typhoid, cholera, and other water-borne diseases are prevalent, because human waste has nowhere to go and drinking water is unsafe. Indeed, residents of slums may often be the victims of environmental injustice, as they receive "the city's nuisances, including industrial effluent and noxious waste, and the only land accessible to slum dwellers is often fragile, dangerous or polluted—land that no one else wants."[73] Given these conditions, unrest can result. Slums can be the site of protests—violent and nonviolent—as they have been in South Africa. In 2005, South African slums were home to about 900 protests, half of which were violent.[74]

There is no universal pattern of slums and no universal prescription for slum improvement, but states have tried several measures.[75] One of the measures states have taken to address slums is to restrict migration from rural to urban areas to slow the growth of cities. These policies are misguided and likely to fail, because most urban growth comes from natural increase. Instead, states should plan for urban growth and work to provide land, infrastructure, and services for the poor. Policies known to reduce fertility, such as women's education and a better health infrastructure, would be a win–win situation for these cities. They would slow urban growth by lowering fertility and also provide a better quality of life for urbanites.[76]

"Slum-upgrading" is another option. For example, in an effort to improve its image, Mumbai's leaders have been trying to turn Mumbai into the "Shanghai of India" by upgrading the city's slums. Through public–private partnerships, Mumbai is trying to build roads, public housing, and a subway system.[77] Some argue that slum upgrading can work, as it did with Indonesia's *Kampung* Improvement Program, supported by the World Bank from 1974 to 1988.[78] Others, however, argue that slum upgrading fails to address the underlying cause of slums: poverty. They argue that the real solution is to institute "policies to support the livelihoods of the urban poor by enabling urban informal-sector activities to flourish and develop, by linking low-income housing development to income generation, and by ensuring easy geographical access to jobs through pro-poor transport and more appropriate location of low income settlements."[79] In Mumbai, the first step in the upgrading plan was to demolish the slums, and between December 2004 and March 2005 the government tore down more than 90,000 dwellings.[80] This policy removed the slum, but not the poverty that caused the slum in the first place. Living in a slum is clearly about more than just location of one's dwelling. Slum dwellers are often kept outside the formal economy by the stigma attached to their social position and the geographic isolation of slums. Yet, urban slums have their own "micro- and small enterprises within the retail, manufacturing, service, repair, and distribution sectors."[81] These could perhaps provide at least some foundation for improving the living conditions of individuals.

Brazil's cities are well known for their crime, corruption, and slums, or *favelas*, a term coined to describe a type of low-income settlement in which residents do not have claims of ownership to the land.[82] In Sao Paulo, slum upgrading was successful because of the particular strategy used by those in government. Brazil's traditional approach to *favelas* was to declare them *Zonas Especiais de Interesse Social* (special zones of social interest) and to work to improve their physical infrastructure, like streets and sewage systems, but without consulting or considering the needs of residents. When a slum-upgrading approach was adopted later, it involved a more comprehensive plan for improvement and turned the *favelas* into regular neighborhoods. Under the traditional approach to *favelas* that tried to turn them into special economic zones and upgrade their infrastructure, Daniel Budny says, "these informal neighborhoods did not officially exist."[83] Yet in some Brazilian cities, urban areas have been used to model the civil society foundations of democracy and use participatory democracy for their urban planning. Since 1996, the Brazilian city of Porto Alegre, capital of the southernmost state, Rio Grande do Sul, has had the highest standards of living and highest life expectancy of all Brazilian metropolitan areas. One author believes that the city's success is the result of the "popular administration" (*administração popular*) model of city management that has been in place since about 1990. Characteristics of this model include "the adoption of techniques for participatory democracy, a high level of citizen involvement in allocating the municipal budget, the reorientation of public priorities by citizens, the integration of public environmental management policies and the regeneration of public spaces."[84] In Porto Alegre, almost all homes have running water, good-quality sanitation, and garbage collection, including a separate collection of recyclables.[85]

There are drawbacks to the participatory democracy model, however. In Sao Paulo, efforts to introduce participatory democracy to help the urban Master Plan had mixed results. Although the model was supposed to enforce the principle of social justice, the process became a platform for the privileged and elite in society to air their concerns. Of the three main coalitions that spoke out during the urban planning debates, two represented rich and powerful interests: real estate developers and affluent upper middle-class neighborhoods. Only one was meant to represent the popular movement. The result was what Budny calls the "legalization of inequality." After the process, the city's more affluent areas have higher land use standards, whereas poorer areas have much lower standards.[86]

Experiences with the *favelas* demonstrate that physical infrastructure is useful, but one of the disadvantages of a slum is its lack of democratic connection to the larger state. Although they are home to a large part of the world's population, in practice slums exist on the margins of society. As Allison Garland et al. note: "Slum dwellers have been denied civic engagement and have no effective means to protect themselves, to make demands for goods and services, or to force accountability of those who represent them."[87] Experience with the *favelas* demonstrates that urbanization could potentially be a force for democratization. Tim Dyson has found a positive relationship between the two variables and attributes the positive relationship to the fact that urbanization focuses attention on the distribution of political power in society.[88]

## Natural Disasters

According to the United Nations Environment Program, between 1980 and 2000, 75 percent of the world's population lived in areas affected by a natural disaster.[89] The scale of human suffering from natural disasters is immense. Between January 1975 and October 2008, the International Emergency Disasters Database, EMDAT, recorded 8,866 events killing 2,283,767 people, excluding

disease epidemics. Of these, just 23 disasters killed 1,786,084 people.[90] When tragedy strikes a densely populated and crowded city, the damage is magnified, not
only in terms of human life but also economic impact. In urban areas, property
values are higher and communication and commerce cease when the complex
infrastructure is damaged. There were more than 700 major natural disasters in
1999 alone, and they caused more than $100 billion in economic losses and thou-
sands of victims.[91] One of the biggest problems is that some of the world's biggest or most important cities are vulnerable to repeated natural disasters. Kobe,
Japan, for example, is prone to earthquakes. The 1995 earthquake there killed
6,000 people and cost more than $100 billion.[92] In Iran, the 2003 earthquake in
the city of Bam killed an estimated 30,000 people and injured another 30,000.
According to the Iranian government, out of a population of 115,000, at least
45,000 were homeless in the immediate aftermath of the quake, and the government expected the number to increase to 75,000 after those who were staying out of town with relatives or in hospitals returned to the city.[93] Essentially,
then, this earthquake wiped out an entire city. Almost a decade earlier, in 1995,
another earthquake there killed 35,000.[94] In general, Iran is extremely vulnerable
to earthquakes, because the country sits on a network of fault lines. Tehran, the
capital, sits on *hundreds* of fault lines.[95] China, too, has had large portions of its
population affected by earthquakes. In May 2008, the most powerful earthquake
in China since 1976 affected Sichuan and parts of several other provinces. The
quake killed at least 87,556 people and injured more than 365,000. Around five
million buildings collapsed and more than 21 million buildings were damaged.[96]

Natural disasters make all cities vulnerable to destruction, but cities in
poor countries may have a harder time recovering. One problem is that in
cities of developing states, damage is often intensified because buildings are
not constructed to conform to strict earthquake codes. However, earthquakes
are only one threat. Several of the world's key cities are subject to landslides,
including Rio de Janeiro, Caracas, and Hong Kong. Others are prone to river
floods: Bangkok, Khartoum, Phnom Penh, Tijuana, Seoul, and Dhaka. Manila,
Shanghai, and Taipei are vulnerable to tropical storms, and Sydney and Los
Angeles are frequently plagued by wildfires.[97] Disasters in poor countries can
also be a problem because private property rights may be unsettled and insurance coverage is not as widespread. The government may not have the means to
deliver aid to needy people, much less to begin the arduous process of rebuilding. Slums face particular vulnerabilities. As the UN describes: "Many slums
are located on land not deemed appropriate for permanent habitation because
of its steep terrain or geological characteristics that make it prone to subsid-
ence, landslides or mudslides."[98] The unstable building materials, crowded
conditions, and means of cooking by open flame also make slums vulnerable
to fires and floods. Society's most vulnerable groups—women, migrants, children, and the elderly—are particularly at risk. After Bangladesh's 1991 cyclone,

women's mortality was more than three times that of men's.[99] Disaster relief costs drain development resources from productive investments to support consumption over short periods. Emergency loans have questionable value as vehicles for long-term investment, and contribute to country indebtedness without necessarily improving economic growth or reducing poverty, although they can certainly help relieve immediate suffering for many in the aftermath of a catastrophic event.[100]

Keeping urban areas secure after natural disasters is a major problem for all cities. After the levees broke in New Orleans as a result of Hurricane Katrina, the flooded city was subject to looting. However, in the dense, poor slum areas of the world, many of which already face competing claims of government legitimacy, there is a greater potential for crime after a disaster. After Haiti's 2010 earthquake, one reporter argued that the danger of crime and violence after disaster "is multiplied in Haiti, where self-designated rebels and freedom fighters—or simply neighborhood toughs—have consistently threatened the country's fragile stability with a few weapons, some spare money for handouts and the ire of disaffected throngs."[101] Vulnerability to natural disasters is also a military security issue, as militaries are often called upon to respond to disasters, given that they are the only organized and mobile resource that could potentially respond. The U.S. and Canadian governments responded to the 2010 earthquake in Haiti, and about 10,000 U.S. troops and 2,000 Canadian troops were expected to respond to the disaster.[102]

In additional to natural disasters, cities are also prone to what we might term "unnatural disasters," or environmental issues exacerbated by urban life. For example, because cities concentrate population and its waste, pollution can be a major problem. China is home to 16 of the 20 most polluted cities on the planet, and some estimate that environmental degradation costs China up to 12 percent of its GDP annually. Every year about 400,000 Chinese die prematurely of respiratory illnesses, and 30,000 children die from diarrhea caused by drinking unclean water.[103] Lastly, climate change may increase the frequency and magnitude of natural disasters. In particular, climate change is likely to exacerbate urban water supplies greatly, which are already stressed in terms of supply, distribution, and quality.[104]

A running theme in this book is that *how* a state deals with its demographic situation—or any other situation for that matter—is more important than the trends themselves. Though resilience is a concept applicable to a range of political challenges, it is perhaps particularly appropriate to the issue of natural disasters in urban areas. The UN has taken note of this as well:

Resilience has been defined as the capacity of an individual, household or community to adjust to threats, to avoid or mitigate harm, as well as to recover from risky events or shocks. Resilience is partly dependent upon the effectiveness of risk response, as well as the capability to respond in the future. Pathways towards greater resilience have to address issues of institutional effectiveness, application of international human rights law and involvement of civil society.[105]

Rebuilding after disasters and planning for urban growth or expansion must be done with vulnerability in mind. Demography is a useful tool for pre-positioning assets and the knowledge that urban centers are vulnerable to disaster can help prepare to meet the challenges. According to Arthur Lerner-Lam, Associate Director of Geology and Geophysics at Columbia University, "There are hot spots around the world where poverty and natural-hazard risk are going to continue to produce these high-level disasters with high casualties, but we know where those hot spots are. So there's a lot more we can do before the fact to mitigate the human suffering."[106]

## CONCLUSION

Cities are strategic assets to the global economy, to the states they are a part of, and to the individuals for whom they provide opportunities. As such, cities should receive significant attention in national security planning. Given their vulnerability, analysis of demographic and environmental challenges of cities can serve as an indicator of potential instability and allow militaries to pre-position assets or at least plan for future aid needs. In spite of their vulnerability, cities have the potential to create economies of scale, encourage new opportunities for economic growth, and foster innovation. With smart planning, cities can provide citizens with access to education, jobs, and a better standard of living. In this sense, cities can be responsible for creating military security, through economic power, and structural security, through better standards of living. As we saw with Brazil, cities can also be a site of democratization and therefore increase the stability and regime security of states. With globalization, large cities are "the principal nodes generating and mediating the flows of capital, people, trade, greenhouse gases, pollutants, diseases, and information."[107] As urban growth continues, "cities will carry a heavy charge of responsibility for political stability, openness, economic progress, and the quality of life in many nations."[108] In fact, many believe that urbanization is the answer to pulling less developed countries out of extreme poverty, given the connection between urbanization and economic growth. In Africa, the countries urbanizing the fastest are also the ones with the best economic performance.[109] Although states should be aware of the vulnerabilities urbanization and urban areas cause for national security, they should also seize opportunities to ensure that these demographic trends increase state power and security.

# 7
## Chapter

# Other Challenges
# of Composition

And you, be ye fruitful, and multiply; bring forth abundantly in the earth,
and multiply therein.

—Genesis 9:7 (www.gospel.com)

Go forth and multiply. Pronounced millennia ago, these words—or ones like
them in other faiths—cemented for many the practice of ensuring the continuation of one's group through numbers. For some, though, such words
were about more than just survival. Demography could be a tool of warfare, a
strategy to ensure long-term victory over the enemy by "outbirthing" them. In
these cases, the demographic practice reflected already existing hatreds, where
groups used demography to increase their own security.

Even in cases where shifts in demographic composition are unintentional,
they can still create insecurity and play a role in the eruption of both violent and nonviolent conflict. This chapter describes the security challenges of
four categories of composition: age structure challenges from high mortality; gender imbalances; and differential growth among ethnic and religious
groups. Age structure is, of course, one of the major categories of composition.
Chapters 2, 3, and 4 covered a number of the links between age structure and
national security, focusing on the relative composition of youth, working-age,
and elderly members of society created, for the most part, by shifts in fertility. This chapter alters the lens and looks briefly at the ways that mortality
creates changes in composition. The cases of HIV/AIDS throughout Africa
and numerous health problems in Russia illustrate how death can amend age
structure in ways that create challenges to national security. In addition to age
structure, the composition of males and females within a society can also create conditions conducive to insecurity. Gender ratio imbalance is a relatively

new area of political demography research, but one that has implications for two of the world's most strategic states: India and China. Differential growth among identity groups, such as religions or ethnicities, is a final category of compositional shift. Countries from Israel, to Russia, to the United States have experienced hostilities arising from the differential growth among their religious or ethnic groups.

Composition is distinct from size, growth, and distribution, but each of these population attributes creates multiple challenges and opportunities for national security.[1] This chapter rounds out the analysis of these attributes. As we have seen, the size of the population is mostly correlated with measurements of power. Growth has similar connections to power, particularly when there is differential growth among countries at the international level. Growth also creates concerns about the government's ability to meet the needs of the population, because absolute size matters. Distribution issues arise mostly through movements of people, and increased density can either strain services or facilitate access to them, depending on the circumstances. Composition is a distinct category with a range of political consequences. Despite its importance, composition, particularly the four themes of this chapter, has been underappreciated in political science and policy approaches. Including these four areas—high mortality, gender imbalance, and differential growth among ethnic and religious groups—can illuminate military, regime, and structural insecurities.

The way that high mortality alters the composition of a population is primarily by creating military and structural insecurity. HIV/AIDS in Africa is changing the composition of African states' populations and poses threats in all three realms of security. Military forces are often devastated by high infection rates, as is the civil service and skilled labor force. From a structural standpoint, HIV/AIDS is robbing these countries of teachers, doctors, and parents, and leaving orphans in its wake who may not have the socialization and care they need to serve as the next generation of their country's teachers, doctors, and parents. In Russia, alcoholism and infectious disease are affecting the quality and effectiveness of the population. High mortality has particularly devastated the male population, which limits the number of military-eligible young men and creates a different sort of military insecurity. In Russia's case, the gender imbalance is also the manifestation of structural insecurity, because high mortality among what would normally be the most productive segments of society reflects the inability of the society to create conditions that would allow the population to flourish.

In other cases, a surplus, not a dearth, of young men is the problem. Cultural practices, such as abortion, lead to imbalanced sex ratios at birth. These societies end up with high proportions of young men, which creates military security implications for reasons similar to those described in the chapter on youthful age structures. In these societies, higher proportions of males raise the possibility that the state will mobilize these restless young men into military service, or that two enemy states will mobilize their respective forces against each other. From a security standpoint, this problem is most acute in China and India. Gender imbalances also create regime security implications because of the correlation between high proportions of unmarried males and high crime rates.

Differential growth among ethnic and religious groups is mostly correlated with regime insecurity. There are always differences in fertility and mortality among groups in a society; these may vary according to socioeconomic class, geographic region, or identity group.[2] Over time, these differences produce major changes in the composition of the society as relative proportions of these groups change. Yet, unlike shifts in age structure, which take place over time, changes in ethnic or religious composition can become problematic when they are unusually rapid or are perceived as driven by unlawful, intentional, or illegitimate forces, such as immigration. Democracies that have major differences in growth rates between different ethnic or religious groups may face regime security issues as factions resist or exploit the ways that changing compositions of the electorate affect the political leadership. In authoritarian states, similar changes in composition have the potential to motivate rebellion in a push for more representative government. At the same time, a multiethnic society by itself need not mean conflict is inevitable. On the contrary, multiethnic societies can be positive when they mix creative people of different backgrounds and give birth to new ideas.

For all the challenges of composition, there are still policy responses that can temper the effects. Political variables can often explain why similar composition issues have different security outcomes. As health security scholar Andrew Price-Smith points out, political capacity and good governance have been the major factors in why Zimbabwe's AIDS epidemic is ruining the country, whereas Botswana has been relatively successful at stabilizing HIV/AIDS rates.[3] In particular, Botswana has nearly halted mother-to-child transmission.[4] China's gender imbalance, like most of their demographic issues, is tempered by the heavy hand of the state. A surplus of young males can actually be seen as the engine that drives China's manufacturing economy. Even in cases of differential growth of identity groups, institutions are important. As the Arab Human Development Report states: "Clashes that may appear on the surface to stem from identity in fact often originate in skewed access to political power or wealth, in a lack of channels for representative political participation, and in the suppression of cultural and linguistic diversity."[5] Having peaceful, permanent channels to redress grievances, such as through regular, fair elections, certainly helps provide an outlet. As we will see, political access may be one reason why differential growth among ethnic groups in democratic

Canada has led to nonviolent conflict, whereas composition changes have exploded into ethnic violence in numerous other nondemocratic cases.

# HIGH MORTALITY
## HIV/AIDS

Worldwide improvements in mortality have been an essential part of the demographic transition to lower fertility, as declining infant mortality rates have encouraged families to have fewer children, with the confidence that more of them will survive to adulthood. A high prevalence of HIV/AIDS creates new and unique issues with regard to mortality, because it reduces life expectancy for adults and creates a distinct age structure with wide-ranging security implications. HIV/AIDS is present in countries around the world, but the problem has been most serious in the African region as a whole, and has had the greatest impact on these states' population profiles. At times, in some Southern African countries, HIV has affected more than a third of the population.[6] HIV/AIDS can undermine any benefit a country might reap from progress along the demographic transition. For example, in Botswana, which has the second highest prevalence rate in the world, 24 percent of the population is infected,[7] and the population older than 30 years of age is noticeably devastated (see Fig. 7.1). This pattern of mortality is typical of states with high HIV/AIDS prevalence. Ninety percent of fatalities associated with HIV infection occur among people of working age and are concentrated between the ages of 25 to 39 years.[8]

Whenever large segments of the population are decimated, particularly those of productive ages, there are multiple security implications. For the militaries of states with high prevalence rates, readiness, unit cohesion, and peacekeeping efforts may suffer. In many cases, the HIV/AIDS infection rates for soldiers are several times higher than for civilians.[9] For example, infection rates are three to four times higher for the military in Zimbabwe and Cameroon than they are for civilians.[10] Soldiers often have higher infection rates because they are of prime sexually active age, are away from home and family for long periods of time, and have access to money and prostitutes. The risk-seeking culture of the military may also play a role.[11] In 1999, HIV/AIDS prevalence rates in the armed forces were estimated to be 55 percent in Zimbabwe, 50 percent in Angola, 50 percent in Malawi, 33 percent in Botswana, and 21 percent in South Africa.[12] Such high rates mean that HIV/AIDS kills more than combat. According to figures released in 2002, seven out of ten military deaths in South Africa are AIDS-related.[13] Seventy percent of deaths in the South African National Defense Force are from HIV/AIDS-related complications.[14] HIV/AIDS disrupts military command structures by decimating middle- and high-ranking officers; HIV levels among the upper middle ranks

**Figure 7.1** Population tree for Botswana, 2005. (Population Action International)

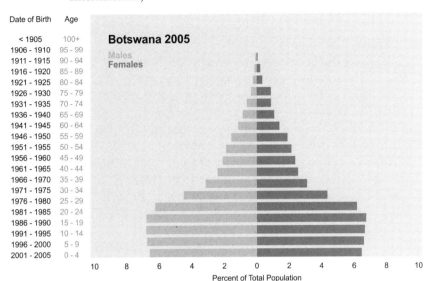

are often in excess of 40 percent.[15] In some cases, governments are promoting inexperienced junior officers to these command positions, which can have implications for the effectiveness of the armed forces.[16] In Western countries, although there is often discussion of how HIV/AIDS will affect peacekeeping forces, UN peacekeepers do not seem to be as affected by HIV/AIDS as national militaries are, in part because of major efforts by the UN to control the spread of HIV. HIV/AIDS is still present among peacekeepers, though, and many of the same concerns are present as with national militaries, including the risk of spreading the disease to surrounding populations through prostitution or rape.[17]

Economic challenges associated with the disease can also affect state power and thus military security. Alex de Waal argues that AIDS not only causes the economy of a state with high prevalence to contract, it causes a "structurally changed economy" that affects development. In particular, high AIDS infection rates in a country affect savings, investment, and capital accumulation.[18] Foreign investors are not likely to want to invest in countries where the disease is so prevalent. The lack of economic development sets up a spiral in which these states must continue to rely on humanitarian aid, rather than develop economies of their own. Which segments of the population are dying matters as well. Highly or semiskilled workers can have a disproportionately high economic impact, because they represent an investment in

training and are harder to replace than unskilled workers. Professional classes
are especially valuable. Another area is access to resources. AIDS in Africa
even affects wealthy states with low infection rates, because it is driving up
the costs of mining for precious metals, and could drive up the costs of petro-
leum as well.[19]

There may also be some regime security implications if HIV/AIDS affects
governance, particularly institutional capacity and political participation.
Certainly, the high mortality caused by AIDS means that the state loses human
resources, including the experience and professional networks that citizens
may have formed. The disease can also affect grassroots civil society, an important part of a functioning democracy. A study in KwaZulu–Natal found that
HIV/AIDS losses of staff members and volunteers undermined the capacities
of local civil society organizations.[20] The effects on civil society are serious. In
many African countries, nongovernmental organizations have been the predominate channels through which social action takes place, in part because of
governance issues.[21] Police, an essential part of maintaining law and order in
a democracy, are not immune to the devastation of the disease. Laurie Garrett
assesses that in countries where the general population's HIV infection rate
exceeds five percent, the police will have infection rates similar to the general
population.[22] In the Kenyan police force, HIV/AIDS is responsible for 75 percent
of all deaths.[23] Therefore, the ability of the state to have a monopoly on violence is also disrupted in cases of high prevalence.

Other regime security connections are less certain and will unfold over
time. The numerous AIDS orphans, who grow up with poor supervision and
socialization, may be at higher than average risk of engaging in criminal activity.[24] There is also evidence that minority white populations are being cast
as scapegoats in some countries, and violence against these populations may
increase as infection rates and mortality climb.[25] In countries where HIV/
AIDS weakens the state, the outcome in some cases could be an improvement
in governance. In what is perhaps good news for those who want to displace
the leadership in Zimbabwe, Price-Smith assesses that leader Robert Mugabe's
"military strength, which serves as an instrument of control over legitimate
democratic processes, will slowly and almost invisibly erode over the next
decade."[26] Eventually, social and political processes could lead to the overthrow
of the government as the disease progresses, if citizens perceive the state as
weak in a context of increasing deprivation.[27] Destabilization in the shortrun
could be a positive development for Zimbabwe if a more capable leader comes
to power.

There may also be competing health priorities in states with high prevalence, because so much needs to be spent on HIV/AIDS as opposed to other
public health services and structures. Emigration of skilled health professionals only adds to the problem.[28] Agricultural laborers in Africa have also been hit

hard, increasing the risk of famine.[29] In most cases, significant income is lost from the illness during the 12 months before dying. Data from Botswana suggest that HIV reduces per-capita household income by 10 percent, with average income losses almost twice as high for households in the lowest income level.[30] Of course, there are many tragic structural security implications. The burden of caring for orphaned children often falls on the elderly, who may have reduced capacity to work because of senescence, and may lack any sort of state-funded pension system. Grandmothers care for 40 to 60 percent of orphans in Namibia, the United Republic of Tanzania, and Zimbabwe.[31]

HIV/AIDS is a threat to national security because it is a threat to the total nation. Like many population issues, the "actions taken to confront the disease as matters of domestic policy or foreign aid may differ markedly from those taken to address threats to national security," as Laurie Garrett says.[32] The danger with seeing HIV/AIDS as a national security threat is that it securitizes infected people and may paint them as enemies of the state. Securitizing them could justify their repression in the name of national defense.[33] Stefan Elbe lists some other dangers with securitizing the disease, in particular that it "allows states to prioritize AIDS funding for their elites and armed forces who play a crucial role in maintaining security" and that "portraying the illness as an overwhelming 'threat' works against ongoing efforts to normalize social perceptions regarding HIV/AIDS."[34] Many of the African states with a high prevalence of HIV/AIDS continue to have high fertility rates, meaning that AIDS mortality is not having a significant impact on population growth, but is straining educational opportunities for children left behind.[35] The combination of disease, high population growth, and strained resources, in the context of lack of political capacity, means that future prospects for many African states are dim, barring major changes in one of these variables.

The political variable could lead the way. Although HIV/AIDS is devastating, many countries around the world have made admirable strides in stemming the epidemic. As devastated as its working-age population is, Botswana has done relatively well in dealing with its epidemic as a result of political leadership and state capacity.[36] Thailand is another of these success stories. In Thailand, the government and civil society have played important roles in slowing the spread of the disease. In the 1980s, Thailand looked poised to have one of the world's worst outbreaks of HIV/AIDS. Some projected that the virus would spread rapidly and infect as many as four million of the country's 65 million people by 2000. In a quick response, though, the government launched a comprehensive education and prevention campaign; after infection peaked at 143,000 in 1991, the annual number of new cases of HIV infection fell to 19,000 in 2003. Although Thailand still has a serious problem with HIV/AIDS, the government's quick response saved many lives.[37] Aid commitments and partnerships between governments and civil society can go far in reducing the impact of HIV/AIDS. Thus far, as UNAIDS notes, "The epidemic has not shattered national economies or threatened the viability of any national government."[38] As prevalence intensifies, however, the implications could become more severe.

### Russia's Lack of Adult Males

High mortality in Russia has created both age structure and gender imbalance issues, with far more females, especially of older ages, than males. Female life expectancy, on the other hand, is more than 13 years higher. Differences in lifestyle account for the gap. Russia's serious demographic issues make it hard to believe the country was once in competition with the United States for global dominance during the Cold War. Russia's crude death rate, the measure of deaths per 1,000 people, has been on the rise, going from 9.5 per 1,000 in 1950 to 15 per 1,000 in 2010. Life expectancy has followed in tandem. The average male born during 1985 to 1990 could expect to live 63.8 years. Less than 20 years later, the average male born between 2000 and 2005 had a life expectancy of only 59.5 years.[39] Russia's male life expectancy is more like that of a developing state than a great power, leading many, including U.S. Secretary of Defense Robert Gates, to write off Russia publicly as a legitimate threat.[40] At 60.3 years, Russia's male life expectancy is not too much higher than Ghana's or Guinea's, both at 55.6.[41]

As has been widely reported, alcohol is the major killer. Alexander Nemtsov, a senior researcher at the Institute of Psychiatry, estimates that excess alcohol consumption is directly or indirectly responsible for nearly 30 percent of all male deaths and 17 percent of female deaths in Russia. This percentage translates to more than 400,000 deaths a year from drink-related causes, including heart disease, accidents, suicides, and murders.[42] In a population of 140 million, with a very low fertility rate of 1.4 children per woman, such numbers represent nationally significant losses.[43] According to Russia's leading demographer, Russia's health problems are, in part, a result of the government's choices during the Cold War to invest money in Russia's external security and national defense, instead of in a health care system that would address the main problems plaguing Russia.[44] Today's leaders seem similarly misguided. In his publicized remarks on Russia's population from the 2006 annual address to the nation, Putin emphasized programs that will facilitate childbearing, and only barely mentioned Russia's high mortality rate, which is arguably a much bigger issue for the country, because any babies born today would have a low life expectancy and would thus contribute little to reversing Russia's population decline.[45] In January 2010, Russia reported a four percent decline in mortality rates, but optimism about a permanent turnaround should be modest, because Putin and other leaders seem to send a signal that they consider Russia's population problem as primarily one of birthrates, not death rates.[46]

In general, the government's response to the health crisis has been inadequate. Demographer and economist Nicholas Eberstadt has claimed that Russia's dire health situation is tantamount to ethnic self-cleansing.[47] Poor lifestyle choices have led to high incidences of cardiovascular disease. Other diseases, like tuberculosis (TB), are serious as well. The TB mortality rate reached 22 cases per 100,000 in 2002 and remains high. An even more serious problem is multidrug-resistant TB. The proportion of new TB cases that were multidrug-resistant in the civilian sector increased from 8.1 percent in 2004 to 9.5 percent in 2005. In the prisons, however, TB infection rates have improved. Adding to its mortality woes, Russia has one of the fastest growing HIV/AIDS epidemics in the world.[48] Finally, abortion rates are comparable with birthrates. According to Health Minister Tatyana Golikova, in 2009, Russia registered 1.7 million births and 1.2 million abortions.[49]

Although not as severe as that of Russian men, the health situation for women is also precarious. In 2005, a Russian woman's risk of death in childbirth was more than six times higher than her peer in Germany or Switzerland. Consequently, mortality for women in their twenties has been increasing in recent decades.[50] In some ways, then, Eberstadt's assessment is right; but, rather than Russia as a whole, it may actually be that Slavic Russians are the ones committing ethnic self-cleansing. Muslim men face far fewer health challenges, possibly because of the lifestyle choices encouraged by their religion, which include staying sober and staying married.[51]

There are, of course, many security implications of Russia's demographic situation. Harley Balzer of Georgetown University argues that there is intense competition among the military, the education system, and employers for the declining number of healthy working-age people.[52] Primary school enrollment is down to just 91 percent in 2004, from 99 percent in 1991, and 1 in 70 children is in a children's home, orphanage, or state boarding care.[53] Those children are the country's future workforce, meaning that long-term economic prospects are dimmed, particularly if Russia tries to diversify its energy-based economy to industries that rely on human capital. Although considered part of the BRIC economies, Russia clearly stands out from a demographic perspective. Brazil, India, and China all have a fairly favorable demographic prognosis, and factors covered in other chapters indicate that their global political power is increasing in tandem. Russia is a different story. The connection between economic growth and working-age population is just one part of Russia's dire prognosis. The other is the obvious lack of a health care infrastructure, which has been shown to contribute to the effectiveness of the population in cases of other states, like those in East Asia, that went through the demographic transition.

Russia's high male mortality rate creates a unique age structure that reflects serious challenges for the well-being of elderly women. Women's life expectancy is 13 years more than men's, meaning that many women are left without companions or caretakers in their old age. Because women are left to care for themselves at older ages, they need more help; the combination of low life expectancy for men and low fertility means that these women do not have extended family networks to help with their care. Instead of family, then, they turn to the state for help. In a series of interviews with elderly Russian women, reporter Luke Harding found that the women see the Soviet era as a golden age. One woman interviewed, named Tamara, said: "The '70s and early '80s were best. We didn't have to pay for anything. There was free education and free hospitals. But after this things fell apart. At some point all the people left."[54] Today there are at least 34,000 villages that are home to 10 people or fewer, almost all of them elderly women. There are more than 30 million pensioners in Russia, and many live in poverty.[55] These demographic patterns create conditions that encourage support for a stronger and more pervasive Russian state. Revenues from oil have allowed the government to provide somewhat higher living standards, but pensions are still meager and many women are just scraping by.

There are direct military implications of Russia's high male mortality rate, because most of the deaths are of military-age males. Although the life expectancy for this group is 59.5 years, that figure is an average, and it disguises how young many males are when they die. In 2003, the BBC reported that for at least the fifth year in a row, more Russian servicemen were killed in noncombat situations than in fighting.[56] In September of that year, the Russian Ministry of Defense released figures that showed that from January through August 2003, 1,200 military personnel were killed in noncombat circumstances. The main causes were accidents, carelessness, bullying, and suicide.[57] Alcohol likely played a role in many deaths. According to the Russian Ministry of Defense, the latest decisions by the Russian government render the prior system of manning inadequate to maintain Russia's military strength, in part because of the shortage of the draft-age manpower and because of the liberal legislation allowing about 90 percent of eligible young men to avoid conscription. They say that 2005 marks the year the Russian federation starts its slide into a "demographic pit." The ministry also expresses concern about the future quality of recruits. Ministry members bemoan the move to a contract-based system, because they claim that the contract servicemen "do not represent the best segment of the country's youth. At present, the majority of contract enlistees comprise people who have, for various reasons, failed to fulfill themselves in civil life."[58] They have been working on programs to recruit higher quality soldiers and to improve the public's perception of the armed forces, as well.

Russian leadership seems to expect that they will be able to have an energy-based economy and that their international power will come from their energy sources. Despite the severity of Russia's internal problems, demography receives little attention in the most recent Russian defense strategy, but the strategy does mention a need for preventive health care for HIV and other potential epidemics and pandemics. Although perhaps out of place, the strategy also mentions a role for the military to "create conditions . . . for stimulating fertility."[59] Russia is also streamlining its armed services, with plans to cut the officer corps by more than half—from 360,000 to 150,000.[60] How Russia will be able to keep the country intact with so many border skirmishes and a declining military is a major challenge to the Russian leadership. However, Russia continues to act aggressively in international politics, placing a flag of ownership on the North Pole, cutting off energy supplies to its Western neighbors, and speaking out against what it sees as NATO encroachment into its former republics. They should not be counted out yet.

## GENDER IMBALANCE

The differential mortality rates between males and females in Russia illustrate the challenges of a surplus of elderly females, who often need help with making ends meet, and a dearth of prime-age males, whose absence weakens the military establishment. How are the security implications different when there is a dearth of young women and a surplus of young males?[61] According to a relatively new line of research, such societies may have a higher risk of both international conflict and civil disorder. The most influential of these works has been the article and subsequent book *Bare Branches* by Valerie M. Hudson and Andrea M. den Boer. These scholars portray exaggerated gender inequality and skewed sex ratios as national security concerns, because rootless males can challenge the state.[62] The term "bare branches" refers to the Chinese label for men who end the genealogical line when they are unable to find a partner to marry and have children with. Women tend to marry up in social status, a practice called "hypergyny," leaving the least educated and poorest males without partners. These "surplus males" can become a threat to the state—"regime security" in the parlance of this book—because they lack the socialization of marriage and lack economic opportunities, given their low educational attainment.

"Marrying up" by itself is only part of the problem. The other part of the story is Asia's "missing females." Preference for male children has led to sex-selective abortion and female infanticide in many parts of the world. In most societies, the normal sex ratio at birth is around 105 boys born for every 100 girls. The slightly higher number of male births is possibly an evolutionary adaptation to the higher survival probabilities of females. As Dudley Poston and

Karen Glover explain: "Since at every year of life males have higher age-specific death rates than females, around 105 or so males are required at birth for every 100 females for there to be about equal numbers of males and females when the groups reach the marriageable ages."[63] In China, the imbalanced ratios are primarily driven by sex-selective abortion, not infanticide.[64] The same is true for India's low sex ratio at birth, where prenatal sex determination is followed by selective abortion of female fetuses. Conservative estimates are that sex selective abortion in India accounts for half a million missing females a year, or 10 million abortions of female fetuses during the past two decades.[65] Because of this problem, India and China have banned the use of sex-selective technologies, which have been available at a fairly low cost since the mid 1980s.[66] Yet, technology has only made an existing cultural practice easier. There is a long history of the problem in India, as even British colonial authorities tried to find ways to address the issue. According to the literature, couples choose to abort female fetuses because they view females as less valuable to their families for both social and economic reasons.[67] For India as a whole, the government estimates its birth sex ratio as approximately 113 boy babies born for every 100 girl babies, but some areas of India have registered ratios as high as 156:100.[68] It is possible that, in China, the national data on sex ratio at birth may be biased upward, because the one-child policy encourages the underreporting of the births of girls,[69] but most agree that the imbalance is real and severe.

It is important to understand the extent to which an imbalanced sex ratio at birth translates to a bride shortage, because the literature assumes that the lack of socialization from marriage is part of the causal link between young men and national security. Several researchers dispute the severity of the problem. Using data on age of first marriage, Poston and Glover assume that if Chinese males born in 1978 decide to marry when they are 22 and look for brides who are age 20, there will be a surplus of more than 23.5 million males looking for wives between the years of 2000 and 2021. According to these scholars, "there will not be enough Chinese women in the marriage market for them to marry."[70] Richard Cincotta, in his review of Hudson and den Boer's work, considers delayed marriage as a solution. Like Poston and Glover, Cincotta chooses to look at sex ratio at marriage, instead of sex ratio at birth, as Hudson and den Boer do. Unlike Poston and Glover, Cincotta expands the available pool of marriage-age women and estimates the sex ratio at marriage as equal to the number of males age 25 to 29 divided by the number of females age 20 to 24, because he says that in many societies men marry women more than five years their junior when they delay marriage to pursue other goals, such as obtaining skills, education, or accumulating wealth. He finds that the sex ratio at marriage using these five-year intervals fluctuates between extreme highs (about 135 males to 100 females) and extreme lows (fewer than 80 males to 100 females) from 1950 to 2000.[71] Poston and Glover use a two-year difference, because that is the current average age difference for first marriages in China, but certainly we must allow for cultural changes that meet the demographic reality. Therefore, Cincotta's estimates of a more flexible marriage market may be more accurate.

There are many states in the world with surplus males and missing females, including South Korea, India, Pakistan, Bhutan, Vietnam, Afghanistan, and China, but the ones that concern national security scholars the most, and the ones on which Hudson and den Boer focus, are India and China.[72] If there is a link between internal violence (especially against women) and violence between societies, bare branches in these two states are especially dangerous. Animosities between China and India over disagreements about the status of the Dalai Lama or territorial disputes could escalate. Bare branches, although not the cause of the disagreement, could play a role in heightening the tension between China and Taiwan, as well. Hudson and den Boer's book, and their article in *International Security* that preceded it, drew attention to an understudied, but potentially important, security problem.[73] Yet, there has been little follow-up in the security community on the issues they raised. Although Hudson and den Boer argue that because of sex selection in China and India democracy is threatened, and authoritarianism may be needed to combat instability, there is little evidence that gender imbalance is the cause of political problems there. Likewise, their claims that skewed sex ratios may exacerbate conflict between India–Pakistan and China–Taiwan are thus far unsupported.

There are many potential regime security implications of gender imbalance that are similar to arguments about youth bulge. There is evidence that unwed men are predisposed to substance abuse, violent crime, and collective aggression.[74] Hudson and den Boer argue, "men who are not provided the opportunity to develop a vested interest in a system of law and order will gravitate toward a system based on physical force, in which they hold an advantage over other members of society."[75] However, if they are given economic opportunities—migrating to the city, for example—they should be able to find some worth in economic success.

China, a country of surplus males, abuts Russia, a country with a surplus of females. The international marriage market is one policy response to mediating the sex ratio imbalance and the possible security challenges stemming from it. Some of this is legal, but some of it is not. One potential implication of the bride shortage is that domestic trafficking could increase. Thus far, there are no signs that an increase in human trafficking is occurring, because of the differential growth of males in China. In China, the majority of trafficking has been internal, and there are between 10,000 and 20,000 cases annually. Most of the trafficking is for sexual exploitation, forced labor and begging, and forced marriage. Ninety percent of reported trafficking cases are women and children, who are often trafficked from poorer rural areas. They are usually abducted or lured to urban centers under the pretence of employment, only to be forced into prostitution or labor. As part of the global total, however, China's domestic trafficking is not a large proportion. The International Labor Organization estimates that 2,450,000 persons are being exploited as victims of human trafficking worldwide, but China has less than 20,000 cases annually. Given the country's large population of 1.3 billion, this number means that trafficking does not affect a large percentage of the total population.[76] Although the problem is growing elsewhere, a recent report by the UN Office on Drugs and Crime paints human trafficking as still a European.[77] Rather than a market at home, increasingly, Chinese female victims are showing up in European countries; in 2008, Chinese were the largest foreign group involved in sexual exploitation in Italy and in the Netherlands.[78]

Differential growth in the male population could also be a way for China to increase its national security through mobilizing surplus males for the economic benefit of the state. In the past, some governments have recruited excess males into large-scale public works projects.[79] China has many of these in both urban centers and in its more remote regions. Using excess males to fuel the large public works projects in the country would increase China's economic growth rather than cause conflict and regime instability.[80] China has also been sending its males abroad to harvest natural resources on other continents, instead of using local labor. China is not likely to recruit these surplus males into the army. Doing so would conflict with their goal of downsizing and streamlining the ground forces, which is necessary in part because pension benefits are so costly, the ground forces are expensive to maintain in general, and because China is reallocating resources toward more expeditionary capabilities.

## DIFFERENTIAL GROWTH AMONG ETHNIC GROUPS

Differential growth among ethnic and religious groups also presents major challenges to national security. Although there is some overlap between these two categories, they are distinct and will be covered in separate sections. There are fewer than 200 sovereign states, but thousands of nations and ethnic groups, so ethnically homogeneous states are rare, as Monica Duffy Toft has pointed out.[81] Because obviously not every country is embattled in civil war, we know that most of the time groups of different religions or cultures resolve their differences peacefully. Why some states are able to deal peacefully with their differential demographics whereas others explode into civil war, engage in genocide, or collapse is important to understand. This section will emphasize the role that demography plays, but there is a large literature on ethnic conflict that looks at a multitude of factors. In general, the context within which changes in composition take place matters most, as we saw with the discussion of age structure in previous chapters.

Theories of ethnic conflict are quite complex, combining *how* differences in identity are created or made salient, *who* does so, and *what* issues identity groups are mobilized around. They also factor differently the roles of elites and the state itself. Management of ethnic conflict is another branch of the literature, positing assimilation, consociation, federation, and other tactics and political arrangements to foster peace. Most theories generally fall into two broad categories—rationalist and psychological–constructivist approaches—although many bridge or combine the two. Theories stemming from the rationalist approach tend to focus on material factors and the role of information and perception. Economic rivalry theories assume that ethnic war is a function of individuals' pursuit of material benefits. Coalitions can form around ethnic differences, and individuals will engage in rent-seeking behavior on behalf of their group.[82] The concept of the ethnic security dilemma also comes from the rationalist approach. According to this theory, actions by one group can lead to feelings of insecurity by the other, potentially escalating to the point of violence.[83] The psychological–constructivist approach includes theories that have been mostly dismissed, like primordial arguments about ancient hatreds, and also theories that draw from social science more broadly and examine the roles of myths and symbols, which can lead to ethnic conflict when manipulated to create differences.[84] Political elites may manipulate ethnic differences to further their interests. Several scholars have examined the relationship of different groups, their number, sizes, and characteristics. Tanja Ellingsen found that wars are more likely in two cases: when the largest group is less than 80 percent of a state's population and in multinational states with fewer groups.[85] Marie Besançon found that greater economic inequality more profoundly affects revolutions, and greater social and political inequality affects ethnic-driven wars.[86] Power transition theory may be a useful framework to help us better understand the conditions under which declining powers within a state would go to war, but thus far the application of this theory has been limited.[87]

There are also several plausible causal mechanisms that can link ethnic violence to international conflict. Leaders can unite their diverse societies by attacking an external adversary—a "rally 'round the flag." Second, internal ethnic conflict can weaken the state so much that it is vulnerable to external attack. Third, efforts to diffuse ethnic tension at home could backfire by undermining military effectiveness. One example given by Ronald Krebs and Jack Levy is the pre-1914 Russian strategy of widely dispersing troops of the same ethnic background throughout the country so as not to concentrate troops of any one ethnicity in a single location. "The spread of the troops slowed mobilization and encouraged the Germans in thinking they could quickly defeat France before turning their attention eastward." Finally, in cases when minorities with ties external to the country are treated poorly, outside interests may threaten or engage in conflict with the host state on their behalf.[88] As we will see, the 2008 Russia–Georgia conflict is an example of this.

Although these ties between differential demographics among ethnic groups and civil or international conflict have some support in the literature, there are several theoretical problems when assessing composition from a purely demographic perspective. First, demography, particularly differential growth, overpredicts ethnic conflict because, in most instances, multiethnic societies do not have large-scale ethnic violence. Second, identity is mutable, and a demographic perspective does not explain why some identities are mobilized into violence and others are not.[89] Identities shift over time; one that is politically mobilized today may not be salient in the future. Third, focusing on demography could cause us to exclude the important role of the state, particularly the degree of state weakness or strength.

## Ethnic Differences and Violent Outcomes

Although many multiethnic states are peaceful, there is no denying that millions have died in ethnic-based civil war and genocide on continents from Africa to Europe. One violent example, and the subject of much ethnic conflict research, is Yugoslavia. Although there were a multitude of factors that contributed to tensions there, demography played a large role. From 1961 to 1991, Albanians grew far faster than Serbs. The consequences of this differential growth turned bloody when Serb leader Slobodan Milosevic launched an ethnic cleansing campaign to make up for the population shortfall.[90] Eventually, the conflict abated after, but not necessarily due to, controversial action by NATO. Because international norms encourage inter-governmental organizations, like the UN and NATO, to continue to intervene in ethnic conflicts like Yugoslavia's, these organizations can expect continued and perhaps increased need for intervention. In the future, calls for intervention may increasingly come from the African continent, where population growth will continue to be high while land and resources per capita dwindle. Some ethnic leaders are also likely to continue to encourage differential growth purposely that benefits their group. Myron Weiner and Michael Teitelbaum refer to these practices as "demographic engineering," which they define as "the full range of government policies intended to affect the size, composition, distribution, and growth rate of a population."[91] Demography will also likely continue to be used as a tool to fight against encroachment, as the opening paragraphs of this chapter described. Intentional or unintentional, both actual and perceived differences in the size or growth rates of different ethnic groups can be a driver of conflict.

Russia has long had differential growth among its ethnic and religious groups. Judyth Twigg assesses that, today, "fertility in the most heavily Muslim regions is significantly and consistently higher than in Russia as a whole, and quite decisively higher than in the most heavily Slavic regions."[92] Since 1999, though, the gap in fertility between Muslims and Slavs has narrowed. Because the Russian census does not ask religion, Twigg infers religion from ethnicity, which is an imperfect method; still, the numbers are useful. In the 2002 census, Muslims comprised about 10 percent of the total Russian population, but they dominate certain regions, such as Dagestan, Tatarstan, North Ossetia, and Ingushetia, which lies to the West of primarily Muslim Chechnya. Fertility is not the only difference, though. Muslims have higher unemployment and a lower standard of living, which could create even more animosity toward the Russian majority.[93] Differential growth among these groups is not a new trend. Historically, there were major fertility differentials within the Soviet Union. In 1980 and 1981, the TFR for the Russian federation and Ukraine was as low as 1.9, but for Tajikistan, Turkmenistan, and Uzbekistan, it was between 4.8 and 5.6 children per woman, and was between four and five a decade later when the Soviet Union was breaking up.[94] Scholarship from the late 1970s is filled with questions about whether the Slavic population would become a minority, and such questions remain.[95]

Russia's Muslims are primarily concentrated in the North Caucasus region, and some militant groups in those regions have acted violently to assert their independence. Given their majority status in those regions, some Muslims feel that they should not be governed by the Russian Slavs.[96] The regime security implications of Russia's differential growth are serious, because the country has been embroiled in several skirmishes on its border regions and with former republics during the past couple decades. According to Toft, one way that differential demographics becomes a problem concerns the new creation of states. "When a dispersed group grows in proportion to its fellow nationalities in a new state, it may gain enough influence to cause that state to pressure a neighboring state about the treatment of fellow nationals within that state."[97] Such a situation recently happened in Georgia, a country with a demographic composition that is a source of contention between the former Soviet republic and the Russian state. In 2008, the separatist region of South Ossetia accused Georgia of firing mortars on them after six Georgian policemen were killed in the border area by a roadside bomb, and Russia conducted airstrikes on Georgian targets, escalating the conflict.[98] The Caucasus region has been the site of many of the tensions and is a security threat for Russia's European neighbors to the West, because the region is an important conduit for the flow of oil from the Caspian Sea to world markets. Georgia's differential demographics mainly concern South Ossetia and another separatist region, Abkhazia, which gained de facto independence from Georgia after the collapse of the Soviet Union.

Both regions have a high concentration of Russians, and one of Russia's goals seems to be to annex South Ossetia and Abkhazia. Given their declining population, this would give Russia a boost in population and in prestige.

Chechnya has also been plagued by violence since 1991, when they declared independence from Russia. Various wars and skirmishes have taken place since then. Chechnya is the region with the strongest degree of homogeneity, at 93 percent ethnic Chechen and just less than six percent non-Muslim.[99] Some of the more radical Chechens hope to start a holy war and create an Islamic state in the North Caucasus.[100] Violence from Chechnya has at times spilled over the border into Ingushetia, as it did in 2004, when the Ingush acting interior minister was attacked and killed, along with others. In 2009, militants renewed their attacks and, in the deadliest attack in the republic since 2005, a suicide bombing at a police station killed at least 25 people. There was also an attempt on the life of President Yunus-Bek Yevkurov.[101] The absolute number of Slavs has decreased along with Russia's general population decrease.[102] Thus, Russia's conscription pool will be increasingly Muslim. Combined with Russia's high mortality and armed forces crisis, this change could further destabilize the Russian military and impede the ability of the state to field a unified and effective ground force.

Experiences with the Republic of the Congo, Democratic Republic of the Congo, and Uganda also support the argument that there is a relationship among population growth, ethnic diversity, and conflict. In Uganda's case, through his examination of local conflict in the district of Kibaale in Western Uganda, Elliot Green found that conflict was sparked by population growth and resultant internal migration, but has more to do with nativism and the failure of nation building in postcolonial Uganda than with ethnic diversity per se. As he says, population growth plus ethnic salience, rather than ethnic diversity, are part of the cause of the ongoing conflict in Kibaale.[103] From a policy standpoint, this is an actionable finding, especially because so many states are ethnically fragmented. Green's research points to the important role nation-building institutions can play in mediating demographic structures.

### Ethnic Differences and Lack of Violence

Regime type may be one of the most influential factors in the link between differential growth and violence. Unlike democracies, authoritarian governments do not have to worry about being voted out of power by growing minorities. However, they may face rebellion and revolution as minorities demand representation, and divisions are more likely to turn violent because the norms of peaceful resolution of conflict are often absent. Although ethnic differences in the United States and Canada have caused tensions, neither case has seen the degree of violence present in Uganda, Yugoslavia, or even Russia,

**Figure 7.2** Age profile of U.S. Immigrants, 2004. (Population Action International)

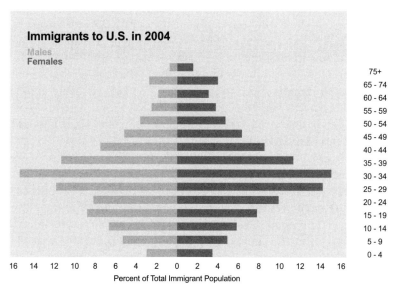

where democratic norms are much weaker. The following paragraphs explore some of the debates over ethnic composition in these two North American democracies.

Immigrants to the United States are primarily of working age, and the implications of immigration for the military have been discussed in Chapter 5. Focusing on the differential growth aspect allows us to explore effects on national cohesion. Hispanic minorities in the United States have fertility rates of about three children per woman, whereas for non-Hispanic white women, the rate is about 1.9.[104] About one-quarter of kindergarteners in the United States and one-fifth of all school-age children, kindergarten through secondary school, are Hispanic, meaning that the group as a whole is a growing proportion of the school-age population.[105] Given that only about 15 percent of the total U.S. population is Hispanic, the minority itself is a growing proportion of the total population. Immigrants are mainly of working ages, but their higher fertility means that subsequent generations have younger age structures (Fig. 7.2).

In the Western United States, the proportions of Hispanic minorities are even higher. There, minority students exceed non-Hispanic whites at the precollege grade levels; about 37 percent of the students are Hispanic. In New Mexico, 54 percent of the students are Hispanic, and in Arizona, the site of 2010's controversial legislation, 40 percent are Hispanic.[106] By 2042, the

United States will be a "majority minority" country, meaning that the white population, which holds the vast majority of the powerful political positions, will be less than 50 percent of the total U.S. population. Even before that, minority children will become the majority in 2023, seven years earlier than a previous estimate made in 2004. Immigration of Hispanics and Asians, and declining birthrates among non-Hispanic whites were the major factors in the revised estimate.[107] Immigration trends are constantly in flux, however, because so many factors motivate migration. The U.S. Hispanic population increased four percent between 2000 and 2001, but only 3.2 percent between 2007 and 2008, because of a drop in immigration to the United States for a variety of economic and political reasons.[108]

Certainly, one of the political reasons for the decline is the harsher climate toward immigrants. A 2010 Arizona immigration law has highlighted the animosity some voters and lawmakers feel toward immigrants. The law is controversial because it requires that police conducting routine traffic stops or other checks ask about immigration status if there is "reasonable suspicion" that the person stopped is in the country illegally. Some are concerned that the law encourages racial profiling of Hispanics, whereas others see the law as enforcing the "illegality" of illegal immigration, because, among other things, the law also makes it a crime for illegal immigrants to solicit work.[109] There have been some news reports that many Hispanics are leaving the state for other parts of the United States before the law goes into effect.[110] There is some precedent for exodus in the face of strict Arizona immigration law. According to the Department of Homeland Security, nearly 100,000 illegal immigrants left Arizona after it passed a 2007 law that penalized businesses that hired them. Yet, even this law is not likely to halt immigration from Mexico to the United States completely. As Professor David Gutierrez of the University of California at San Diego says, the century-old historical trend of northward migration is not likely to be reversed just because some legislators hope it will.[111]

Such political division likely has few implications for the United State's ability to defend itself, but there are foreign policy implications, particularly the United State's ability to project power in the Western Hemisphere. The Arizona law triggered a backlash from Mexico, and led President Obama of the United States to stand alongside Mexican President Felipe Calderon in condemning this law, which Calderon called discriminatory and Obama, "a misdirected effort."[112] Echoing former Mexican leader Vicente Fox before him, Calderon asked that the United States and Mexico work together to establish less discriminatory immigration policy. To the extent that the changing profile of the U.S. population challenges the sovereignty of lawmakers' decisions, differential growth affects military security.

A potentially more serious issue is the regime insecurities created by the state-on-state and federal–state battles over the immigration law. In protest of

Arizona's new immigration law, the Los Angeles City Council voted to boycott travel to Arizona and halt future contracts with the state. In a move that seemed more like politics in Eastern Europe than the United States, an Arizona state official threatened to return the economic dig and shut off Los Angeles' Arizona-based electricity supply. One estimate is that the boycott could cause Arizona to lose $52 million in contracts from Los Angeles.[113] Given the scale of the state economies in the United States, such economic battles are as serious as interstate battles on other continents. U.S. democratic principles and the peaceful resolution of conflict are the norm, but past experiences with civil conflict and protest in the 1960s show that ethnic differences in the United States, as elsewhere, can be politically divisive and have regime security implications, although these protests turned out to create greater political representation and freedom for minorities, and thus were a positive development for American democracy. Domestic political divisions among states within the United States are currently mild. However, this is an area to watch for two reasons. The federal structure of the United States affords individual states a good deal of autonomy in policy making. Second, the differential growth in ethnic groups among states within the United States means that the political issues among states may also increasingly diverge. States within the U.S. have very different demographic profiles and are rapidly changing. Minorities of all backgrounds comprise more than 50 percent of the population in Texas.[114] The majority of these minorities are Hispanic (about 37 percent); the Anglo population is less than 47 percent of the total population.[115] The United States has not had such a high degree of differential ethnic growth in recent history, so we cannot be sure the degree to which these differences will have political regime security implications. Most likely, though, democratic norms and institutions will work to facilitate the peaceful resolution of differences.

Experiences in Canada can also shed light on how democracies deal with their differential growth, but in Canada's case, one of the ultimate national security challenges is on the table: total secession of a portion of the country itself. During the 18th century, Quebec fertility rates were nearly the highest of recorded human history, second only to the religious Hutterites, but during the 1960s and '70s, they became close to the lowest in the world. Fertility rates in the rest of Canada were comparatively high. Leaders of the Quebec separatist movement, including Parti Québécois founder René Levesque, were alarmed at the prospect that Quebec could disappear. Immigration strengthened the Québécois numbers and was accompanied by strong nationalist movements to fight the creeping Anglophone influence. The fertility gap between Quebec and the rest of Canada narrowed during the 1980s and '90s.[116] The Meech Lake Accord, which would have amended Canada's Constitution with the intention to persuade Quebec to sign it and remain within the federation, failed to pass in 1990, and in essence prolonged the fight for separatism.[117] Later, when a 1995 referendum on sovereignty for Quebec failed to pass, with "no" votes receiving 50.6 percent, many thought the issue disappeared, in part because of demographic defeat, yet the issue continues to resurface in Canadian politics and remains unsettled.[118] Canada's experiences with differential growth between the Québécois and Anglophones demonstrates how groups can act within democratic institutions to work through their political differences. Although there are many on each side who are likely dissatisfied with the outcome of some of these referenda, both sides seem committed to working through institutions for peaceful resolution of conflict.

There are some global trends in ethnicity and politics that may mean demography is becoming even more important for determining the distribution of political power within states. As the principles of democracy and popular sovereignty have come to dominate the international agenda and have become essential parts of what it means to be "modern," the time of dominant minorities may have come to an end.[119] The world may be transitioning to dominant majority ethnicity. In this modern world, then, demography matters more than ever, and we can expect that anytime a subpopulation—be it ethnic or religious—becomes a majority, it will dominate politics. In this postcolonial age, the number of cases where minorities govern subordinate majorities, as the Alawis in Syria and the Tutsi in Burundi have done, are dwindling. Just as power shifts in the international community are often violent, power shifts within a state are not guaranteed to be peaceful either. When the minority loses its dominance, or when the majority becomes the minority, change is most likely resisted, and the outcome could be violent. In a democracy, however, these groups are more likely to hammer out their differences through the legal system, as in the cases of the United States and Canada.

## DIFFERENTIAL GROWTH AMONG RELIGIOUS GROUPS

Anytime identity groups grow at different rates, the potential for conflict is there. When groups that are already at war grow at different rates, the situation is even more intense. Major changes in composition in an environment of hostility is what makes Israel one of the key cases of differential demographic growth and one that illustrates how ethnicity and religion can combine to create conditions that exacerbate conflict. The different ethnic and religious groups within the country—primarily secular Jewish Israelis, ultraorthodox Jews, and Muslim Arab Israelis, although there are others—have vastly different fertility rates, and thus very different growth rates, meaning that the composition of the country is constantly in flux. Although we most often associate the Arab–Israeli conflict as territorial, it is demographic as well; insecurities over territory and population together create the perception by each group that it faces an existential threat.[120]

In general, there are two issues with differential demographic growth in Israel. The first issue is the shrinking proportions of Jews and the growing proportions of Arabs. Although total fertility is 2.8, secular Jewish fertility is about replacement level whereas Muslim Arab fertility is about 4.5.[121] In 1948, Israel was 82 percent Jewish and nearly 18 percent Arab, but by 2007, it was 76 percent Jewish and 20 percent Arab, with four percent non-Arab Christians and other religious denominations.[122] Immigration of Jews to Israel has slowed tremendously during the past couple decades and in general plays much less of a role in boosting the Jewish population now. In 1950, 35 percent of the Jews in Israel were Israeli born; in 2007, 70 percent were.[123] The differences in these fertility rates, plus the slowdown of Jewish immigration to Israel, mean that current population trends will continue. The state certainly uses demography as a weapon by pushing Jewish Israelis farther from population centers and into Arab regions. Settlement policy, in general, aims at "creating a physical Jewish presence in regions of conflict, enhancing territorial control, and contributing to demographic parity, and even majority."[124] As the internal composition of Israel changes, the very nature of the state as a Jewish homeland is in question. Israel expends a lot of effort defending the state from outside encroachment, but domestic trends will negate these efforts over time. From a regime security perspective, Israel's democratic system provides the institutional channels for representation, and we should expect that Arab Muslim interests will increasingly be represented politically. If the Jewish majority resists these changes by suppressing Arab rights or acting violently, resulting conflict could spill into the region, creating military security implications for surrounding states. Those states that support Israel even outside the region, such as the United States, may also be drawn into the conflict.

The second demographic issue is differences in the Jewish Israeli population. Although fertility is low for the secular Jewish population, it is extremely high—eight or nine children per woman—for the ultraorthodox Jewish population.[125] The ultraorthodox, or *haredim,* are between 7 percent and 11 percent of Israel's total population, but are rapidly growing at about four percent annually.[126] In 1960, only 15 percent of primary school students were either Israeli Arabs or *haredim,* but in 2009, the proportion had increased to about 46 percent. By 2020 these two groups—the *haredim* and the Arabs—will comprise the majority of primary school students. If current trends continue, by 2030 these two groups will dominate the Israeli electorate and will be nearly half of all 18- and 19-year-olds eligible for conscription. The Israeli Defense Forces may have a very hard time recruiting, then, because ultraorthodox Jews do not serve in the armed forces. Arab conscripts, who will also make up a larger share of the conscription pool, may not be enthusiastic about serving in conflicts against Arab Palestinian neighbors. These demographic trends call into question the ability of the Israeli state to continue to defend its interests and pursue an aggressive foreign policy in a tumultuous region surrounded by hostile states.

Given that Israel is a democracy, with proportional representation and a low threshold for seats, such population changes will have major political implications. Richard Cincotta and Eric Kaufmann have argued that the increasing proportion of ultraorthodox Jews is making the political landscape more conservative. "Once peace-process-disinterested members of various coalition governments, ultra-Orthodox politicians now rank among the most hawkish in the Knesset, defending haredi settlements on the West Bank and in East Jerusalem."[127] Toft, on the other hand, argues that as the ultraorthodox become a larger proportion of the electorate, they will actually make Israel more dovish, because they may believe that prayer, not force, is the way to settle disputes.[128] The *haredim* have not always been a very politically active group, choosing instead to focus on their religion, but as their numbers grow, Cincotta and Kaufmann may be correct in that they will seek to make Israel's politics more in line with their interests. Not only their attitudes, but their lack of military service potentially weaken Israel.

At the structural security level there are many economic implications of the growing *haredim* minority that threaten the budget of the Israeli state, because cultural norms discourage many from seeking gainful unemployment and, instead, encourage them to pursue religious study. As a result, many live off of state resources: education, welfare assistance, and child allowances to support their large families. Ultraorthodox young men are able to get draft deferments and student stipends for decades, by extending their study in state-subsidized religious schools (*yeshiva*).[129] If current demographic trends continue, there will be fewer employed taxpayers to support *haredim*, and the imbalance will be economically unsustainable.

## CONCLUSION

Population proportions—age structure, gender, or identity—play a large role in the many conflicts worldwide, particularly in mixed ethnic and religious states. Whenever multiple groups share and compete over resources, physical or political, they run the risk of coming into conflict. When these groups are growing or changing at different rates, the balance of power they have established can be upset, just as happens with competing states in the international system. In democracies, norms and rules mean that changeovers in power between majorities and minorities should be peaceful, but do not guarantee that they will not meet with resistance, as the economic tussling between Arizona and Los Angeles demonstrates. In nondemocracies, absent legal protections for changeover of power and in a restrictive political and social climate, such differential growth can turn deadly. Russia's experiences with its ethnic minorities are one example. How Israel's national security will be affected by the major changes taking place among its religious and ethnic groups remains to be seen, but will be a major challenge not only for them, but also for their allies and states in the region.

Differential growth can be an important warning sign for future conflict and should be included in security assessments for strategic states. Unofficially, Muslims now constitute a majority of the Lebanese population, but are underrepresented in government. Maronite Christians have been steadily losing their demographic position throughout the decades because their fertility has been comparatively low. If scholars Eric Kaufmann and Oded Haklai are correct, it is only a matter of time before the Maronites need to give up the presidency and assume their minority position.[130] As far as demography can be used for warning and risk assessment, we should closely watch political developments in several countries with differential growth rates: Sudan, 27 percent non-Muslim; Indonesia, 12.8 percent; Brunei, 35.8 percent; and Bangladesh, 13.4 percent.[131] Continued differential growth in these countries, all of which have a history of civil conflict, could provide fodder for future violence and instability. On the flip side, countries experiencing differential demographic growth, including the United States, should be aware that other states are following their demographic changes closely in their own assessments of risk.

In general, we need more research on how and when demographic change matters. Existing studies have mostly been conducted on a larger scale and, like urbanization, better data need to be collected and more studies done on the subnational level, with the dependent variable open to include conflict that is not large-scale violence or war. Research on the security implications of gender imbalance has just begun to scratch the surface. Policy makers should be cautious when interpreting preliminary findings and not overestimate the ability of these imbalances to destabilize what are otherwise two strong and growing powers—China and India—until further research is done. Differential growth has a greater ability to shape Russia, however. Even with restructuring of its forces, Russia's military-age males will decline tremendously during the next several decades, and high mortality and disease—including alcoholism—among those males that are of age will impair the ability of Russia to wield a strong military. Unsettled political disputes within its border regions also contribute to instability. Yet, Russia cannot be counted out. The country's recent aggressive behavior, strong leadership, and energy reserves demonstrate that Russia is still powerful in other ways.

For powerful industrialized democracies, the HIV/AIDS epidemic in Africa can seem only remotely connected to national security. For the most part, it is true that HIV/AIDS poses no military threat to the powerful states, that the economies of some of the most affected African states are well outside of the global economy, and that the deprivation caused by structural insecurity stemming from AIDS has not been shown to increase the risk of radicalization. However, HIV/AIDS in African states connects to security for the Global North at a couple of points. The first is the increasing cost of resources. The second is its role in destabilizing political capacity. As the Global North continues to intervene in conflicts in Africa, they will run up against the aftermath of the disease. Finally, the humanitarian crisis created by AIDS means that there continues to be a role for international aid efforts both through governments and civil society organizations.

# 8
Chapter

# Challenges and Opportunities for the 21st Century

## GENERAL CHALLENGES AND OPPORTUNITIES

The chapters on age structure, movement of people, and challenges with composition demonstrate that demography can serve many roles—in particular, as an indicator, a multiplier, and a resource. The first role to consider is demography as an indicator of both challenge and opportunity. Certain demographic issues are associated with a greater risk of conflict. In general, the higher the proportion of youth in a population, the greater the chances that a country will face civil conflict. In many cases, youth who face dismal prospects in the labor market turn their grievances against the state. Sometimes, the conflict does not escalate beyond nonviolent protest; in others, youth may stage a formal rebellion and ignite a civil war. If the correlation between conflict and age structure holds into the 21st century, we can expect that those regions that continue to have high fertility and younger age structures will have a higher likelihood of civil conflict, and we can therefore use our knowledge of demographic stress factors to anticipate instability. Most states in Africa are likely at risk according to this factor, with the exception of South Africa. Angola, Botswana, Burundi, Central African Republic, Chad, the Democratic Republic of Congo, Sierra Leone, Somalia, Timor-Leste, and Uganda are likely to have 60 to 67 percent of their population younger than the ages of 29 in 2025.[1] In North Africa and the Middle East, the age structures of Saudi Arabia, Syria, Jordan, and Algeria will all mature to a transitional age structure, whereas Yemen and Afghanistan, in Central Asia, will remain very young.

On the other hand, age structure can also indicate potential ability to build partnership capacity. When countries with transitional age structures take advantage of their window of opportunity, they can see major benefits in economic growth. For some, such as India, Brazil, and South Africa, economic growth is translating to a greater desire to play a role in global politics. To the extent that these states wish to contribute more to development efforts in poor countries, police international waterways, and send troops to conflict-ridden areas, advanced industrial states should welcome opportunities to share the burden. Capable partners are especially important for aging states to pursue foreign policy goals like peace building and security of transport routes. Aging states may not have enough eligible military-age men and women, and will likely face strained budgets that hinder their ability to fund such projects. Right now, aging states are each other's closest allies. There is great benefit in keeping these alliances strong, because states have a history of working together on economic and security issues. However, aging states should also foster partnerships with states that have younger age profiles, because they will have different comparative advantages. If aging states—in particular, the United States, states in the EU, and Japan—do not foster these partnerships, they risk being excluded from liaisons that younger states will make among themselves. Reaching out to successfully developing states by reforming global institutions that tend to favor the interests of aging countries, like the UN Security Council and World Bank, is one way to engage rising powers.

Like age structure, other demographic composition characteristics can pose challenges for security. In particular, differential growth among ethnic and religious groups can serve as an indicator of potential conflict. Migration and urbanization, which also mix people of different backgrounds, generally create great benefits for individuals by giving them opportunities to earn a living or access education and health care, but they can be a source of conflict under some circumstances. In particular, some refugees are subject to militarization, which exacerbates existing tensions. Most of the world's states are multiethnic but peaceful; in other cases, differential growth among groups can be used by elites to factionalize politics further and encourage rebellion. Tracking demographic patterns is therefore useful in a comprehensive assessment of risk. Urbanization can be a clear indicator of risk because of the vulnerability of urban areas to devastating natural disaster. Urbanization in general has tended to be heavily concentrated in coastal regions, which are already vulnerable to natural disasters and will increasingly be so as climate change affects weather patterns and sea levels. Given the enormous economic importance of cities, such as those on China's East coast, the ramifications of a natural disaster that affects a city across the world will still be felt by all. Demographic trends in urbanization, differential growth, or age structure should be part of plans for global posture and needed capabilities, like naval capabilities.

The second theme is demography as a multiplier. If a state already has weak governance, demography can exacerbate conditions for instability. As the Fund for Peace and *Foreign Policy Magazine* point out in their annual *Failed States Index*, when combined with economic strains and ineffective governance, demographic pressures are often part of the cause of failed states.[2] Demography can also be a multiplier for other governance trends, particularly democratization. Along with economic growth and capable leadership, prospects are positive for states that are making the permanent transition to more mature age structures because of improvements in fertility and mortality. With a greater number of consolidated democracies worldwide, the world may be a more peaceful place, if liberal democratic peace holds. Certainly, the world could be more prosperous, because democracies also tend to be more open to trade. The combination of open trade, increased cooperation, and reduced commitment to fighting civil conflict could mean that the 21st century will be characterized by prosperity.

Finally, the chapters point to the theme of demography as a resource. A healthy and productive population can contribute to economic growth, military strength, and social cohesion. Those states that have favorable age structures with high proportions of a working-age population are particularly suited to experience economic growth and internal security. States that accept skilled migrants are also in a position to draw on population as a resource for labor. On the other hand, as part of an index of power, an adverse age structure can create conditions for insecurity. Population aging forces difficult choices about how to raise and spend revenue. In states that already have mature age structures, the social welfare institutions were not set up in a way that would take account of the increases in spending required by an elderly population with fewer workers. These states must reform their systems and increase the labor force participation rates of underrepresented groups, such as women, older persons, and even youth. States that have somewhat younger age structures, especially those for whom the demographic window of opportunity has not yet closed, can position themselves to weather the aging storm. Many states in Latin America, like Chile, have instituted private pension systems that will be more sustainable than pay-as-you-go systems in place across Europe and the U.S.

## REGIONAL PERSPECTIVES

The themes of demography as an indicator, multiplier, and resource emerge from a global overview of population and national security. It is also useful to consider how demographic trends within key states and broad regions of the world converge to create different challenges and opportunities for security. The chapters in this book are organized according to trends, but most states and regions experience multiple demographic issues simultaneously. A state-level or regional viewpoint, then, allows us to see how these trends interact with each other and with other trends in governance, economics, or the environment, to name but a few. Additionally, what happens in one region affects others. According to the 2010 U.S. Quadrennial Defense Review, "as a global power, the strength and influence of the United States are deeply intertwined with the fate of the broader international system—a system of alliances, partnerships, and multinational institutions that our country has helped build and sustain for more than sixty years."[3] This "intertwining" means that demographic, governance, and conflict trends and developments in other parts of the world are keys to the future of U.S. safety and national security and that of other states as well.

## United States

Analysis of demographic security brings to light some important lessons for the United States when set in a global political context. The first lesson is that the United States should widen its web of alliances and partnerships, and strengthen existing ones. Most books on national security published during the past 20 years have been able to assume American primacy, and have accordingly offered policy suggestions that take advantage of America's strong global influence and unmatched economic and political power. Times have changed for a number of reasons, including unsustainable debt, a damaged international reputation because of involvement in Iraq, and other unpopular foreign policies. No longer can the United States assume that its wishes will be carried out throughout the world and that it will remain unchallenged in the foreseeable future. Some of the damage has been to long-standing alliances with European states, but for the most part these relationships continue to be strong. To support its goals and missions, the United States should strengthen these existing relationships and demonstrate a continued commitment to European and Japanese security. Doing so is especially important to balance the growing strength of China and the continued influence of Russia in multilateral forums.

At the same time, the United States should not be afraid to seek new partnerships and strengthen relationships with emerging powers or its regional neighbors. America's closest formal allies, some of whom the United States relies on for military missions—are aging rapidly. Although these states may be able to compensate for their aging through increased military efficiency and better policies to take advantage of the labor force, the United States should earnestly pursue a wider network of allies and partners with more favorable age structures. States in Latin America and the Caribbean, and several in the Middle East and South Asia are in the midst of a demographic transition. If these states take full opportunity of their favorable age structures, they will have increased capacity to provide for their own security and to project force in surrounding areas, and will have valuable potential to become beacons of regional stability. The 2010 U.S. National Security Strategy recognizes this need for capable partners: "The burdens of a young century cannot fall on American shoulders alone—indeed, our adversaries would like to see America sap our strength by overextending our power."[4] As the strategy notes, the United States should invest now in the capable partners of the future. Age structure is one indicator of potential future partners. Those that have a favorable age structure, with increased proportions of working ages, are likely to have the ability to become good partners. Whether they have the willingness is something that United States policy makers will have to cultivate actively through diplomatic engagement. Some states in the Middle East have seen declining fertility and are moving to transitional age structures. These states, including Qatar and Kuwait, can also be partners to the United States.

## Latin America

Most states to the south of the United States have the type of favorable age structures that have, in the past, created conditions for economic growth, civil peace, and democratization. To take full advantage of its demographic bonus, each state needs to ensure that its health and education systems are robust. Latin American states will want to develop even closer trading ties with one another to take advantage of their comparative strengths and the reduced transportation costs of trading regionally. As each grows economically, the region as a whole can benefit. Those states in Latin America further along the demographic transition should work to become leaders in combating instability, particularly the regime instability that the international drug trade poses. Chile, as the least corrupt country in Latin America, should work with other states to spread the model of transparency and how it can be economically beneficial to the state, in part because it creates an open environment for investment. States that are only at the beginning stages of the demographic transition, such as Bolivia, should continue on that path so that they, too, can experience the demographic bonus that comes from reduced fertility. Bolivia faces many governance challenges that, unless they are fixed, will impede the advantages of the demographic bonus. There are already many formal partnerships and regimes in Latin America, such as Mercosur, that can serve as a foundation for future broadening and deepening of cooperation. The countries of the region will have to overcome their different forms of governance, levels of development and commitment, and, especially, visions of what a strong Latin America should look like.

But the window always closes. Because population aging is inevitable in a country that has reduced fertility, Latin American states should shape their social security institutions in a way that will be sustainable as the workforce ages and there are fewer new entrants to the labor market each year. Many states have already taken solid steps toward this by implementing private pension schemes. In this sense, they are actually ahead of the United States and Europe, who rely on unsustainable public schemes.

Although declining U.S. hegemony may complicate the ability of the United States to find support for its foreign policy objectives, it also provides political opportunity for other states to take on a greater international role. Many states in Latin America are already showing an increased desire to forge external ties. Their economic growth and increased governance capacity may make them more attractive international partners both in trade and in defense, not only to the United States, but to states such as China, India, and South Africa. Consequently, many rising powers, including Brazil, want to reform international institutions, like the World Trade Organization and the UN Security Council, to make them more equitable and representative of interests of developing countries.

## Asia

Similar to Latin America, many states within South and East Asia have favorable age structures and are seeing concurrent increases in international influence and economic growth. China is, of course, the major success story of the post-Cold War era thus far. With high proportions of a working-age population, China has been able to fuel an explosive manufacturing sector. At the same time, their intentional efforts to create large-scale building projects in coastal cities, and even entirely new cities all around the country, have been a way to put that large labor force to work. Employing so many people serves two goals of the regime: make the most of the demographic bonus and avoid a growing sense of resentment among citizens who would otherwise experience low standards of living and a lack of economic engagement that could motivate grievances against the state. Yet the Chinese government has long viewed its large population as a burden, as evidenced in part by the one-child policy, which is designed to decrease family size and slow population growth. As standards of living have risen in China, it has been necessary to seek resources outside the state, leading to a growing presence on other continents, including South America and Africa, and in regions like Central Asia. To the United States, this increased presence has been a source of angst, as evidenced by the growing attention to China in recent U.S. defense planning documents.[5]

Many countries to China's south, including Indonesia, Vietnam, and Thailand, have also reduced fertility to the point that they are experiencing a demographic bonus. There are still many political problems in several of these states that hinder their ability to take full advantage of their demographic windows of opportunity. India, despite its regional variations in development and uneven fertility, has reaped some of the benefits of its demographic transition. It is possible that as Indian leadership increasingly values economic growth, it will seek the stability that sets conditions favorable for continued growth, meaning that it will work to promote internal stability and peace within the region, particularly with Pakistan. Still, high fertility within some of the poorer regions in India, gender imbalances, and the growth of slum areas are holding India back from reaching its full potential.

## Africa

The continent of Africa is projected to see a near doubling of its population during the next several decades. Africans will face a great number of demographic challenges, including intercontinental refugees and IDPs, population growth, differential growth of ethnic and religious groups, and disease. In addition, the population issues on the continent cannot be separated from the environmental stresses, which may only exacerbate Africa's problems. Poor or weak governance provides the political opportunities for these problems to turn into violence against the state or rival groups within the state. Corrupt leaders may take advantage of the differences among groups highlighted by differential growth or migration. Africa's leaders in government, business, and civil society will need a comprehensive approach to solve the continent's problems. The approach must include tasks at high levels, such as establishing inclusive governance institutions and stabilizing governments to attract investment and create job opportunities. They must also address the citizens' individual needs through poverty reduction, health care, education, and family planning. Countries that are doing comparatively better, such as those in West Africa and the country of South Africa, can play leadership roles and work through diplomatic channels to foster peace and stability in the more conflict-ridden areas. They can also work to establish partnerships with countries abroad with which they share interests, as South Africa is doing with India and Brazil.

As demand for resources increases worldwide as a result of both population growth and higher standards of living, Africa will find many markets for its energy resources and raw materials. The average citizen currently sees little of the spoils. Of late, China has been notorious for establishing relationships with unsavory leaders to acquire the materials they need to fuel their growth, but they are hardly alone, as long-term outside involvement in Nigeria's oil market can attest. On the whole, unfortunately, African states are low on the priority list of advanced industrial states when it comes to national security. Even though the continent has been plagued by civil conflict in several regions, and HIV/AIDS has devastated segments of the population in several states, in general Africa is peripheral from the perspective of the U.S. defense community. The United States sees domestic instability and poverty in the Middle East and Central Asia as much more of a U.S. national security threat than Africa's issues. There are likely many factions within Africa that are pleased to be excluded, as the backlash against the establishment of Africa Command attests.[6] However, being low on the priority list also means that resources to make improvements to poverty and disease are not being directed to the continent. Even the attention of European states may start to flag, as they potentially scale back their humanitarian efforts in the face of the strains of an aging population. Africans can rely on one another, but also may have willing allies in the fight against poverty among rising powers, as the partnership of India, Brazil, and South Africa demonstrates. IBSA wants to play a greater role in addressing the needs of least developed countries. To the extent that developed states plan to become involved on the continent through peacekeeping or even development efforts, demographic and environmental trends will thwart their efforts.

## Europe

European states should continue efforts to streamline their defense by focusing on efficiency and looking to technology. Population aging need not spell their complete demise, but they will need to be much more ambitious in reforming retirement. France's 2010 vote to increase retirement age from 60 to 62, for example, will do little to improve their fiscal situation. As these countries shrink, the logical step would be to pursue deeper integration to have strength in numbers. Broadening the EU is also an option, although that decision also has consequences. The most recent expansion of the EU eastward actually brought on countries with even lower fertility and more rapid aging than Western Europe. Including Turkey is one option that would bring more people of working ages into the EU, but doing so is not an easy policy choice. Europe's cohesion is at risk because of divergent views over the future of the EU, and some political interests are using cultural differences as part of the debate. Bringing Turkey into the EU may only exacerbate those tensions by antagonizing the far Right and creating a greater mix as Turks migrate westward for new economic opportunities. Europe already has problems integrating immigrants and their descendents, and should actively work on integration to promote stability and peace. Turkey's accession into the EU could actually help with this last goal, if it improves the image of Europe as more welcoming to immigrants of different backgrounds and faiths, particularly Muslim.

## Middle East and Central Asia

Although culturally distinct, the Middle East and Central Asia have two important commonalities: they are very young and very tumultuous. These regions are high on the national security priority list of many states. In particular, Iraq, Israel, Iran, Saudi Arabia, Pakistan, and Afghanistan are often singled out as targets of foreign policy. Many states in these regions continue to have high population growth rates, even though fertility in most has declined. Iran has completed the demographic transition, but is at the stage when a high proportion of the population consists of young adults, an age structure correlated with civil conflict under certain conditions. Israel is experiencing differential growth along ethnic and religious lines that are already fraught with tension. Conflict in these two regions has also created large numbers of refugees and IDPs. The Middle East is likely to be the site of environmental stresses, particularly water, at the same time that the region's population remains one of the fastest growing in the world. There is a significant body of research that suggests strained environmental resources can actually be an impetus for cooperation, rather than leading to "water wars," as many would assume.[7] This research means that the growing imbalance between population and resources could actually be a potential foundation upon which to build peace in the turbulent region. Central Asia, including Afghanistan and Pakistan, is also expected to have high future population growth rates, which will diminish prospects for democratization and economic growth. These patterns indicate that Central Asia will continue to be a turbulent region that requires the attention of policy makers.

## POLICY OPTIONS

Certain demographic trends, like youthful age structures, carry greater risks for conflict, whereas others, like urbanization, create more favorable conditions for increasing security. Yet, no demographic issue has a predetermined relationship to national security. To meet the challenges and take advantage of the opportunities to strengthen security that demography provides, a comprehensive approach to building national security is necessary—one that addresses issues not only with military efficiency and effectiveness, but also with family planning, democratic accountability, poverty reduction, and education. First, countries with high fertility have been shown to be at greater risk of conflict and undemocratic governance, so family planning programs that include contraception and education should be included as part of broader state-building efforts. Certainly, the main mission of the military is not family planning, but the connection between the three realms of national security—military, regime, and structural—demonstrates that states will have to use a "whole-of-government" approach to meet 21st-century challenges. U.S. Secretary of Defense Robert Gates has argued for pooled funds between the Department of Defense and the State Department, in the model of the United Kingdom, because he believes this is the best way to meet challenges.[8] There will be important domestic debates regarding whether militaries should be involved in civilian assistance activities or whether those tasks are best left to civilian agencies. National security is the task of all government agencies, but we cannot deny that often the military is the only agency with the resources, scale, organization, and access to complete tasks that increase security. However, other agencies can play important roles, as well. There may also be a role for the private sector in women's empowerment, which will help to lower fertility and increase female labor force participation—both beneficial to the state and to individuals.[9] Women's empowerment is not just an issue for less developed countries; it makes economic sense for developed countries, as well. Anytime powerful states in the world act to help unstable states gain security, powerful states gain soft power, and therefore greater national security for themselves. As Christine Parthemore writes for the Center for New American Security: "Bolstering agricultural production is certainly not a traditional security mission—and, in particular, not a [Department of Defense] mission—yet in conflicts such as the one in Afghanistan today it can become a key variable to success." The U.S. government's capacity for nonmilitary security assistance is relatively weak.[10] This, then, is an area where partnership capacity can make a difference.

Second, postconflict reconstruction is exceedingly important to help other states build the capacity to govern well. Disarmament, demobilization, and reintegration programs are one way to build stability. Often, reintegration is the hardest part, mainly because of the need for justice and reconciliation, but shifts away from exclusively focusing on ex-combatants to helping the wider population are a good step.[11] Building the capacity of states to govern is important for neighboring states, because they hope to avoid conflict spillover, refugees, and disruption in regional trade and travel.

USAID's integrated population–health–environment approach is one way to address structural insecurities. Environmental issues are tied to many population stresses, especially in less developed countries. These programs try simultaneously to improve a community's access to health services, manage their natural resources, and protect the environment.[12] As USAID says: "Population, health and environment . . . projects acknowledge and address the complex connections between humans, their health, and their environment." Some integrated population, health, and environment programs include sustainable agriculture to improve both child nutrition and a community's food security, community credit groups or community health insurance schemes, improved access to latrines and promotion of hygienic behavior, and malaria prevention through bio-environmental controls and promotion of insecticide-treated bed nets.[13]

At the fall 2009 Global Water Institute symposium in Brussels, representatives from intergovernmental organizations, including the African Union and the UN, civil society, and research institutes discussed ways to employ former soldiers in the water sector to "create peace dividends, bridge divided societies, and improve water security in countries recovering from conflict."[14] Population pressures can place tremendous stress on the environment. In many parts of Ethiopia, rural communities may have an average TFR of more than six children per woman, and as they try to work the land to earn a living and survive, many times their unsustainable practices worsen their situation. In particular, families may be forced to cut trees for fuel and to sell timber for food and housing.[15]

The varied challenges of demography require a range of policy responses. A military solution is not always the best or most appropriate one and, indeed, demographic trends of advanced industrialized states show that, in the future, these militaries may have reduced capacity to become involved in external conflicts. If the state's ability to deal with the breadth of national security challenges at the military, regime, and structural levels is strengthened, increased political capacity will alleviate the burden on the military by drawing on all the resources of the state and society.

## RISKS OF SECURITIZING

The point of national security is ultimately to protect the population of the nation, but this book has flipped the lens and considered how population can itself create insecurity. This exercise necessitated accepting certain assumptions—namely, that the interests of the state (as the collective embodiment of the population) are paramount. Privileging the state in this way creates certain risks. As one group of authors notes: "*In naming a certain development a security problem, the 'state' can claim a special right*, one that will, in the first instance, always be defined by the state and its elites [emphasis in original]."[16] Painting demography as a threat to national security risks legitimizing oppression in the name of defending the state. If we say that young people are a threat because of their correlation with conflict, then the state may feel justified in restricting their civil liberties. Similar risks exist when migrants and refugees, ethnic minorities, or any subpopulation, whether identity group or age group, is made out to be a threat. As Myron Weiner and Michael Teitelbaum point out: "It is essential to distinguish between demography as explanation and demography as justification. Governments have often justified their aggression on demographic grounds—the classic example is the Nazi doctrine of *lebensraum*, the right asserted by Germany to expand and extend its territory in order to acquire greater living space for its people."[17] They argue that when demography is embedded in political ideology, it can become the instrument of a form of aggressive nationalism. Several examples of manipulating population in a coercive manner to further the goals of the state come to mind, including Ceausescu in Romania and China's one-child policy. To what extent are arguments to reduce fertility in countries like Uganda or Afghanistan similarly viewing the population as something to be manipulated as a means to an end, particularly when the calls come from Western scholars and aid agencies?

There are also multiple gender implications of "problematizing" population. First, women, as bearers of children, may be blamed for "producing" too many or too few. For example, when a population has too few children, women may be seen as making a choice to pursue a career instead of having children.

Monetary incentives, such as tax breaks or bonuses, target them to encourage fertility, but may not address the underlying societal disincentives to have children, such as when work and family life are culturally incompatible. Even in states where women are seen as having "too many" children, merely providing contraception may be the major policy goal instead of addressing underlying cultural conditions that disempower women to take charge of their own fertility, whether through birth spacing or contraception, many of which education would address. Second, young males may be the object of blame for conflict. As Nicole Detraz points out:

> [T]he issue of population has specific gendered implications. Impacts may be different if populations have "youth bulges" typically made up of young males. This group disproportionately engages in crime, commits suicide, or joins militias, all of which are important security concerns. . . . When issues are securitized, certain actions are seen as justifiable, and it is likely that men and women will experience these actions differently.[18]

These issues should be part of the conversation about the links between demography and security.

Because the umbrella of national security gives license to the state, Wæver argues that instead of broadening national security to include issues like disease, population growth, or the environment, we should be working to desecuritize issues.[19] I remain unconvinced that securitizing issues is always a bad thing. As David Mutimer says: "The invocation of security in relationship to an issue allows the state to take extraordinary measures to combat whatever threat is thereby identified."[20] Such measures could include suspending rights and civil liberties. Alternatively, securitizing an issue may direct resources *toward* it. Bringing attention to those links between population and national security can be the impetus for action to promote education and health to reduce fertility, strengthen protections for migrants or ethnic minorities, or even institute more sustainable employment policies to include older workers. Any of these measures would do more good than harm.

A final risk of securitizing population, or even environmental and health issues, is that solving these problems may be seen as a means to an end rather than an end themselves. It is true that it is potentially problematic to treat these missions as a means to an end. The human security paradigm asks us to move away from this way of thinking and to see helping humanity as an end in itself. Taxpayers who fund militaries, though, often do not agree, and governments that are accountable to their citizens have to be stewards of their country's resources, and spend and use them in a way that benefits the citizens. What I've tried to show in this book is that helping other states with structural and regime security can boost the helper's national security, if it counters threats directly relevant to the latter's security. Not all instabilities abroad affect U.S. national security, so planners should be able to prioritize and avoid overextending.

## THE FUTURE

If the defining population trend of the 20th century was the growth in world population from one billion to six billion, what will the 21st century bring? During the past century land and resources remained finite, but population density, the number of people, and consumption levels all increased. In tandem, there were many positive developments. The hallmarks were certainly vastly improved technology and innovation. As Esther Boserup argues, population density may have been a driving force behind this progress.[21] Increased food production allowed for larger family sizes, and improvements in health care and disease prevention dramatically lowered mortality for most of the world. The explosion in global population was so influential in part because of the way it shaped the behavior of individual nation-states. The changing balance between population and resources made a major impact on national security and defense during the 20th century. Just as the desire for resources and riches drove royal-backed explorers out of Europe to seek new lands centuries ago, invasions of the 20th century, like Japanese imperialism and Germany's *lebensraum*, also tied population needs to the pursuit of national security. There were some negatives of innovation as well, of course, one of which took the form of nuclear weapons of mass destruction. Population is even relevant here, as the ability to carry out mass destruction is unnecessary if there is not a massive number of people to destroy.

The role of government also changed. During the past century, governments increasingly used a range of nonmilitary tools to meet foreign policy goals, including foreign aid. Many governments also deployed the military for humanitarian missions to meet foreign policy goals. The 1991 Gulf War, and resource wars and civil conflict in Africa are just two examples of ways that resources contributed to conflict. Globalization has also played a role in securitizing population and environmental issues. In general, globalization turns what were once national security issues into transnational threats. Although there is a long history of transnational threats like disease, including the Black Plague, few deny that globalization has accelerated or increased these threats. Today, increased globalization means increased movement of people and goods, and increased potential threats, because these are harder to regulate.

Population will continue to grow in the 21st century, particularly among the world's least developed countries. Will the increasing divide between the shrinking and aging Global North and the young and growing Global South be the defining population trend of the 21st century? We can envision a scenario in which the North's inability to adapt to population aging means that centers of economic activity move away from the most advanced industrial countries to those that are really neither in the North nor the South, but in the middle, transitional age structure states. Certainly, as economic power shifts, so, too, would other forms of power, including political influence and possibly even military power. As the populations of many countries in the Global South double every few decades, while land and resources deteriorate from the strain of a growing population to feed plus new generations of consumers, the civil conflicts that plague many of these states are likely to grow more frequent or intense. As world population increases to between 9 billion and 11 billion by 2050, stresses on the planet's resources will mount. Population growth will be uneven throughout the world, mostly taking place in the states least equipped to deal with a doubling of their population. How aging developed states or a new crop of powerful states that benefited from economic growth and their demographic bonuses help manage the conflicts and clashes that arise will be a major part of national security in the 21st century.

But perhaps population size will not be the defining trend. The 1996 UN "State of the World's Population Report" predicted: "The growth of cities will be the single largest influence on development in the 21st century."[22] At the global level, all future population growth will be in towns and cities.[23] Instead of dealing with other states, then, some states might deal with cities. Because of globalization, Arjun Appaduri argues that we are witnessing new forms of globally organized power within states. One example is that "wealthier 'world cities' [will] increasingly operate like city states in a networked global economy, increasingly independent of regional and national mediation, and where poorer cities—and the poorer populations within them—seek new ways of claiming space and voice."[24] This new model of governance will challenge international institutions, which were established for the framework of the Westphalian nation state system. Will cities increasingly have their own city-funded militaries? Or will the development of city-states encourage the further privatization of the military?

Assessments of national security need to continue to give demography a prominent place, because population issues are fundamentally related to traditional defense concerns about alliances, weapons, and war, and to broader national security issues including environmental and energy challenges, disease, and civil conflict. There are many plausible scenarios about how population will shape international relations during the 21st century, and we should be humble enough to know that we are incapable of guessing which one will play out. What we can be more sure of is that how population trends in fertility, mortality, and migration develop throughout the next several decades will play a major role in shaping national security and international relations during the 21st century.

# Notes

## CHAPTER 1

1. United Nations Population Division, "World Population Prospects: The 2008 Revision Population Database" (New York: United Nations, 2009), http://esa.un.org/UNPP/.

2. William Drozdiak, "The Brussels Wall," *Foreign Affairs* 89, no. 3 (2010): 9.

3. Several scholars mention how demography overpredicts conflict, including Ronald R. Krebs and Jack S. Levy, "Demographic Change and the Sources of International Conflict," in *Demography and National Security*, ed. Myron Weiner and Sharon Stanton Russell (New York: Berghahn Books, 2001), 62–105. Urdal mentions that the motive literature on youth bulge and political violence tends to overpredict violence. See Henrik Urdal, "A Clash of Generations? Youth Bulges and Political Violence," *International Studies Quarterly* 50, no. 3 (2006): 607–630.

4. The three-prong framework around which this book organizes the discussion of demographic security was originally introduced by international relations scholar Nazli Choucri. Nazli Choucri, "Migration and Security: Some Key Linkages," *Journal of International Affairs* 56, no. 1 (2002): 99–100.

5. The religious element is noted by Richard Jackson and Neil Howe, *The Graying of the Great Powers: Demography and Geopolitics in the 21st Century* (Washington, DC: Center for Strategic & International Studies, 2008), 20.

6. Hans J. Morgenthau and Kenneth W. Thompson, *Politics among Nations: The Struggle for Power and Peace*, 6th ed. (New York: Alfred A. Knopf, 1985).

7. Harold Sprout and Margaret Sprout, *Foundations of National Power* (Princeton, NJ: Princeton University Press, 1945), 39.

8. Katherine Organski and A. F. K. Organski, *Population and World Power* (New York: Alfred Knopf, 1961), 3–4.

9. See Neil W. Chamberlain, *Beyond Malthus: Population and Power* (New York: Basic Books, 1970), 174.

10. John J. Mearsheimer, *The Tragedy of Great Power Politics* (New York: W.W. Norton, 2001).

11. Krebs and Levy, "Demographic Change and the Sources of International Conflict," 74.

12. Nazli Choucri and Robert C. North, "Lateral Pressure in International Relations," in *Handbook of War Studies*, ed. Manus I. Midlarsky (London: Allen and Unwin, 1989), 289–326.

13. See A. F. K. Organski, *World Politics* (New York: Alfred A. Knopf, 1958); Dale C. Copeland, *The Origins of Major War* (Ithaca, NY: Cornell University Press, 2000); Ronald L. Tammen et al., *Power Transitions: Strategies for the 21st Century* (New York: Chatham House Publishers, 2000).

14. Thomas R. Malthus, *An Essay on the Principle of Population* (London, Reeves and Turner, 1888), 4–6.

15. Colin H. Kahl, *States, Scarcity, and Civil Strife in the Developing World* (Princeton, NJ: Princeton University Press, 2006), 9.

16. For example, see Jack A. Goldstone, *Revolution and Rebellion in the Early Modern World* (Berkeley, CA: University of California Press, 1991); Thomas F. Homer-Dixon, *Environment, Scarcity, and Violence* (Princeton, NJ: Princeton University Press, 2001).

17. Philip M. Hauser, "Demographic Dimensions of World Politics," in *The Population Crisis and the Use of World Resources*, ed. Stuart Mudd (The Hague: Dr. W. Junk, 1964); Richard N. Gardner, "The Politics of Population: Blueprint for International Cooperation," in *The Population Crisis: Implication and Plans for Action*, ed. Larry K. Y. Ng and Stuart Mudd (Bloomington: Indiana University Press, 1965); J. C. Hurewitz, "The Politics of Rapid Population Growth in the Middle East," *Journal of International Affairs* 19, no. 1 (1965); Paul R. Ehrlich, *The Population Bomb* (New York: Ballantine Books, 1968); Chamberlain, *Beyond Malthus*.

18. Henry Kissinger, "National Security Study Memorandum 200 Directive," (Washington, DC: National Security Council, 1974), http://www.population-security.org/11-CH3.html#1.

19. Terry L. McCoy, "Political Scientists as Problem-Solvers: The Case of Population," *Polity* 5, no. 2 (1972): 250 259.

20. Department of Defense, "National Defense Strategy of the United States of America," (Arlington, VA: Department of Defense, 2008), 4–5.

21. Although I take Choucri's general frame as a basis, I very liberally interpret what she means by these three categories. By adding detail and extending Choucri's formulation, I may depart from her intention, but I think her framework is an excellent starting point for organizing the connections between population and security. Another benefit of her definition is that it lends itself well to empirical measurement, which we will see in the book's individual chapters.

22. Choucri, "Migration and Security," 99–100.

23. Sean Kay, *Global Security in the Twenty-First Century: The Quest for Power and the Search for Peace* (Lanham, MD: Rowman & Littlefield, 2006), 258.

24. Choucri, "Migration and Security," 100.

25. Robert M. Gates, "Helping Others Defend Themselves," *Foreign Affairs* 89, no. 3 (2010): 2.

26. See, for example, "National Defense Strategy of the United States of America," "An Initial Long-Term Vision for European Defence Capability and Capacity Needs," (European Defence Agency, 2006); Keir Giles, "Review: Russia's National Security Strategy to 2020," *Russia Review Series*, ed. Andrew C. Monaghan (Rome, Italy: NATO Defense College, 2009), http://www.ndc.nato.int/research/publications.html.

27. The Fund for Peace, "Failed States Index Scores 2007," The Fund for Peace, 2007, http://www.fundforpeace.org/web/index.php?option=com_content&task=view&id=229&Itemid=366.

28. Colin S. Gray, "The 21st Century Security Environment and the Future of War," *Parameters* Winter (2008): 19.

29. Department of Defense, "Quadrennial Defense Review Report," (Arlington, VA: US Government Printing Office, 2010).

30. Mary M. Kent and Carl Haub, "Global Demographic Divide," *Population Bulletin* 60, no. 4 (2005).

31. United Nations Population Division, "World Population Prospects: The 2008 Revision Population Database."

32. United Nations Department of Economic and Social Affairs, "World Urbanization Prospects: The 2009 Revision," (United Nations Department of Economic an Social Affairs, Population Division, 2010).

33. "John Hajnal on the Prospect for Population Forecasts," *Population & Development Review* 35, no. 1 (2009): 189.

## CHAPTER 2

1. Paul R. Ehrlich, *The Population Bomb* (New York: Ballantine Books, 1968), 15.

2. Population Division Department of Economic and Social Affairs, "The World at Six Billion," (New York: United Nations, 1999), 14.

3. United Nations Population Division, "World Population Prospects: The 2008 Revision Population Database," (New York: United Nations, 2009), http://esa.un.org/UNPP/.

4. Ibid.

5. Elizabeth Leahy, Robert Engelman, Carolyn Gibb Vogel, Sarah Haddock, and Tod Preston, *The Shape of Things to Come: Why Age Structure Matters to a Safer, More Equitable World* (Washington, DC: Population Action International, 2007), 25–26.

6. Elizabeth Leahy, "Beginning the Demographic Transition: Very Young and Youthful Age Structures," *Environmental Change and Security Program* 13 (2009): 40.

7. Henrik Urdal, "The Demographics of Political Violence: Youth Bulges, Insecurity, and Conflict," in *Too Poor for Peace? Global Poverty, Conflict, and Security in the 21st Century*, ed. Lael Brainard and Derek Chollet (Washington, DC: Brookings Institution Press, 2007), 96.

8. United Nations, "Youth Development Indicators," United Nations, http://www.un.org/esa/socdev/unyin/youthindicators2.htm, accessed September 22, 2009.

9. Carl Haub and Mary Mederios Kent, "World Population Data Sheet," (Washington, DC: Population Reference Bureau, 2009), 2.

10. "World Population Prospects: The 2008 Revision Population Database."

11. Ibid.

12. Jason Bremner et al., "World Population Highlights: Key Findings from PRB'S 2009 World Population Data Sheet," *Population Bulletin* 64, no. 3 (2009): 2.

13. "World Population Data Sheet," 6.

14. "World Population Prospects: The 2008 Revision Population Database."

15. Hosni Mubarak. "President Hosni Mubarak on Egypt's Population," *Population & Development Review* 34, no. 3 (2008): 585.

16. "World Population Prospects: The 2008 Revision Population Database."

17. "President Hosni Mubarak on Egypt's Population," 584.

18. Richard Cincotta, "Iran's Chinese Future," *Foreign Policy*, June 25, 2009, http://www.foreignpolicy.com/articles/2009/06/25/irans_chinese_future.

19. Diane J. Macunovich, "Relative Cohort Size: Source of a Unifying Theory of Global Fertility Transition?," *Population & Development Review* 26 (2000): 236. Originally from Richard A. Easterlin, "Easterlin Hypothesis," in *The New Palgrave: A Dictionary of Economics, Volume 2*, ed. John Eatwell, Murray Milgate, and Peter Newman (New York: Stockton Press, 1987), 1–4.

20. Urdal, "The Demographics of Political Violence," 93.

21. Jonathan Finer and Omar Fekeiki, "Tackling Another Major Challenge in Iraq: Unemployment," *The Washington Post*, June 20, 2005, A: 10.

22. Joaquin M. Fuster, "Frontal Lobe and Cognitive Development," *Journal of Neurocytology* 31, no. 3–5 (2002): 373–385.

23. Jamil Anderlini, "China's Angry Youth Drown Out Dissent," *Financial Times*, May 3, 2008, www.ft.com.

24. Steven Lee Myers, "Youth Groups Created by Kremlin Serve Putin's Cause," *The New York Times*, July 8, 2007, http://www.nytimes.com/2007/07/08/world/europe/08moscow.html.

25. Ibid.

26. Cincotta, "Iran's Chinese Future."

27. Bremner et al., "World Population Highlights," 6.

28. "Behind the Protests Spreading across Greece," *The Economist*, December 9, 2008, http://www.economist.com/node/12756043.

29. Richard Curtain, "Where There Are No Jobs," Presented at Youth Exclusion and Political Violence Conference (Oslo: PRIO, 2008).

30. Ibid.

31. Travis Hirschi and Michael Gottfredson, "Age and the Explanation of Crime," *American Journal of Sociology* 89, no. 3 (1983): 552–584.

32. John Archer, "Violence between Men," in *Male Violence*, ed. John Archer (New York: Routledge, 1994), 121–140.

33. "Youth Development Indicators."

34. M. Bedoui and G. Ridha, "Les Politiques de Lutte Contre L'Exclusion Sociale en Tunisie," (Geneva: International Institute of Labour Studies, International Labour Office, 1996); Hilary Silver, "Social Exclusion: Comparative Analysis of Europe and Middle East Youth," *Middle East Youth Initiative Working Paper* (Washington, DC: Wolfensohn Center for Development and Dubai School of Government, 2007), 30.

35. Fred C. Pampel and Elizabeth H. Peters, "The Easterlin Effect," *Annual Review of Sociology* 21 (1995): 163–194.

36. Raymond Gilpin, "Counting the Costs of Somali Piracy," *Working Paper* (Washington, DC: United States Institute of Peace, 2009), 3.

37. John C. K. Daly, "Somalia: Pirates of the Gulf," *International Relations and Security Network,* 2009, http://www.isn.ethz.ch/isn/Current-Affairs/Security-Watch/Detail/?id=97585&lng=en.

38. UN Office on Drugs and Crime, *The Globalization of Crime: A Transnational Organized Crime Threat Assessment* (Vienna: United Nations Office on Drugs and Crime, 2010), 7.

39. Ibid., 14.

40. Ibid.

41. Ibid., 227.

42. Ibid., 221.

43. "World Population Prospects: The 2008 Revision Population Database."

44. Hilary Silver, "Social Exclusion," 20.

45. Hilary Silver, "Social Exclusion," 20–21.

46. Navtej Singh Dhillon and Tarik Yousef, *Generation in Waiting: The Unfulfilled Promise of Young People in the Middle East* (Washington, DC: Brookings Institution Press, 2009), 4.

47. John R. Calvert and A. S. Al-Shetaiwi, "Exploring the Mismatch between Skills and Jobs for Women in Saudi Arabia in Technical and Vocational Areas: The Views of Saudi Arabian Private Sector Business Managers," *International Journal of Training and Development* 6, no. 2 (2002): 112–124.

48. Inter-Agency Information and Analysis Unit, "Iraq Labour Force Analysis 2003–2008," (New York: United Nations Office for the Coordination of Humanitarian Affairs, 2009), 1.

49. Nader Kabbani and Ekta Kothari, "Youth Employment in the Mena Region: A Situational Assessment," (Washington, DC: World Bank, 2005), 36, in Silver, "Social Exclusion," 11.

50. "World Population Prospects: The 2008 Revision Population Database."

51. Inter-Agency Information and Analysis Unit, "Iraq Labour Force Analysis 2003–2008," 4.

52. Silver, "Social Exclusion," 9–10.

53. Imelda Dunlop, *Business and Youth in the Arab World* (London: International Business Leaders Forum, 2006), 13; Silver, "Social Exclusion," 23.

54. Salwa Ismail, *Political Life in Cairo's New Quarters: Encountering the Everyday State* (Minneapolis: University of Minnesota Press, 2006), 105–106; Roel Meijer, "Introduction," in *Alienation or Integration of Arab Youth: Between Family, State and Street,* ed. Roel Meijer (Richmond, Surrey: Curzon, 2000), in Silver, "Social Exclusion," 14.

55. Dhillon and Yousef, *Generation in Waiting,* 3.

56. Dhillon, "The Arab Marriage Crisis," Newsweek, 2007, http://www.msnbc.msn.com/id/17303203/site/newsweek; Silver, "Social Exclusion," 29.

57. Bremner et al., "World Population Highlights," 7.

58. Department of Economic and Social Affairs, "United Nations World Youth Report 2005," (New York: United Nations, 2005).

59. United Nations High Commissioner for Refugees, Division of Programme Support and Management, "2009 Global Trends," (Geneva: United Nations High Commissioner for Refugees, 2007), 1.

60. Leahy et al., *The Shape of Things to Come,* 30.

61. Sabrina Tavernise, "Pakistan's Islamic Schools Fill Void, but Fuel Militancy," *The New York Times,* May 3, 2009, http://www.nytimes.com/2009/05/04/world/asia/04schools.html.

62. Michael Kugelman, "Look beyond Islamabad to Solve Pakistan's 'Other' Threats," in *The New Security Beat,* ed. Meaghan Parker (Washington, DC: Environmental Change and Security Program, Woodrow Wilson International Center for Scholars, 2010), http://newsecuritybeat.blogspot.com/2010/05/guest-contributor-michael-kugelman.html.

63. Urdal, "The Demographics of Political Violence," 97.

64. United Nations Development Programme, "Arab Human Development Report 2009: Challenges to Human Security in the Arab Countries," (New York: United Nations Development Programme, 2009), 60.

65. Paul Collier, "Doing Well out of War: An Economic Perspective," in *Greed & Grievance: Economic Agendas in Civil War,* ed. Mats Berdal and David M. Malone (Boulder, CO: Lynne Rienner, 2000).

66. Rachel Brett and Irma Specht, *Young Soldiers: Why They Choose to Fight* (Boulder, CO: Lynne Rienner, 2004), 3.

67. M. Crill, *The Demobilisation and Reintegration of Former Child Soldiers in the Democratic Republic of Congo* (London: Save the Children UK, 2000); in Brett and Specht, *Young Soldiers: Why They Choose to Fight,* 14.

68. Dexter Filkins, "Afghans Offer Jobs to Taliban Rank and File If They Defect," *The New York Times* (2009), http://www.nytimes.com/2009/11/28/world/asia/28militias.html.

69. Brett and Specht, *Young Soldiers,* 10.

70. Ibid., 12–13.

71. Henrik Urdal, "A Clash of Generations? Youth Bulges and Political Violence," *International Studies Quarterly* 50, no. 3 (2006): 610.

72. Richard P. Cincotta, "Half a Chance: Youth Bulges and Transitions to Liberal Democracy," *Environmental Change and Security Program* 13 (2009): 10.

73. On this theory, see John A. Doces, "Feisty Youths and Freedom: The Effect of Youth Populations on Civil Liberties and Political Rights," Presented at *Midwest Political Science Association* (Chicago, 2009).

74. Cincotta, "Half a Chance," 11.

75. Ibid.

76. Ibid., 14.

77. Associated Press, "Lebanon's Parliament Rejects Lowering Voting Age," *Jpost.com,* Febrary 23, 2010, http://www.jpost.com/MiddleEast/Article.aspx?id=169430.

78. Håvard Hegre et al., "Toward a Democratic Civil Peace? Democracy, Political Change, and Civil War, 1816–1992," *American Political Science Review* 95(2001): 33–48.

79. Democratic Party of Japan, "Creating a Dynamic Japan: Towards a Secure Society," (Tokyo: Democratic Party of Japan, 2003), 16.

80. Lael Brainard, Derek Chollet, and Vinca LaFleur, "The Tangled Web: The Poverty–Insecurity Nexus," in *Too Poor for Peace? Global Poverty, Conflict, and Security in the 21st Century*, ed. Lael Brainard and Derek Chollet (Washington, DC: Brookings Institution Press, 2007), 1.

81. Ibid., 13.

82. The World Bank, "Girls' Education," Last updated April 1, 2009. Accessed September 8, 2010, from http://go.worldbank.org/1L4BH3TG20.

83. United States Agency for International Development, "Unmet Need for Family Planning," *Issue Brief* Washington, DC: USAID, 2006, 1.

84. The World Bank, "World's Progress on Maternal Health and Family Planning Is Insufficient," Last updated July 9, 2009. Accessed September 8, 2010, from http://go.worldbank.org/70P0CCPUF0.

85. Megan Catley-Carlson, "Foreword," in *Do Population Policies Matter? Fertility and Politics in Egypt, India, Kenya, and Mexico*, ed. Anrudh Jain (New York: Population Council, 1998), x.

86. Leahy, "Beginning the Demographic Transition," 44.

87. Farzaneh Roudi, "Youth, Women's Rights, and Political Change in Iran," Population Reference Bureau, 2009, http://www.prb.org/Articles/2009/iranyouth.aspx.

88. "World Population Prospects: The 2008 Revision Population Database."

89. Catley-Carlson, "Foreword," xii.

90. Ben Block, "Family Planning Aid Drops in Priority," (Washington, DC: Worldwatch Institute, July 10, 2009), http://www.worldwatch.org/node/6193.

## CHAPTER 3

1. For example, Mark L. Haas, "A Geriatric Peace? The Future of U.S. Power in a World of Aging Populations," *International Security* 32, no. 1 (2007): 112–147; Richard Jackson and Neil Howe, *The Graying of the Great Powers: Demography and Geopolitics in the 21st Century* (Washington, DC: Center for Strategic & International Studies, 2008).

2. See, for example, Department of Defense, "2006 Quadrennial Defense Review Report," (Arlington, VA: US Government Printing Office, 2006).

3. Vladimir Putin, "Vladimir Putin on Raising Russia's Birth Rate," *Population & Development Review* 32, no. 2 (2006): 385–388.

4. Robert M. Gates, "A Balanced Strategy: Reprogramming the Pentagon for a New Age," *Foreign Affairs* 88, no. 1 (2009), www.foreignaffairs.org/20090101faessay88103/robert-m-gates/how-to-reprogra, m-the-pentagon.html.

5. Carl Haub and Mary Mederios Kent, "2008 World Population Reference Sheet," (Washington, DC: Population Reference Bureau, 2008), http://www.prb.org/pdf08/08WPDS_Eng.pdf.

6. See, for example, Dirk J. van de Kaa, "Europe's Second Demographic Transition," *Population Bulletin* 42:1 (Washington, DC: Population Reference Bureau, 1987); David Coleman, "Why We Don't Have to Believe without Doubting in the 'Second Demographic Transition'—Some Agnostic Comments," *Vienna Yearbook of Population Research* (2004): 11–24.

7. United Nations Population Division, "World Population Prospects: The 2008 Revision Population Database," (New York: United Nations, 2009), http://esa.un.org/UNPP/.

8. Ibid.

9. Jean-Claude Chesnais, "Below-Replacement Fertility in the European Union (EU-15): Facts and Policies, 1960–1997," *Review of Population and Social Policy* 7 (1998): 84.

10. See Harold Sprout and Margaret Sprout, *Foundations of National Power* (Princeton, NJ: Princeton University Press, 1945), 29; Hans J. Morgenthau and Kenneth W. Thompson, *Politics among Nations: The Struggle for Power and Peace*, 6th ed. (New York: Alfred A. Knopf, 1985), chap. 9.

11. See A. F. K. Organski, *World Politics* (New York: Alfred A. Knopf, 1958), chaps. 6 and 7, 116–184. On the general argument, see also Dale C. Copeland, The Origins of Major War (Ithaca, NY: Cornell University Press, 2000); Ronald L. Tammen et al., *Power Transitions: Strategies for the 21st Century* (New York: Chatham House Publishers, 2000).

12. Jonathan M. DiCicco and Jack S. Levy, "Power Shifts and Problem Shifts: The Evolution of the Power Transition Research Program," *Journal of Conflict Resolution* 43, no. 6 (1999): 675–794.

13. Anne-Marie Slaughter, "America's Edge: Power in the Networked Century," *Foreign Affairs* 88, no. 1 (2009): 94–113.

14. Using constant fertility variant. United Nations Population Division, "World Population Prospects: The 2008 Revision Population Database," (New York: United Nations, 2009), http://esa.un.org/UNPP/.

15. Julia Preston, "Mexican Data Show Migration to U.S. in Decline," *The New York Times*, May 14, 2009, http://www.nytimes.com/2009/05/15/us/15immig.html; Jeffrey Passel and D'Vera Cohn, "U.S. Unauthorized Immigration Flows Are Down Sharply since Mid-Decade," (Washington, DC: Pew Hispanic Center, September 1, 2010). Accessed September 8, 2010, from http://pewhispanic.org/reports/report.php?ReportID=126.

16. P. W. Singer, "Robots at War: The New Battlefield," *The Wilson Quarterly* Winter (2009), http://www.wilsonquarterly.com/article.cfm?aid=1313.

17. European Defence Agency, "Defence Data 2007," (Brussels: European Defence Agency, 2007), 4.

18. Singer, "Robots at War."

19. Mark Mazzetti, "The Downside of Letting Robots Do the Bombing," *The New York Times*, March 21, 2009, http://www.nytimes.com/2009/03/22/weekinreview/15MAZZETTI.html?pagewanted=1&_r=1.

20. Headquarters, Department of the Army, "Counterinsurgency," (Washington, DC: Headquarters, Department of the Army, 2006).

21. Department of Defense, "Quadrennial Defense Review Report," (Arlington, VA: US Government Printing Office, 2010), iv-vi.

22. German Federal Ministry of Defence, "White Paper on German Security Policy and the Future of the Bundeswehr 2006," (Berlin: German Federal Ministry of Defence, 2006), 7.

23. Vlasta Parkanova, "A Role to Play," *EDA Bulletin* no. 10 (February 2009): 8.

24. "World Population Prospects: The 2008 Revision Population Database."

25. Organski, *World Politics*; Woosang Kim, "Alliance Transitions and Great Power War," *American Journal of Political Science* 35, no. 4 (1991): 833–850.

26. See, for example, Jeffrey Simon, "NATO's Uncertain Future: Is Demography Destiny?," *Strategic Forum* 236 (2008): 1–8.

27. Shanghai Cooperation Organization, "Brief Introduction to the Shanghai Cooperation Organisation," Shanghai Cooperation Organization (2010), http://www .sectsco.org/EN/index.asp.

28. Mark N. Katz, "Russia and the Shanghai Cooperation Organization: Moscow's Lonely Road from Bishkek to Dushanbe," *Asian Perspective* 32, no. 3 (2008): 183–187.

29. Dimitrios Moutsiakis, "The European Air Transport Fleet Gets Off to Flying Start," *EDA Bulletin* no. 10 (February 2009): 4.

30. Edward N. Luttwak, "Where Are the Great Powers? At Home with the Kids," *Foreign Affairs* 72, no. 4 (1994): 27.

31. Gerhard Kummel and Nina Leonhard, "Casualty Shyness and Democracy in Germany," *Themenschwerpunkt* 3 (2004): 119.

32. "White Paper on German Security Policy and the Future of the Bundeswehr 2006," 9.

33. Xiaobing Li, "The Impact of Social Changes on the PLA," in *Civil–Military Relations in Today's China: Swimming in a New Sea*, ed. David Michael Finkelstein and Kristen Gunness (Armonk, NY: M.E. Sharpe, 2007), 28–29.

34. Ibid., 27–31.

35. Anita U. Hattiangadi, Gary Lee, and Aline O. Quester, "Recruiting Hispanics: The Marine Corps Experience Final Report," (Alexandria, VA: Center for Naval Analysis, 2004), 1.

36. Christopher Dandeker and David Mason, "Diversifying the Uniform? The Participation of Minority Ethnic Personnel in the British Armed Services," *Armed Forces & Society* 29, no. 4 (2003): 481–507.

37. Brian Mockenhaupt, "The Army We Have," *The Atlantic Monthly* June (2007), http://www.theatlantic.com/doc/print/200706/mockenhaupt-army.

38. Stefan Bergheim, "Live Long and Prosper! Health and Longevity as Growth Drivers," in *Current Issues: Global Growth Centres*, ed. Stefan Schneider (Frankfurt: Deutsche Bank Research, 2006), 6.

39. One study by Deutsche Bank, however, found that, in Germany, household members have continued to accumulate savings in their old age, although at slower rates than they did during working years. See Bernhard Gräf and Marc Schattenberg, "The Demographic Challenge," in *Current Issues: Demography Special*, ed. Stefan Schneider (Frankfurt: Deutsche Bank Research, 2006), 13.

40. "World Population Prospects: The 2006 Revision Population Database."

41. Organization for Economic Co-operation and Development, "OECD Employment Outlook 2010: Moving Beyond the Jobs Crisis," (Paris: OECD Publishing, 2010), 271–285.

42. "Robotic Baby Seal Wins Top Award," *BBC News*, December 22, 2006, http:// news.bbc.co.uk/2/hi/technology/6202765.stm.

43. World Intellectual Property Organization, "World Patent Report: A Statistical Review," (Geneva, Switzerland: World Intellectual Property Organization, 2008), 7.

44. Slaughter, "America's Edge," 108.

45. Office of Management and Budget, "Historical Tables: Budget of the United States Government," (Washington, DC: US Government Printing Office, 2009), 21.

46. Gerard O'Dwyer, "World Military Spending Rose by 5.9% in '09: Sipri," *DefenseNews. com*, June 8, 2010, http://www.defensenews.com/story.php?i=4661977.

47. Japan Ministry of Defense, "Defense of Japan 2008," (Tokyo: Japan Ministry of Defense, 2008), 3.

48. O'Dwyer, "World Military Spending."

49. "Japan Seeks to Increase Defense Spending," *DefenseNews.com*, August 31, 2005, http://dfn.dnmediagroup.com/story.php?F=1069707&C=asiapac.

50. Sewell Chan and Jackie Calmes, "U.S. Keeps Command of Military in Seoul," *The New York Times*, June 26, 2010, http://www.nytimes.com/2010/06/27/world/asia/27prexy.html?hp.

51. Elizabeth Leahy, Robert Engelman, Carolyn Gibb Vogel, Sarah Haddock, and Tod Preston, *The Shape of Things to Come: Why Age Structure Matters to a Safer, More Equitable World* (Washington, DC: Population Action International, 2007), 55.

52. Jeffrey D. Sachs, "The Strategic Significance of Global Inequality," *The Washington Quarterly* 24, no. 3 (2001): 191.

53. United Nations Population Division, "World Population Prospects: The 2008 Revision Population Database."

# CHAPTER 4

1. Dudley Kirk, "Population Changes and the Post-War World," *The American Sociological Review* 9 no. 1 (1944): 33.

2. This was the case in 2005, mainly because China has a transitional age structure, but if fertility stays extremely high in Africa and China and India, which together are home to almost one-third of the world's population, regardless of age, this statistic would no longer be accurate. Mary M. Kent and Carl Haub, "Global Demographic Divide," *Population Bulletin* 60, no. 4 (2005): 4.

3. On fertility, see Kent and Haub, "Global Demographic Divide," 4.

4. Jacques Vallin, "The Demographic Window," *Asian Population Studies* 1, no. 2 (2005): 165.

5. A. F. K. Organski, Bruce Bueno de Mesquita, and Alan Lamborn, "The Effective Population in International Politics," in *Political Science in Population Studies*, ed. Richard L. Clinton, William S. Flash, and R. Kenneth Godwin (Lexington, MA: Lexington Books, 1972), 83.

6. Ibid., 81.

7. Ibid., 87.

8. There are many ways to define the window of opportunity: support ratios, dependency ratios, a threshold of the population younger than age 15 and older than 60, or even younger than 20 and older than 65. Such specificity is necessary

for statistical analyses, but our purpose is a general understanding of the national security challenges and opportunities in states with age structures that have relatively more workers than dependents, so this is the definition that will be used for this chapter.

9. Birthrates take a while to catch up, because people still want a lot of children.

10. United Nations Population Division, "World Population Prospects: The 2008 Revision Population Database," (New York: United Nations, 2009), http://esa.un.org/UNPP/.

11. "World Population Prospects: The 2008 Revision Population Database."

12. Wang Feng and Andrew Mason, "Demographic Dividend and Prospects for Economic Development in China," Presented at *UN Expert Group Meeting on Social and Economic Implications of Changing Population Age Structures* (Mexico City: United Nations, 2005), 4.

13. Andrew Mason, "Capitalizing on the Demographic Dividend," in *Population and Poverty, Population and Development Strategies*, ed. United Nations Population Fund (New York: United Nations Population Fund, 2003), 39–48.

14. Megan Catley-Carlson, "Foreword," in *Do Population Policies Matter? Fertility and Politics in Egypt, India, Kenya, and Mexico*, ed. Anrudh Jain (New York: Population Council, 1998), x.

15. David E. Bloom, David Canning, and Pia N. Malaney, "Demographic Change and Economic Growth in Asia," *CID Working Paper* (Boston: Center for International Development at Harvard University, 1999), 3.

16. David E. Bloom, David Canning, and Jaypee Sevilla, *The Demographic Dividend: A New Perspective on the Economic Consequences of Population Change: Population Matters* (Santa Monica, CA: RAND, 2003), 35.

17. Ester Boserup, *Population and Technological Change: A Study of Long-Term Trends* (Chicago, IL: The University of Chicago Press, 1981), 101.

18. Livi-Bacci, *A Concise History of World Population*, 138.

19. Bloom et al., "Demographic Change and Economic Growth in Asia," 3.

20. Ibid., 7.

21. The World Bank, "Open Data," (Washington, DC: The World Bank, 2010), http://data.worldbank.org, accessed June 20, 2010.

22. Kent and Haub, "Global Demographic Divide," 16.

23. Naohiro Ogawa, Makoto Kondo, and Rikiya Matsukura, "Japan's Transition from the Demographic Bonus to the Demographic Onus," *Asian Population Studies* 1, no. 2 (2005): 207.

24. Xizhe Peng and Yuan Cheng, "Harvesting the Demographic Bonus: The Impact of Migration in Shanghai," *Asian Population Studies* 1, no. 2 (2005): 191.

25. Eduard B. Vermeer, "Demographic Dimensions of China's Development," in *The Political Economy of Global Population Change, 1950–2050*, Population and Development Review Supplement to Vol. 32, ed. Paul Demeny and Geoffrey McNicoll (New York: Population Council, 2006), 116.

26. The World Bank, "Open Data," (Washington, DC: The World Bank, 2010), http://data.worldbank.org, accessed June 20, 2010.

27. "Speak Softly and Carry a Blank Cheque," *The Economist*, July 15, 2010, http://www.economist.com/node/16592455.

28. Ibid.

29. Peng and Cheng, "Harvesting the Demographic Bonus," 191.

30. Ibid.

31. Richard P. Cincotta, "Half a Chance: Youth Bulges and Transitions to Liberal Democracy," *Environmental Change and Security Program* 13 (2009): 10.

32. Aris Ananta, "Demand for Democracy in Indonesia: A Demographic Perspective," *Asian Population Studies* 2, no. 1 (2006): 1.

33. "World Population Prospects: The 2008 Revision Population Database."

34. Kua Wongboonsin, Philip Guest, and Vipan Prachuabmoh, "Demographic Change and the Demographic Dividend in Thailand," *Asian Population Studies* 1, no. 2 (2005): 245.

35. The World Bank, "Open Data."

36. Kua Wongboonsin, "Labor Migration in Thailand," Presented at *International Conference on Migrant Labor in Southeast Asia* (Armidale, Australia: UNE Asia Center and School of Economics, University of New England, December 1–3, 2003) in Wongboonsin, Guest, and Prachuabmoh, "Demographic Change and the Demographic Dividend in Thailand," 249–251.

37. Bloom, Canning, and Sevilla, *The Demographic Dividend*, 57.

38. Ronald Lee and Andrew Mason, "What Is the Demographic Dividend?," *Finance and Development* 43, no. 3 (2006).

39. Bloom, Canning, and Sevilla, *The Demographic Dividend*, 59.

40. Vallin, "The Demographic Window," 160.

41. "World Population Prospects: The 2008 Revision Population Database."

42. Virgilio Partida-Bush, "Demographic Transition, Demographic Bonus and Ageing in Mexico," Prepared for United Nations Expert Group Meeting on Social and Economic Implications of Changing Population Age Structures (Mexico City, Mexico: Population Division, Department of Economic and Social Affairs, United Nations, 2005), 292.

43. Ibid.

44. Thomas Black, "Mexico Has 85 Organized-Crime Deaths, Bloodiest Day of Calderon Presidency," *Bloomberg.com*, June 12, 2010, http://preview.bloomberg.com/news/2010-06-12/mexico-has-85-organized-crime-deaths-bloodiest-day-of-calderon-presidency.html.

45. "Thirteen Killed in Crime Wave in Mexico's Acapulco," *Reuters.com*, March 13, 2010, http://www.reuters.com/assets/pritn?aid=USTRE62C1ET20100313.

46. Ibid.

47. United Nations Office on Drugs and Crime, "The Globalization of Crime: A Transnational Organized Crime Threat Assessment," (Vienna: United Nations Office on Drugs and Crime, 2010), 4.

48. Vallin, "The Demographic Window," 160.

49. World Bank, "Open Data."

50. "World Population Prospects: The 2008 Revision Population Database."

51. Barbara E. Kritzer, "Chile's Next Generation Pension Reform," *Social Security Bulletin* 68, no. 2 (2008): 69.

52. Ibid.

53. Eduardo Gallardo, "Chile's Private Pension System Adds Public Payouts for Poor," *The New York Times*, March 10, 2008, http://www.nytimes.com/2008/03/10/business/worldbusiness/10iht-pension.4.10887983.html.

54. "World Population Prospects: The 2008 Revision Population Database."

55. Kritzer, "Chile's Next Generation Pension Reform," 69.

56. Gallardo, "Chile's Private Pension System Adds Public Payouts for Poor."

57. Dieter Zinnbauer, Rebecca Dobson, and Krina Despota, eds., *Global Corruption Report 2009: Corruption and the Private Sector* (New York: Cambridge University Press, 2009), 217.

58. Ibid., 396.

59. "World Population Prospects: The 2008 Revision Population Database."

60. Kritzer, "Chile's Next Generation Pension Reform," 76.

61. *The Globalization of Crime*, 82.

62. Simon Romero, "Economies in Latin America Race Ahead," *The New York Times*, June 30, 2010, http://www.nytimes.com/2010/07/01/world/americas/01peru.html.

63. Ibid.

64. Francis A. Kornegay, "Global Governance & Foreign Policy: The South African Dimension of IBSA," in *Emerging Powers: India, Brazil and South Africa (IBSA) and the Future of South–South Cooperation*, edited by Brazil Institute, Woodrow Wilson International Center for Scholars (Washington, DC: Woodrow Wilson International Center for Scholars, 2009), 13.

65. "World Population Prospects: The 2008 Revision Population Database."

66. Ibid.; World Bank, "Open Data."

67. Kornegay mentions some of these issues in Kornegay, "Global Governance & Foreign Policy," 15.

68. Paolo Sotero, "Introduction," in *Emerging Powers: India, Brazil and South Africa (IBSA) and the Future of South–South Cooperation*, edited by the Brazil Institute, Woodrow Wilson International Center for Scholars (Washington, DC: Woodrow Wilson International Center for Scholars, 2009), 2.

69. Carey Carpenter, "Global Governance, South–South Economic Relations, and Foreign Policy Strategies," in *Emerging Powers: India, Brazil and South Africa (IBSA) and the Future of South–South Cooperation*, edited by the Brazil Institute, Woodrow Wilson International Center for Scholars (Washington, DC: Woodrow Wilson International Center for Scholars, 2009), 4.

70. Again, Kornegay mentions some of these issues in Kornegay, "Global Governance & Foreign Policy," 15.

71. Francisco Figueiredo de Souza, "IBSA: A Brazilian Perspective," in *Emerging Powers: India, Brazil and South Africa (IBSA) and the Future of South–South Cooperation*, edited by Brazil Institute, Woodrow Wilson International Center for Scholars (Washington, DC: Woodrow Wilson International Center for Scholars, 2009), 10; "Indian Navy Escorted 900 Foreign Ships in Gulf of Aden," *The Times of India*, June 18, 2010,

http://economictimes.indiatimes.com/news/politics/nation/Indian-Navy-escorted-900-foreign-ships-in-Gulf-of-Aden/articleshow/6065236.cms.

72. Ministério da Defesa, "National Strategy of Defense: Peace and Security to Brazil," (Brasil Governo Federal, 2008), 10.

73. Ibid.

74. Department of Defence, "FY 2007–2008 Annual Report," (Department of Defence, Republic of South Africa, 2008), xiii.

75. Sotero, "Introduction," 3.

76. Umma Salma Bava, "India's Foreign Policy in the Regional Context," in *Emerging Powers: India, Brazil and South Africa (IBSA) and the Future of South–South Cooperation,* edited by Brazil Institute, Woodrow Wilson International Center for Scholars (Washington, DC: Woodrow Wilson International Center for Scholars, 2009), 17.

77. Sotero, "Introduction," 2.

78. Quoted in Frederick F. Fenech, "The Factor of Ageing in International Development Co-operation," *BOLD* 15, no. 3 (2005), 4.

79. "World Population Prospects: The 2008 Revision Population Database."

80. Albert I. Hermalin, Mary Beth Ofstedal, and Rebbeca Tesfai, "Future Characteristics of the Elderly in Developing Countries and Their Implications for Policy," *Asian Population Studies* 3, no. 1 (2007): 6.

81. Ibid., 16.

82. World Health Organization, "Core Health Indicators," World Health Organization (2006), http://www.who.int/countries/en/.

83. Richard Jackson and Neil Howe, "The Graying of the Middle Kingdom: The Demographics and Economics of Retirement Policy in China," (Washington, DC: Center for Strategic and International Studies, 2004), 13.

84. See, for example, "An Initial Long-Term Vision for European Defence Capability and Capacity Needs," (European Defence Agency, 2006).

85. "World Population Prospects: The 2008 Revision Population Database."

86. World Bank, "Open Data."

## CHAPTER 5

1. Kelly O'Donnell and Kathleen Newland, "The Iraqi Refugee Crisis: The Need for Action," (Washington, DC: Migration Policy Institute, 2008), 3, 6.

2. William J. Durch, "Keepers of the Gates: National Militaries in an Age of International Population Movement," in *Demography and National Security,* ed. Myron Weiner and Sharon Stanton Russell (New York: Berghahn Books, 2001), 112.

3. Population Reference Bureau, "World Population Highlights 2007: Migration," (Washington, DC: Population Reference Bureau, 2007), http://prb.org/Articles/2007/623Migration.aspx.

4. Fiona B. Adamson, "Crossing Borders: International Migration and National Security," *International Security* 31, no. 1 (2006): 185.

5. Stephen John Stedman and Fred Tanner, "Refugees as Resources in War," in *Refugee Manipulation: War, Politics, and the Abuse of Human Suffering,* ed. Fred Tanner and Stephen John Stedman (Washington, DC: Brookings, 2003), 1–2.

6. Population Division, Department of Economic and Social Affairs, "International Migration Report: A Global Assessment," (New York: United Nations, 2006), 2.

7. UN Development Programme, "Arab Human Development Report 2009: Challenges to Human Security in the Arab Countries," (New York: UN Development Programme, 2009), 9.

8. Ibrahim Hejoj, "A Profile of Poverty for Palestinian Refugees in Jordan: The Case of Zarqa and Sukhneh Camps," *Journal of Refugee Studies* 20, no. 1 (2007): 120.

9. For 2005 statistics, see United Nations High Commissioner for Refugees, *Statistical Yearbook 2005* (Geneva: United Nations High Commissioner for Refugees, 2007), 78–79. For 2010, see United Nations High Commissioner for Refugees, "2010 UNHCR Country Operations Profile–Jordan," (Geneva: United Nations High Commissioner for Refugees, 2010), retrieved September 17, from http://www.unhcr.org/cgi-bin/texis/vtx/page?page=49e486566; United Nations High Commissioner for Refugees, "2010 UNHCR Country Operations Profile–Syrian Arab Republic," (Geneva: United Nations High Commissioner for Refugees, 2010), retrieved September 17, from http://www.unhcr.org/cgi-bin/texis/vtx/page?page=49e486a76.

10. United Nations High Commissioner for Refugees, "Internally Displaced People," (Geneva: United Nations High Commissioner for Refugees, 2010), http://www.unhcr.org/pages/49c3646c146.html.

11. Internal Displacement Monitoring Centre, "Global IDP Estimates (1990–2009)," (Geneva: Internal Displacement Monitoring Centre, 2009), http://www.internal-displacement.org/8025708F004CE90B/%28httpPages%29/10C43F54DA2C34A7C125 73A1004EF9FF?OpenDocument&count=1000.

12. Philip Martin and Gottfried Zurcher, "Managing Migration: The Global Challenge," *Population Bulletin* 63, no. 1 (2008): 15.

13. Stedman and Tanner, "Refugees as Resources in War," 8.

14. Ibid., 3.

15. Ibid.

16. Aristide Zolberg, Astri Suhrke, and Sergio Aguayo, *Escape from Violence: Conflict and the Refugee Crisis in the Developing World* (Oxford: Oxford University Press, 1989), 275.

17. Stedman and Tanner, "Refugees as Resources in War," 5.

18. Sarah Kenyon Lischer, *Dangerous Sanctuaries: Refugee Camps, Civil War, and the Dilemmas of Humanitarian Aid* (Ithaca, NY: Cornell University Press, 2005), 14.

19. Daniel L. Byman and Kenneth M. Pollack, "Iraqi Refugees: Carriers of Conflict," Washington, DC: *The Atlantic*, November 2006, http://www.theatlantic.com/magazine/archive/2006/11/carriers-of-conflict/5268/.

20. Lischer, *Dangerous Sanctuaries*, 13.

21. Byman and Pollack, "Iraqi Refugees: Carriers of Conflict."

22. Lischer, *Dangerous Sanctuaries*, 23.

23. Hejoj, "A Profile of Poverty for Palestinian Refugees in Jordan," 123; Dawn Chatty, "Researching Refugee Youth in the Middle East: Reflections on the Importance of Comparative Research," *Journal of Refugee Studies* 20, no. 2 (2007): 270.

24. Adamson, "Crossing Borders," 192.

25. Stedman and Tanner, "Refugees as Resources in War," 2.

26. Paul Collier, *Economic Causes of Conflict and Their Implications for Policy* (Washington, DC: World Bank, 2000), 6. Adamson, "Crossing Borders," 192.

27. James D. Fearon and David D. Laitin, "Sons of the Soil, Migrants, and Civil War," Draft chapter dated January 8, 2004. Forthcoming in *World Development Review*. Cited with author's permission, *iicas.ucsd.edu/papers/GTCconf/**soil**11.pdf*.

28. O'Donnell and Newland, "The Iraqi Refugee Crisis," 10.

29. Ibid., 1.

30. Patricia Weiss Fagen, "Iraqi Refugees: Seeking Stability in Syria and Jordan" (Institute for the Study of International Migration, Georgetown University, and Center for International and Regional Studies, Georgetown University School of Foreign Service in Qatar, 2007), Abstract.

31. O'Donnell and Newland, "The Iraqi Refugee Crisis: The Need for Action," 2.

32. Ibid., 11.

33. O'Donnell and Newland, "The Iraqi Refugee Crisis," 15; Tom A. Peter, "Iraqi Refugees Spill into Jordan, Driving Up Prices," *The Christian Science Monitor*, November 29, 2006, http://www.csmonitor.com/2006/1129/p04s01-woiq.html.

34. Fagen, "Iraqi Refugees," Abstract.

35. O'Donnell and Newland, "The Iraqi Refugee Crisis," 13.

36. Ibid., 1.

37. Stedman and Tanner, "Refugees as Resources in War," 3.

38. Chatty, "Researching Refugee Youth in the Middle East," 272.

39. Durch, "Keepers of the Gates," 145.

40. Lischer, *Dangerous Sanctuaries*, 11.

41. Ibid., 28.

42. Jean Raspail, *The Camp of the Saints* (Petoskey, MI: The Social Contract Press, 1973), xiv.

43. Jack A. Goldstone, "Demography, Environment, and Security: An Overview," in *Demography and National Security*, ed. Myron Weiner and Sharon Stanton Russell (New York: Berghahn Books, 2001), 48. Goldstone references the argument of Michael S. Teitelbaum and Jay Winter, *A Question of Numbers: High Migration, Low Fertility, and the Politics of National Identity* (New York: Hill and Wang, 1998).

44. Stephen Castles and Mark J. Miller, *The Age of Migration*, 2nd ed. (New York and London: Guilford Press, 1998).

45. Aristide R. Zolberg, "Managing a World on the Move," in *The Political Economy of Global Population Change, 1950–2050*, ed. Paul Demeny and Geoffrey McNicoll, Population and Development Review Supplement to Volume 32 (New York: Population Council, 2006), 232.

46. Population Division, Department of Economic and Social Affairs, "International Migration Report: A Global Assessment," xiv–xv.

47. Zolberg, "Managing a World on the Move," 225.

48. William M. Bowsky, "Siena: Stability and Dislocation," in *The Black Death: A Turning Point in History?*, ed. William M. Bowsky (New York: Holt, Rinehart and Winston, 1971), 120. Bowsky notes that this information really only appears in one historical document, but at other points in the chapter he describes other incentives, such as tax breaks for immigrants who agreed to farm the land.

49. See Lega Nord, "Siamo a Rischio Di Poverta," (Milan: Lega Nord, 2008), 1.

50. Jeffrey Simon, "NATO's Uncertain Future: Is Demography Destiny?," *Strategic Forum* 236 (2008): 1.

51. Department of Defense, "Quadrennial Defense Review Report," (Arlington, VA: US Government Printing Office, 2010), 62.

52. Martin and Zurcher, "Managing Migration," 11.

53. Katya Vasileva and Fabio Sartori, "Acquisition of Citizenship in the European Union," *Population and Social Conditions: Statistics in Focus: Eurostat* 108 (2008): 1.

54. Berlin-Institut für Bevölkerung und Entwicklung, "Summary of the Study's Findings," *Unutilised Potentials: On the Current State of Integration in Germany* (Berlin: Berlin-Institut für Bevölkerung und Entwicklung, 2009), 3–4.

55. Martin and Zurcher, "Managing Migration," 11.

56. Durch, "Keepers of the Gates," 128.

57. The United Nations Refugee Agency, "UNHCR Concerned over Humanitarian Situation in Lampedusa, Italy," (Geneva: The United Nations Refugee Agency, 2009), http://www.unhcr.org/news/NEWS/497991064.html.

58. Sylvia Poggioli, "French Minorities Push for Equality Post-Obama," *NPR.org,* January 14, 2009, http://www.npr.org/templates/story/story.php?storyId=99298290.

59. Martin and Zurcher, "Managing Migration," 12.

60. Mary Mederios Kent, "Do Muslims Have More Children Than Other Women in Western Europe?," (Washington, DC: Population Reference Bureau, 2008), http://prb.org/Articles/2008/muslimsineurope.aspx.

61. Anne Goujon, Vegard Skirbekk, Katrin Fliegenschnee, and Pawel Strzelecki, "New Times, Old Beliefs: Projecting the Future Size of Religions in Austria," *Vienna Yearbook of Population Research* (Vienna: Vienna Institute of Demography, 2007), 237.

62. David Coleman, "Immigration and Ethnic Change in Low-Fertility Countries: A Third Demographic Transition," *Population & Development Review* 32, no. 3 (2006): 415.

63. Kent, "Do Muslims Have More Children Than Other Women in Western Europe?"

64. Peder J. Pedersen, Mariola Pytlikova, and Nina Smith, "Migration into OECD Countries, 1900–2000," in *Immigration and the Transformation of Europe,* ed. Craig A. Parsons and Timothy M. Smeeding (Cambridge: Cambridge University Press, 2006), 43–84.

65. Marion Kraske, "Far Right Benefits from Voter Dissatisfaction," *Speigel Online,* September 29, 2008, http://www.spiegel.de/international/europe/0,1518,581098,00.html.

66. Poggioli, "French Minorities Push for Equality Post-Obama."

67. Lorenzo Vidino, "Europe's New Security Dilemma," *The Washington Quarterly* 32, no. 4 (2009): 62.

68. Poggioli, "French Minorities Push for Equality Post-Obama."

69. Lorna Spence, "A Profile of Londoners by Country of Birth: Estimates from the 2006 Annual Population Survey," (London: Data Management and Analysis Group, Greater London Authority, 2008), 1–2.

70. Martin and Zurcher, "Managing Migration," 14.

71. Jørgen Carling, *Migration, Human Smuggling and Trafficking from Nigeria to Europe* (Geneva: International Organization for Migration, 2006), 8.

72. Organisation for Economic Co-operation and Development, "International Migration Outlook: SOPEMI 2009, Summary in English," (Paris: OECD, 2009), 2.

73. Adamson, "Crossing Borders," 189.

74. Martin and Zurcher, "Managing Migration," 10.

75. Yossi Shain, *Frontiers of Loyalty: Political Exiles in the Age of the Nation-State* (Ann Arbor, University of Michigan Press, 2005), xvii.

76. Ibid., xviii–xx.

77. Devesh Kapur and John McHale, *Give Us Your Best and Brightest: The Global Hunt for Talent and Its Impact on the Developing World* (Washington, DC: Center for Global Development, 2005), 25.

78. Delanyo Dolvo and Frank Nyonator, "Migration of Graduates of the University of Ghana Medical School: A Preliminary Rapid Appraisal," *Human Resources for Health Development Journal* 3, no. 1 (1999): 1, in Kapur and McHale, *Give Us Your Best and Brightest*, 29.

79. Celia W. Dugger, "Devastating Exodus of Doctors from Africa and Caribbean Is Found," *New York Times*, October 27, 2005, http://www.nytimes.com/2005/10/27/international/27brain.html; in Kapur and McHale, *Give Us Your Best and Brightest*, 29.

80. Jad Chaaban, "The Impact of Instability and Migration on Lebanon's Human Capital," in *Generation in Waiting: The Unfulfilled Promise of Young People in the Middle East*, ed. Navtej Singh Dhillon and Tarik Yousef (Washington, DC: Brookings Institution Press, 2009), 133.

81. Ibid.

82. Martin and Zurcher, "Managing Migration," 15.

83. Population Division, Department of Economic and Social Affairs, "International Migration Report: A Global Assessment," 6.

84. Kapur and McHale, *Give Us Your Best and Brightest*, 5.

85. Benedict Moran, "US–Ecuador: Luring Migrant Home an Uphill Battle," *IPS*, October 27, 2009, http://ipsnews.net/news.asp?idnews=49015.

86. Aristide Zolberg, "From Invitation to Interdiction: U.S. Foreign Policy and Immigration since 1945," in *Threatened Peoples, Threatened Borders: World Migration and U.S. Policy*, ed. Michael S. Teitelbaum and Myron Weiner (New York: W.W. Norton, 1995), 123–24; Adamson, "Crossing Borders," 190.

87. Adamson, "Crossing Borders," 188.

88. Chris Jennings, "Accelerated Citizenship Available for Active Duty Personnel," *Navy.mil*, August 27, 2002, http://www.navy.mil/search/display.asp?story_id=3295.rhod.

89. "Military Accessions Vital to the National Interest Pilot Recruiting Program," *STAND-TO!*, March 10, 2009, http://www.army.mil/standto/archive/2009/03/10/.

90. Adamson, "Crossing Borders," 189.

91. David Coleman, "Europe's Demographic Future: Determinants, Dimensions, and Challenges," in *The Political Economy of Global Population Change: 1950–2050*, ed. Paul Demeny and Geoffrey McNicoll, Population and Development Review Supplement to Volume 32 (New York: Population Council, 2005), 73.

92. Population Reference Bureau, "World Population Highlights 2007: Migration."

93. Rafael Reuveny, "Climate Change-Induced Migration and Violent Conflict," *Political Geography* 26, no. 6 (2007): 657.

94. Ibid., 658.

## CHAPTER 6

1. Anna Mehler Paperny, "In China, Out-of-Work Migrants Destabilizing," *SFGate. com*, January 23, 2009, http://articles.sfgate.com/2009-01-23/news/17199365_1_migrant-workers-pro-democracy-demonstrations-china.

2. Carl Haub, "What Is a City? What Is Urbanization?," Population Reference Bureau, 2009, http://www.prb.org/Articles/2009/urbanization. aspx?p=1.

3. Arthur Haupt and Thomas T. Kane, *Population Handbook*, 5th ed. (Washington, DC: Population Reference Bureau, 2004), 41.

4. Haub, "What Is a City? What Is Urbanization?"

5. United Nations Department of Economic and Social Affairs, "World Urbanization Prospects: The 2007 Revision, Executive Summary," (New York: United Nations, 2008), 4–7.

6. UN-HABITAT, *State of the World's Cities 2010/2011: Bridging the Urban Divide* (London: Earthscan for UN-HABITAT, 2010), 16.

7. Haub, "What Is a City? What Is Urbanization?"

8. UN-HABITAT, *State of the World's Cities 2010/2011*, x.

9. Ibid., 7.

10. UN-HABITAT, "State of the World's Cities 2006/7: The Millennium Development Goals and Urban Sustainability: 30 Years of Shaping the Habitat Agenda," (London: Earthscan for UN-Habitat, 2006), 46.

11. UN-HABITAT, *State of the World's Cities 2010/2011*, 8.

12. UN-HABITAT and United Nations Economic Commission for Africa, "The State of African Cities 2008: A Framework for Addressing Urban Challenges in Africa," (Nairobi: UN-HABITAT, 2008), 94; UN-HABITAT, *State of the World's Cities 2010/2011*, 8.

13. UN-HABITAT, *State of the World's Cities 2010/2011*, 20.

14. Ibid., x.

15. United Nations Population Fund, "State of World Population 2007: Unleashing the Potential of Urban Growth," (New York: United Nations Population Fund, 2007), 9.

16. Ibid., 10.

17. Ibid., 9.

18. United Nations Human Settlements Programme, "The Challenge of Slums," (Sterling, VA: United Nations Human Settlements Programme, 2003), 25.

19. Ellen Brennen, "Population, Urbanization, Environment, and Security: A Summary of the Issues," *Comparative Urban Studies Occasional Papers Series* (Washington, DC: Woodrow Wilson International Center for Scholars, 1999), 10.

20. United Nations Human Settlements Programme, "The Challenge of Slums," 1.

21. Ibid., 9.

22. Ibid., 5.

23. Carl Haub and Mary Mederios Kent, "World Population Data Sheet," (Washington, DC: Population Reference Bureau, 2009), 12.

24. Raymond J. Struyk and Stephen Giddings, "The Challenge of an Urban World: An Opportunity for U.S. Foreign Assistance," (Washington, DC: International Housing Coalition, 2009), 2.

25. Population Action International, "How Shifts to Smaller Family Sizes Contributed to the Asian Miracle," *FACTSheet* (Washington, DC: Population Action International, 2006), 1–2.

26. Ester Boserup, *Population and Technological Change: A Study of Long-Term Trends* (Chicago: The University of Chicago Press, 1981), 129.

27. Richard Florida, *Who's Your City? How the Creative Economy Is Making Where to Live the Most Important Decision of Your Life* (New York: Basic Books, 2008), 86–87.

28. Roch Legault, "The Urban Battlefield and the Army: Changes and Doctrines," *Canadian Military Journal* Autumn (2000): 39.

29. Thomas Homer-Dixon, *The Upside of Down: Catastrophe, Creativity, and the Renewal of Civilization* (Washington, DC: Island Press, 2006), 10.

30. United Nations Human Settlement Program, "The Urban Penalty: New Threats, Old Fears," (Nairobi, Kenya: UN-HABITAT, 2006), 1.

31. Dean Nelson and Rob Crilly, "Mumbai Attack Masterminds 'Will Never Be Brought to Justice,'" *Telegraph*, April 30, 2010, http://www.telegraph.co.uk/news/worldnews/asia/india/7658529/Mumbai-attack-masterminds-will-never-be-brought-to-justice.html.

32. UN-HABITAT, *State of the World's Cities 2010/2011*, 25.

33. "Global 500," *Fortune*, July 20, 2009, http://money.cnn.com/magazines/fortune/global500/2009/countries/SouthKorea.html.

34. Peter J. Donaldson and Son-Ung Kim, "Dealing with Seoul's Population Growth: Government Plans and Their Implementation," *Asian Survey* 19, no. 7 (1979): 660–673.

35. Legault, "The Urban Battlefield and the Army," 40.

36. Jennifer Morrison Taw and Bruce Hoffman, "The Urbanization of Insurgency: The Potential Challenge to U.S. Army Operations," (Santa Monica, CA: RAND, 1994), x.

37. Ibid., 21.

38. Department of Defense, "Quadrennial Defense Review Report," (Arlington, VA: US Government Printing Office, 2010), 20.

39. Diane Davis, "Urban Violence, Quality of Life, and the Future of Latin American Cities: The Dismal Record So Far and the Search for New Analytical Frameworks to Sustain the Bias towards Hope," in *Global Urban Poverty: Setting the Agenda*, ed. Allison M. Garland, Mejgan Massoumi, and Blair A. Ruble (Washington, DC: Woodrow Wilson International Center for Scholars, 2007), 65.

40. Amita Baviskar, Subir Sinha, and Kavita Philip, "Rethinking Indian Environmentalism," in *Forging Environmentalism: Justice, Livelihood, and Contested Environments*, ed. Joanne R. Bauer (London: M.E. Sharpe, 2006), 189–193.

41. Central Intelligence Agency, "China," *CIA World Factbook* (Washington, DC: Central Intelligence Agency 2010), accessed April 21, 2010, https://www.cia.gov/library/publications/the-world-factbook/index.html.

42. UN-HABITAT, "China's Rising Cities," (Nairobi, Kenya: UN-HABITAT, 2006).

43. International Bank for Reconstruction and Development/The World Bank, *World Development Indicators* (Washington, DC: International Bank for Reconstruction and Development/The World Bank, 2007), 66–68.

44. See, for example, "'Thousands Riot' in China Protest," *BBC News*, March 12, 2007, http://news.bbc.co.uk/2/hi/asia-pacific/6441295.stm; Edward Cody, "China Grows More Wary over Rash of Protests," *The Washington Post*, August 10, 2005, http://www.washingtonpost.com/wp-dyn/content/article/2005/08/09/AR2005080901323.html.

45. Yuanting Zhang and Franklin W. Goza, "Who Will Care for the Elderly in China? A Review of the Problems Caused by China's One-Child Policy and Their Potential Solutions," *Journal of Aging Studies* 20, no. 2 (2006): 151–164.

46. Robert Stowe England, *The Fiscal Challenge of an Aging Industrial World* (Washington, DC: CSIS Press, 2002), xiii.

47. "China's Migrant Reforms Will Help Economy," *UPI.com*, December 28, 2009, http://www.upi.com/Top_News/International/2009/12/28/Chinas-migrant-reforms-will-help-economy/UPI-17711262006375/.

48. Robert D. Lamb, "Ungoverned Areas and Threats from Safe Havens," (Arlington, VA: Office of the Under Secretary of Defense for Policy, 2008), 1.

49. Taw and Hoffman, "The Urbanization of Insurgency," x.

50. Lamb, "Ungoverned Areas and Threats from Safe Havens," 25.

51. Robert Gay, "From Popular Movements to Drug Gangs to Militias: An Anatomy of Violence in Rio de Janiero," in *Megacities: The Politics of Urban Exclusion and Violence in the Global South*, ed. Kees Koonings and Kirk Fruijt (London: Zed Books, 2009), 31.

52. "London Bombers: Key Facts," *BBC News*, Last updated July 21, 2005, http://news.bbc.co.uk/2/hi/uk_news/4676861.stm.

53. Henrik Urdal and Kristian Hoelscher, "Urban Youth Bulges and Social Disorder: An Empirical Study of Asian and Sub-Saharan African Cities," *Policy Research Working Paper* (Washington, DC: The World Bank, 2009), 9.

54. UNFPA, "State of World Population 2007," 8.

55. Urdal and Hoelscher, "Urban Youth Bulges and Social Disorder," 17.

56. Laura Brewer, "Youth at Risk: The Role of Skills Development in Facilitating the Transition to Work," *InFocus Programme on Skills, Knowledge and Employability* Working Paper No. 19 (Geneva: International Labour Organization, 2004), 4.

57. On the other hand, Alan Gilbert argues that there are few links between urbanization and crime, revolution, and poverty. See Alan Gilbert, "Urbanization and Security," *Comparative Urban Studies Occasional Paper Series* (Washington, DC: Woodrow Wilson International Center for Scholars, 1999), 19.

58. Gary Fuller and Forrest R. Pitts, "Youth Cohorts and Political Unrest in South Korea," *Political Geography Quarterly* 9, no. 1 (1990): 9–22. Richard P. Cincotta, "Demographic Security Comes of Age," *Environmental Change and Security Program* 10 (2004): 24–29.

59. Christopher Johnson, "A Turning Point in Thailand," *The Japan Times Online*, May 13, 2010, http://search.japantimes.co.jp/cgi-bin/eo20100513a1.html.

60. Henrik Urdal, "The Demographics of Political Violence: Youth Bulges, Insecurity, and Conflict," in *Too Poor for Peace? Global Poverty, Conflict, and Security in the 21st Century*, ed. Lael Brainard and Derek Chollet (Washington, DC: Brookings Institution Press, 2007), 96.

61. Gilbert, "Urbanization and Security," 9.

62. Urdal and Hoelscher, "Urban Youth Bulges and Social Disorder," 2.

63. United Nations Population Fund, "State of World Population 2007," 27.

64. Anna Kajumulo Tibaijuka, "Introduction: The Challenge of Slums," in *Global Report on Human Settlements*, ed. United Nations Human Settlements Programme (London: Earthscan Publications Ltd., 2003), vi.

65. On sub-Saharan Africa, see United Nations Human Settlements Programme, "Slums: Past, Present, and Future," (Nairobi, Kenya: UN-HABITAT, 2006), 1. On global statistic, see UN-HABITAT, *State of the World's Cities 2010/2011*, 30.

66. UN-HABITAT, *State of the World's Cities 2010/2011*, 30.

67. Struyk and Giddings, "The Challenge of an Urban World," 2.

68. UNFPA, "State of World Population 2007," 6.

69. Beatrice Daumerie and Karen Hardee, "The Effects of a Very Young Age Structure on Haiti: Country Case Study," *The Shape of Things to Come Series* (Washington, DC: Population Action International, 2010), 6.

70. UN-HABITAT, *State of the World's Cities 2010/2011*, 75.

71. Ibid.

72. "The Challenge of Slums," 73.

73. Tibaijuka, "Introduction: The Challenge of Slums," vi.

74. Struyk and Giddings, "The Challenge of an Urban World," 18.

75. UN-HABITAT, *State of the World's Cities 2010/2011*, 38.

76. Allison M. Garland, Mejgan Massoumi, and Blair A. Ruble, eds., *Global Urban Poverty: Setting the Agenda* (Washington, DC: Woodrow Wilson International Center for Scholars, 2007), 3.

77. United Nations Human Settlements Programme, "Mumbai's Quest for 'World City' Status," (Nairobi, Kenya: UN-HABITAT, 2006), 1.

78. Struyk and Giddings, "The Challenge of an Urban World," 22.

79. Tibaijuka, "Introduction: The Challenge of Slums," vi–vii.

80. United Nations Human Settlements Programme, "Mumbai's Quest for 'World City' Status," 1.

81. Struyk and Giddings, "The Challenge of an Urban World," 7.

82. Daniel Nogueira Budny, "Democracy and the City: Assessing Urban Policy in Brazil," (Washington, DC: Woodrow Wilson International Center for Scholars, 2007), 3.

83. Ibid., 4.

84. Rualdo Menegat, "Participatory Democracy and Sustainable Development: Integrated Urban Environmental Management in Porto Alegre, Brazil," *Environment & Urbanization* 14, no. 2 (2002): 181.

85. Ibid.

86. Budny, "Democracy and the City," 3.

87. Garland et al., eds., *Global Urban Poverty*, 5.

88. Tim Dyson, "A Partial Theory of World Development: The Neglected Role of the Demographic Transition in the Shaping of Modern Society," *International Journal of Population Geography* 7, no. 2 (2001): 67–90; Jo Beall, "Urban Governance and the Paradox of Conflict," in *Megacities: The Politics of Urban Exclusion and Violence in the Global South*, ed. Kees Koonings and Dirk Kruijt (London: Zed Books, 2009), 108.

89. United Nations Educational Scientific and Cultural Organization (UNESCO), "Water and Natural Disasters in Celebration of International Day for Natural Disaster Reduction," *UNESCO Water Portal Bi-monthly Newsletter* No 209 (Paris: UNESCO, 2008), http://www.unesco.org/water/news/newsletter/209.shtml.

90. United Nations International Strategy for Disaster Reduction, "2009 Global Assessment Report on Disaster Risk Reduction: Risk and Poverty in a Changing Climate," (Geneva: United Nations International Strategy for Disaster Reduction Secretariat, 2009), 3. The authors include the footnote: "EMDAT does not register reports of small-scale disasters below its threshold of 10 deaths, 100 affected people, or a call for international assistance." 16.

91. UNFPA, "State of World Population 2007," 59.

92. James K. Mitchell, "Megacities and Natural Disasters: A Comparative Analysis," *GeoJournal* 49 (1999): 137.

93. United States Agency for International Development, "Assistance for Iranian Earthquake Victims," (Washington, DC: USAID), last updated January 16, 2004, http://www.usaid.gov/iran/, accessed April 29, 2010.

94. "Iran Earthquake Kills Thousands," *BBC News*, December 26, 2003, http://news.bbc.co.uk/2/hi/3348613.stm.

95. Frances Harrison, "Quake Experts Urge Tehran Move," *BBC News*, March 14, 2005, http://news.bbc.co.uk/2/hi/middle_east/4346945.stm.

96. United Nations International Strategy for Disaster Reduction, "2009 Global Assessment Report on Disaster Risk Reduction," 3.

97. Mitchell, "Megacities and Natural Disasters," 137.

98. United Nations Human Settlements Programme, "The Challenge of Slums," 69.

99. C. Bern, "Risk Factors for Mortality in the Bangladesh Cyclone of 1991," *Bulletin of the World Health Organization* 71, no. 11 (1993), 73–78 in Mark Pelling, "Urbanization and Disaster Risk," Presented at *Population–Environment Research Network Cyberseminar on Population and National Hazards* (Palisades, NY: Population-Environment Research Network, 2007), 3.

100. Maxx Dilley et al., "Natural Disaster Hotspots: A Global Risk Analysis, Synthesis Report," (Washington, DC: International Bank for Reconstruction and Development/The World Bank and Columbia University, 2005), 25.

101. Jonathan M. Katz, "Armed Thugs Filling Haiti's Security Void," *The Seattle Times*, January 18, 2010, http://seattletimes.nwsource.com/html/nationworld/2010828972_haitisecure19.html.

102. Dana Hedgpeth, "U.S. Task Force Commander for Haitian Relief Says Logistics Remain Stumbling Block," *The Washington Post*, January 18, 2010, http://www.washingtonpost.com/wp-dyn/content/article/2010/01/18/AR2010011804059.html.

103. United Nations Human Settlements Programme, "China's Rising Cities," 2.

104. UNFPA, "State of World Population 2007," 58–59.

105. United Nations Human Settlements Programme, "Reducing Urban Crime and Violence: Policy Directions," (London: United Nations Human Settlements Programme, 2007), 4.

106. Jeneen Interlandi, "What We Did Wrong," *Newsweek*, January 14, 2010, http://www.newsweek.com/2010/01/13/what-we-did-wrong.html.

107. Brennen, "Population, Urbanization, Environment, and Security," 19.

108. Ibid.

109. Stephanie Hanson, "Backgrounder: Urbanization in Sub-Saharan Africa," Last updated October 1, 2007 (Washington, DC: Council on Foreign Relations), http://www.cfr.org/publication/14327/urbanization_in_subsaharan_africa.html, accessed December 22, 2009.

# CHAPTER 7

1. On this typology, see Terry L. McCoy, "Political Scientists as Problem-Solvers: The Case of Population," *Polity* 5, no. 2 (1972): 254.

2. Myron Weiner and Michael S. Teitelbaum, *Political Demography, Demographic Engineering* (New York: Berghahn Books, 2001), 32.

3. Andrew Price-Smith, *Contagion and Chaos: Disease, Ecology, and National Security in the Era of Globalization* (Cambridge, MA: The MIT Press, 2009), 95.

4. Maranyane Ngwanaamotho, "Botswana: HIV/AIDS Stabilises in Botswana," *allAfrica.com*, October 14, 2009, http://allafrica.com/stories/200910150161.html.

5. United Nations Development Programme, "Arab Human Development Report 2009: Challenges to Human Security in the Arab Countries," (New York: United Nations Development Programme, 2009), 56.

6. Stefan Elbe, "Should HIV/AIDS Be Securitized? The Ethical Dilemmas of Linking HIV/AIDS and Security," *International Studies Quarterly* 50 (2005): 119.

7. Central Intelligence Agency, "Botswana," *CIA World Factbook* (Washington, DC: Central Intelligence Agency, 2010), accessed August 21, 2010, https://www.cia.gov/library/publications/the-world-factbook/index.html.

8. Elizabeth Leahy, Robert Engelman, Carolyn Gibb Vogel, Sarah Haddock, and Tod Preston, *The Shape of Things to Come: Why Age Structure Matters to a Safer, More Equitable World* (Washington, DC: Population Action International, 2007), 72.

9. Radhika Sarin, "The Enemy Within: Aids in the Military," Online discussion, 2003, http://www.worldwatch.org/node/1550.

10. UNAIDS, "AIDS and the Military: UNAIDS Point of View," (Geneva: Joint United Nations Programme on HIV/AIDS, 1998), 2.

11. Ibid.; John Kemoli Sagala, "HIV/AIDS and the Military in Sub-Saharan Africa: Impact on Military Effectiveness," *Africa Today* 53, no. 1 (2006): 53–77.

12. Lindy Heinecken, "Facing a Merciless Enemy: HIV/AIDS and the South African Armed Forces," *Armed Forces & Society* 29, no. 2 (2003): 281–300.

13. United Nations Integrated Regional Information Networks (IRIN), *HIV/AIDS and the Military*, PlusNews, United Nations Integrated Regional Information Networks (IRIN), 2, www.irinnews.org/pdf/pn/Plusnews-Media-Fact-file-Military.pdf.

14. Gwyn Prins, "AIDS and Global Security," *International Affairs* 80, no. 5 (2004): 931–952.

15. Alex de Waal, "How Will HIV/AIDS Transform African Governance?," *African Affairs* 102 (2003): 16.

16. Lindy Heinecken, "HIV/AIDS, the Military and the Impact on National and International Security," *Society in Transition* 31, no. 1 (2001): 120–128.

17. Laurie Garrett, *HIV and National Security: Where Are the Links?* (New York: Council on Foreign Relations, 2005), 10.

18. de Waal, "How Will HIV/AIDS Transform African Governance?," 9.

19. Garrett, *HIV and National Security*, 11.

20. de Waal, "How Will HIV/AIDS Transform African Governance?," 13.

21. Ibid., 18.

22. Garrett, *HIV and National Security*, 9.

23. "AIDS Accounts for 75 Percent of Police Deaths," *Daily Nation*, November 27, 2000, www.nationaudio.com; Sagala, "HIV/AIDS and the Military in Sub-Saharan Africa."

24. Martin Schonteich, "Age and AIDS: South Africa's Crime Time Bomb?," *Africa Security Review* 18, no. 4 (1999): 57.

25. Andrew T. Price-Smith, *Contagion and Chaos: Disease, Ecology, and National Security in the Era of Globalization* (Cambridge, MA: MIT Press, 2009), 108.

26. Ibid., 110–111.

27. Ibid., 112.

28. de Waal, "How Will HIV/AIDS Transform African Governance?"

29. Garrett, *HIV and National Security*, 11.

30. Robert Greener, "The Impact of HIV/AIDS on Poverty and Inequality," in *The Macroeconomics of HIV/AIDS*, ed. Markus Haacker (Washington, DC: International Monetary Fund, 2004), 177; UNAIDS, "2008 Report on the Global AIDS Epidemic," (Geneva: UNAIDS, 2008), 162.

31. UNAIDS, "2008 Report on the Global Aids Epidemic," 164.

32. Garrett, *HIV and National Security*, 9.

33. Ibid.

34. Elbe, "Should HIV/AIDS Be Securitized?," 119.

35. Leahy et al., *The Shape of Things to Come*, 72.

36. Price-Smith, *Contagion and Chaos*, 95.

37. Christine Gorman, "Sex, AIDS and Thailand," *Time.com*, July 12, 2004, http://www.time.com/time/magazine/article/0,9171,662826,00.html.

38. "2008 Report on the Global AIDS Epidemic," 162.

39. United Nations Population Division, "World Population Prospects: The 2008 Revision Population Database," (New York: United Nations, 2009), http://esa.un.org/UNPP/.

40. Robert M. Gates, "A Balanced Strategy: Reprogramming the Pentagon for a New Age," *Foreign Affairs* 88, no. 1 (2009), www.foreignaffairs.org/20090101faessay88103/robert-m-gates/how-to-reprogram-the-pentagon.html.

41. "World Population Prospects: The 2008 Revision Population Database."

42. "The Incredible Shrinking People," *The Economist*, November 27, 2008, http://www.economist.com/node/12627956.

43. Data from "World Population Prospects: The 2008 Revision Population Database."

44. "The Incredible Shrinking People," *The Economist*.

45. Vladimir Putin, "Vladimir Putin on Raising Russia's Birth Rate," *Population & Development Review* 32, no. 2 (2006): 385–388.

46. Guy Faulconbridge, "Russia Says Population Up for First Year since 1995," *Reuters India* (2010), http://in.reuters.com/article/idINTRE60I2KM20100119.

47. Nicholas Eberstadt, "Drunken Nation: Russia's Depopulation Bomb," *World Affairs* Spring (2009), http://www.worldaffairsjournal.org/articles/2009-Spring/full-Eberstadt.html.

48. United Nations in the Russian Federation, "UN in Russia," (New York: United Nations, 2007), http://www.unrussia.ru/en/about.html.

49. Faulconbridge, "Russia Says Population Up for First Year since 1995."

50. Eberstadt, "Drunken Nation: Russia's Depopulation Bomb."

51. Judyth Twigg, "Differential Demographics: Russia's Muslim and Slavic Populations," in *PONARS Policy Memo* (Washington, DC: Eurasian Strategy Project, 2005), 137, https://gushare.georgetown.edu/eurasianstrategy/Memos/2005/pm_0388.pdf.

52. Harley Balzer, "Demography and Democracy in Russia: Human Capital Challenges to Democratic Consolidation," *Demokratizatsiya* 11, no. 1 (2003): 95–109.

53. Eberstadt, "Drunken Nation."

54. Luke Harding, "No Country for Old Men," *The Guardian*, February 11, 2008, http://www.guardian.co.uk/world/2008/feb/11/russia.

55. Ibid.

56. Stephen Dalziel, "Death Rate High in Russian Army," *BBC*, September 13, 2003, http://news.bbc.co.uk/2/low/europe/3106368.stm.

57. Ibid.

58. The Russian Federation Ministry of Defence, "Recruitment," http://www.mil.ru/eng/1862/12069/index.shtml. Accessed June 20, 2010.

59. Keir Giles, "Review: Russia's National Security Strategy to 2020," in *Russia Review Series*, ed. Andrew C. Monaghan (Rome, Italy: NATO Defense College, 2009), http://www.ndc.nato.int/research/publications.html.

60. Clifford J. Levy, "Russian Military Cuts Leave Soldiers Adrift," *The New York Times*, June 11, 2009, http://www.nytimes.com/2009/06/12/world/europe/12russia.html.

61. I take sex differences to be biological, and gender to be socially constructed, but most of the scholarly literature on sex ratios uses "sex" and "gender" interchangeably, and I follow the original author's lead in using the terms. Both are issues, as it is because of the social construction of unequal gender roles in these societies that the sex ratio at birth is imbalanced.

62. Valerie M. Hudson and Andrea M. den Boer, *Bare Branches: Security Implications of Asia's Surplus Male Population*, BCSIA Studies in International Security (Cambridge, MA: MIT Press, 2004).

63. Dudley L. Poston, Jr., and Karen S. Glover, "Too Many Males: Marriage Market Implications of Gender Imbalances in China," (2004), 6. Unpublished work obtained with permission of the author: dudleyposton@yahoo.com.

64. Ibid., 8.

65. Prabhat Jha et al., "Low Male-to-Female Sex Ratio of Children Born in India: National Survey of 1.1 Million Households," *The Lancet* 367, no. 9506 (2006): 211–218.

66. Monica Das Gupta, "Explaining Asia's 'Missing Women': A New Look at the Data," *Population & Development Review* 31, no. 3 (2005): 529–535.

67. Ibid.

68. India Registrar General, "Census of India, 2001, Series 1: India, Paper of 2001: Provisional Population Totals," (New Delhi: India Registrar General, Office of the Registrar General, 2001), in Valerie M. Hudson and Andrea M. den Boer, "Missing Women and Bare Branches: Gender Balance and Conflict," *Environmental Change and Security Program*, 11 (2005): 20.

69. Poston and Glover, "Too Many Males," 9.

70. Ibid., 12.

71. Richard Cincotta, "Review of Bare Branches: The Security Implications of Asia's Surplus Male Population," *Environmental Change and Security Program* 11 (2005): 71.

72. Valerie M. Hudson and Andrea M. den Boer, "Missing Women and Bare Branches: Gender Balance and Conflict," *Environmental Change and Security Program Report* no. 11 (2005): 20.

73. Valerie M. Hudson and Andrea M. den Boer, "A Surplus of Men, a Deficit of Peace: Security and Sex Ratios in Asia's Largest States," *International Security* 26, no. 4 (2002): 5–38.

74. Allan Mazur and Joel Michalek, "Marriage, Divorce, and Male Testosterone," *Social Forces* 77, no. 1 (1998): 315–330; Hudson and den Boer, "Missing Women and Bare Branches," 22.

75. Hudson and den Boer, "Missing Women and Bare Branches," 21.

76. UNODC, *The Globalization of Crime: A Transnational Organized Crime Threat Assessment* (Vienna: United Nations Office on Drugs and Crime, 2010), 49.

77. Ibid.

78. Ibid., 51.

79. Poston and Glover, "Too Many Males," 14.

80. Ibid.

81. Monica Duffy Toft, "Differential Demographic Growth in Multinational States: Israel's Two-Front War," *Journal of International Affairs* 56, no. 1 (2002): 71–94.

82. See, for example, Francesco Caselli and Wilbur John Coleman, II, "On the Theory of Ethnic Conflict," Discussion Paper No 732 (London: Centre for Economic Performance, 2006).

83. See Barry R. Posen, "The Security Dilemma and Ethnic Conflict," *Survival* 35, no. 1 (1993): 27–47. Distrust and fear also play a role in David A. Lake and Donald Rothchild, "Containing Fear: The Origins and Management of Ethnic Conflict," *International Security* 21, no. 2 (1996): 41–75.

84. See Stuart J. Kaufman, *Modern Hatreds: The Symbolic Politics of Ethnic War* (Ithaca, NY: Cornell University Press, 2001).

85. Tanja Ellingsen, "Colorful Community or Ethnic Witches' Brew?," *Journal of Conflict Resolution* 41, no. 4 (2000): 509–528.

86. Marie L. Besançon, "Relative Resources: Inequality in Ethnic Wars, Revolutions, and Genocides," *Journal of Peace Research* 42, no. 4 (2005): 393–415.

87. Monica Duffy Toft, "Population Shifts and Civil War: A Test of Power Transition Theory," *International Interactions* 33, no. 3 (2007): 71–94.

88. Ronald R. Krebs and Jack S. Levy, "Demographic Change and the Sources of International Conflict," in *Demography and National Security*, ed. Myron Weiner and Sharon Stanton Russell (New York: Berghahn Books, 2001), 85.

89. Ibid., 82.

90. Toft, "Differential Demographic Growth in Multinational States," 80–83.

91. Weiner and Teitelbaum, *Political Demography, Demographic Engineering*, 54.

92. Twigg, "Differential Demographics," 136.

93. Ibid., 137.

94. For 1980 and 1981 figures, see Ellen Jones and Fred W. Grupp, *Modernization, Value Change, and Fertility in the Soviet Union* (Cambridge: Cambridge University Press, 1987), table 2.11. For other figures, see Carl Haub, "Population Change in the Former Soviet Republics," *Population Bulletin* 49, no. 4 (1994), accessed at http://www.ncbi.nlm.nih.gov/pubmed/12346298.

95. Weiner and Teitelbaum, *Political Demography, Demographic Engineering*, 34.

96. Regarding the statistics, see Twigg, "Differential Demographics," 135.

97. Toft, "Differential Demographic Growth in Multinational States," 74.

98. Michael Schwirtz, Anne Barnard, and C. J. Chivers, "Russia and Georgia Clash over Separatist Region," *The New York Times*, August 8, 2008, http://www.nytimes.com/2008/08/09/world/europe/09georgia.html.

99. Twigg, "Differential Demographics," 134.

100. "Q&A: The Chechen Conflict," *BBC News*, July 10, 2006, http://news.bbc.co.uk/2/hi/europe/3293441.stm.

101. "Regions and Territories: Ingushetia," *BBC News*, February 10, 2010, http://news.bbc.co.uk/2/hi/europe/country_profiles/3829691.stm.

102. Twigg, "Differential Demographics," 135.

103. Elliott D. Green, "Demography, Diversity and Nativism in Contemporary Africa: Evidence from Uganda," Presented at *ASEN Conference on Political Demography* (London: London School of Economics and Political Science, 2006), 3.

104. Jamie Wilson, "Ethnic Minorities to Form Majority by 2050," *The Guardian*, August 13, 2005, http://www.guardian.co.uk/world/2005/aug/13/usa.population.

105. Associated Press, "Hispanics Comprise 20% of America's Student Body," *Telegraph-Herald*, March 6, 2009, http://findarticles.com/p/news-articles/telegraph-herald-dubuque-iowa/mi_8023/is_20090306/hispanics-comprise-20-americas-student/ai_n44873940/.

106. Ibid.

107. Ibid.

108. Mark Mather and Kelvin Pollard, "U.S. Hispanic and Asian Population Growth Levels Off," Population Reference Bureau (2009), http://prb.org/Articles/2009/hispanicasian.aspx.

109. Randal C. Archibold, "Arizona Enacts Stringent Law on Immigration," *The New York Times*, April 23, 2010, http://www.nytimes.com/2010/04/24/us/politics/24immig.html.

110. Husna Haq, "Hispanics Abandon Arizona, Fleeing Economy, Immigration Law," *The Christian Science Monitor*, June 10, 2010, http://www.csmonitor.com/USA/Society/2010/0610/Hispanics-abandon-Arizona-fleeing-economy-immigration-law.

111. Ibid.

112. "Obama, Calderon Blast Arizona Immigration Law during White House Visit," *FoxNews.com*, 2010, http://www.foxnews.com/politics/2010/05/19/mexicos-president-blasts-arizona-immigration-law-white-house-visit-1351636523/.

113. Liz Goodwin, "Arizona Official Threatens to Cut Off Electricity to L.A. in Retaliation for Boycott," *Yahoo! News*, May 19, 2010, http://news.yahoo.com/s/ynews/20100519/pl_ynews/ynews_pl2133.

114. Wilson, "Ethnic Minorities to Form Majority by 2050."

115. State of Texas, "Estimates of the Population by Age, Sex, and Race/Ethnicity," (San Antonio, TX: State of Texas, 2008), http://txsdc.utsa.edu/tpepp/txpopest.php, 1.

116. Weiner and Teitelbaum, *Political Demography, Demographic Engineering*, 38–40.

117. "Sovereigntists Pursue Quebec Independence," *CBCNews*, June 21, 2010, http://www.cbc.ca/canada/ottawa/story/2010/06/21/sovereignty-march.html.

118. Gerald L. Gall, "Québec Referendum (1995)," in *The Canadian Encyclopedia* (The Historica Foundation, 2010), http://www.thecanandianencyclopedia.com.

119. Eric Kaufmann and Oded Haklai, "Dominant Ethnicity: From Minority to Majority," *Nations and Nationalism* 14, no. 4 (2008): 743.

120. David Newman, "Population as Security: The Arab–Israeli Struggle for Demographic Hegemony," in *Redefining Security: Population Movements and National Security*, ed. Nana Poku and David T. Graham (Westport, CT: Praeger, 1998), 164.

121. On total fertility, see "World Population Prospects: The 2008 Revision Population Database"; Dov Friedlander, "Fertility in Israel: Is the Transition to Replacement Level in Sight?," in *Completing the Fertility Transition*, edited by United Nations Department of Economic and Social Affairs (New York: United Nations Department of Economic and Social Affairs, 2002), http://www.un.org/esa/population/publications/completingfertility/RevisedFriedlanderpaper.PDF, 440–447.

122. Central Bureau of Statistics, "Israel in Statistics 1948–2007," (Jerusalem: Central Bureau of Statistics, 2009), 2.

123. Ibid.

124. Newman, "Population as Security," 168.

125. Isabel Kershner, "Israel's Ultra-Orthodox Protest Schools Ruling," *The New York Times*, June 17, 2010, http://www.nytimes.com/2010/06/18/world/middleeast/18israel.html.

126. Richard Cincotta and Eric Kaufmann, "The Changing Face of Israel," *Foreign-Policy.com*.

127. Ibid.

128. Toft, "Differential Demographic Growth in Multinational States."

129. Cincotta and Kaufmann, "The Changing Face of Israel."

130. Kaufmann and Haklai, "Dominant Ethnicity: From Minority to Majority," 746.

131. Philippe Fargues, "Demographic Islamization: Non-Muslims in Muslim Countries," *SAIS Review* 21, no. 2 (2001): 107.

## CHAPTER 8

1. Elizabeth Leahy, Robert Engelman, Carolyn Gibb Vogel, Sarah Haddock, and Tod Preston, *The Shape of Things to Come: Why Age Structure Matters to a Safer, More Equitable World* (Washington, DC: Population Action International, 2007).

2. The Fund for Peace, "Failed States Index Scores 2007," The Fund for Peace, 2007, http://www.fundforpeace.org/web/index.php?option=com_content&task=view&id=229&Itemid=366.

3. Department of Defense, "Quadrennial Defense Review Report," (Arlington, VA: US Government Printing Office, 2010), iii.

4. Barack Obama, "National Security Strategy," (Washington, DC: US Government Printing Office, 2010), 2.

5. Some of these references are indirect, referring only to "near-peer competitors," but many are explicit. See for example, Department of Defense, "National Defense Strategy of the United States of America," (Arlington, VA: Department of Defense, 2008); Department of Defense, "Quadrennial Defense Review Report," (Arlington, VA: US Government Printing Office, 2010).

6. Brett D. Schaefer and Mackenzie M. Eaglen, "U.S. Africa Command: Challenges and Opportunities," *Backgrounder* no. 2118 (Washington, DC: Heritage Foundation, March 21, 2008): 6–8.

7. See Aaron T. Wolf, Shira B. Yoffe, and Mark Giordano, "International Waters: Identifying Basins at Risk," *Water Policy* 5, no. 1 (2003): 29–60; Geoffrey D. Dabelko and Karin R. Bencala, "Water Wars: Obscuring Opportunities," *Journal of International Affairs* 61, no. 2 (2008): 21–33.

8. Robert M. Gates, "Helping Others Defend Themselves," *Foreign Affairs* 89, no. 3 (2010): 2–6.

9. See Isobel Coleman, "The Global Glass Ceiling," *Foreign Affairs* 4, no. 88 (2010).

10. Christine Parthemore, "Promoting the Dialogue: Climate Change and U.S. Ground Forces," (Washington, DC: Center for a New American Security, 2010), 8.

11. Adrienne Stork, "Demobilized Soldiers Developing Water Projects—and Peace," *The New Security Beat*, April 9, 2010, http://newsecuritybeat.blogspot.com/2010/04/guest-contributor-adrienne-stork.html.

12. "Population and Environment," USAID, http://www.usaid.gov/our_work/global_health/pop/techareas/environment/index.html.

13. United States Agency for International Development, "Population, Health and Environment (PHE)," USAID, http://www.ehproject.org/phe/phe.html, Accessed April 17, 2010.

14. Stork, "Demobilized Soldiers Developing Water Projects—and Peace."

15. Cassie Gardener, "The Beat on the Ground: Ethiopia's Bale Mountains," *The New Security Beat*, April 14, 2010, http://newsecuritybeat.blogspot.com/2010/04/beat-on-ground-ethiopias-bale-mountains.html.

16. Ole Wæver., "Securitization and Desecuritization," in *On Security*, edited by Ronnie D. Lipschutz. New York: Columbia University Press, 1995: 54.

17. Myron Weiner and Michael S. Teitelbaum, *Political Demography, Demographic Engineering* (New York: Berghahn Books, 2001), 46.

18. Nicole Detraz, "Environmental Security and Gender: Necessary Shifts in an Evolving Debate," *Security Studies* 18, no. 2 (2009): 349.

19. David Mutimer, "Beyond Strategy: Critical Thinking on the New Security Studies," in *Contemporary Security and Strategy*, ed. Craig A. Snyder (New York: Palgrave Macmillan, 2008), 50.

20. Ibid, 49.

21. Esther Boserup, *Population and Technological Change: A Study of Long-Term Trends* (Chicago: The University of Chicago Press, 1981), 101.

22. UNFPA, "The State of World Population 1996: Changing Places: Population, Development and the Urban Future," (New York: United Nations Population Fund, 1996), 1.

23. UNFPA "State of World Population 2007: Unleashing the Potential of Urban Growth," (New York: United Nations Population Fund, 2007), 6.

24. Arjun Appaduri, "Deep Democracy: Urban Governmentality and the Horizon of Politics," *Environment & Urbanization* 13, no. 2 (2001): 25.

# Bibliography

Adamson, Fiona B. "Crossing Borders: International Migration and National Security." *International Security* 31, no. 1 (2006): 165–199.

"AIDS Accounts for 75 Percent of Police Deaths." *Daily Nation*, November 27, 2000, www.nationaudio.com.

Ananta, Aris. "Demand for Democracy in Indonesia: A Demographic Perspective." *Asian Population Studies* 2, no. 1 (2006): 1–2.

Anderlini, Jamil. "China's Angry Youth Drown Out Dissent." *Financial Times*, May 3, 2008, http://www.thefinancialexpress-bd.com/more.php?news_id=33791.

Appaduri, Arjun. "Deep Democracy: Urban Governmentality and the Horizon of Politics." *Environment & Urbanization* 13, no. 2 (2001): 23–43.

Archer, John. "Violence between Men." In *Male Violence*, edited by John Archer, 121–140. New York: Routledge, 1994.

Archibold, Randal C. "Arizona Enacts Stringent Law on Immigration." *The New York Times*, April 23, 2010, http://www.nytimes.com/2010/04/24/us/politics/24immig.html.

Associated Press. "Hispanics Comprise 20% of America's Student Body." *Telegraph-Herald*, March 6, 2009, http://findarticles.com/p/news-articles/telegraph-herald-dubuque-iowa/mi_8023/is_20090306/hispanics-comprise-20-americas-student/ai_n44873940/.

Associated Press. "Lebanon's Parliament Rejects Lowering Voting Age." Jpost.com, Febrary 23, 2010, http://www.jpost.com/MiddleEast/Article.aspx?id=169430.

Balzer, Harley. "Demography and Democracy in Russia: Human Capital Challenges to Democratic Consolidation." *Demokratizatsiya* 11, no. 1 (2003): 95–109.

Bava, Umma Salma. "India's Foreign Policy in the Regional Context." In *Emerging Powers: India, Brazil and South Africa (IBSA) and the Future of South–South Cooperation*, edited by the Barzil Institute, 16-20. Woodrow Wilson International Center for Scholars. Washington, DC: Woodrow Wilson International Center for Scholars, 2009.

Baviskar, Amita, Subir Sinha, and Kavita Philip. "Rethinking Indian Environmentalism."
    In *Forging Environmentalism: Justice, Livelihood, and Contested Environments*,
    edited by Joanne R. Bauer, 189–256. London: M.E. Sharpe, 2006.
Beall, Jo. "Urban Governance and the Paradox of Conflict." In *Megacities: The Politics
    of Urban Exclusion and Violence in the Global South*, edited by Kees Koonings and
    Dirk Kruijt, 107–119. London: Zed Books, 2009.
Bedoui, M., and G. Ridha. "Les Politiques de Lutte Contre l'Exclusion Sociale en
    Tunisie." Geneva: International Institute of Labour Studies, International Labour
    Office, 1996.
"Behind the Protests Spreading across Greece." *The Economist*, December 9, 2008,
    http://www.economist.com/node/12756043.
Bergheim, Stefan. "Live Long and Prosper! Health and Longevity as Growth Drivers."
    In *Current Issues: Global Growth Centres*, edited by Stefan Schneider. Frankfurt:
    Deutsche Bank Research, 2006.
Berlin-Institut für Bevölkerung und Entwicklung. "Summary of the Study's Findings."
    In *Unutilised Potentials: On the Current State of Integration in Germany*, 73–78.
    Berlin: Berlin-Institut für Bevölkerung und Entwicklung, 2009.
Bern, C. "Risk Factors for Mortality in the Bangladesh Cyclone of 1991." *Bulletin of the
    World Health Organization* 71, no. 11 (1993): 73–78.
Besançon, Marie L. "Relative Resources: Inequality in Ethnic Wars, Revolutions, and
    Genocides." *Journal of Peace Research* 42, no. 4 (2005): 393–415.
Black, Thomas. "Mexico Has 85 Organized-Crime Deaths, Bloodiest Day of Calderon
    Presidency." *Bloomberg.com*, June 12, 2010, http://preview.bloomberg.com/
    news/2010-06-12/mexico-has-85-organized-crime-deaths-bloodiest-day-of-
    calderon-presidency.html.
Bloom, David E., David Canning, and Pia N. Malaney. "Demographic Change and
    Economic Growth in Asia." *CID Working Paper*. Boston: Center for International
    Development at Harvard University, 1999.
Bloom, David E., David Canning, and Jaypee Sevilla. *The Demographic Dividend: A
    New Perspective on the Economic Consequences of Population Change: Population
    Matters*. Santa Monica, CA: RAND, 2003.
Boserup, Ester. *Population and Technological Change: A Study of Long-Term Trends*.
    Chicago: University of Chicago Press, 1981.
Bowsky, William M. "Siena: Stability and Dislocation." In *The Black Death: A Turning
    Point in History?*, edited by William M. Bowsky, 114–121. New York: Holt, Rine-
    hart and Winston, 1971.
Brainard, Lael, Derek Chollet, and Vinca LaFleur. "The Tangled Web: The Poverty–
    Insecurity Nexus." In *Too Poor for Peace? Global Poverty, Conflict, and Security in
    the 21st Century*, edited by Lael Brainard and Derek Collet, 1–30. Washington,
    DC: Brookings Institution Press, 2007.
Bremner, Jason, Carl Haub, Marlene Lee, Mark Mather, and Eric Zuehlke. "World Pop-
    ulation Highlights: Key Findings from PRB's 2009 World Population Data Sheet."
    *Population Bulletin* 64, no. 3 (2009).
Brennen, Ellen. "Population, Urbanization, Environment, and Security: A Summary of
    the Issues." *Comparative Urban Studies Occasional Papers Series*. Washington, DC:
    Woodrow Wilson International Center for Scholars, 1999.

Brett, Rachel, and Irma Specht. *Young Soldiers: Why They Choose to Fight.* Boulder, CO: Lynne Rienner, 2004.

Brewer, Laura. "Youth at Risk: The Role of Skills Development in Facilitating the Transition to Work." *InFocus Programme on Skills, Knowledge and Employability* Working Paper No. 19. Geneva: International Labour Organization, 2004.

Budny, Daniel Nogueira. "Democracy and the City: Assessing Urban Policy in Brazil." Washington, DC: Woodrow Wilson International Center for Scholars, 2007.

Byman, Daniel L., and Kenneth M. Pollack. "Iraqi Refugees: Carriers of Conflict." *The Atlantic*, November 2006, http://www.theatlantic.com/magazine/archive/2006/11/carriers-of-conflict/5268/.

Calvert, John R., and A. S. Al-Shetaiwi. "Exploring the Mismatch between Skills and Jobs for Women in Saudi Arabia in Technical and Vocational Areas: The Views of Saudi Arabian Private Sector Business Managers." *International Journal of Training and Development* 6, no. 2 (2002): 112–124.

Carling, Jørgen. "Migration, Human Smuggling and Trafficking from Nigeria to Europe." Geneva: International Organization for Migration, 2006.

Carpenter, Carey. "Global Governance, South–South Economic Relations, and Foreign Policy Strategies." In *Emerging Powers: India, Brazil and South Africa (IBSA) and the Future of South–South Cooperation*, 4–7. Edited by the Brazil Institute, Woodrow Wilson International Center for Scholars. Washington, DC: Woodrow Wilson International Center for Scholars, 2009.

Caselli, Francesco, and Wilbur John Coleman II. "On the Theory of Ethnic Conflict." *Discussion Paper No 732.* London: Centre for Economic Performance, 2006.

Castles, Stephen, and Mark J. Miller. *The Age of Migration.* 2nd ed. New York and London: Guilford Press, 1998.

Catley-Carlson, Megan. "Foreword." In *Do Population Policies Matter? Fertility and Politics in Egypt, India, Kenya, and Mexico*, edited by Anrudh Jain. New York: Population Council, 1998.

Central Bureau of Statistics. "Israel in Statistics 1948–2007." Jerusalem: Central Bureau of Statistics, 2009.

Central Intelligence Agency. "Botswana." *CIA World Factbook.* Washington, DC: Central Intelligence Agency, 2010, Accessed August 21, 2010, https://www.cia.gov/library/publications/the-world-factbook/index.html

Central Intelligence Agency. "China." *CIA World Factbook.* Washington, DC: Central Intelligence Agency, 2010. Accessed April 21, 2010, https://www.cia.gov/library/publications/the-world-factbook/geos/bc.html.

Chaaban, Jad. "The Impact of Instability and Migration on Lebanon's Human Capital." In *Generation in Waiting. The Unfulfilled Promise of Young People in the Middle East*, edited by Navtej Singh Dhillon and Tarik Yousef, 120–141. Washington, DC: Brookings Institution Press, 2009.

Chamberlain, Neil W. *Beyond Malthus: Population and Power.* New York: Basic Books, 1970.

Chan, Sewell, and Jackie Calmes. "U.S. Keeps Command of Military in Seoul." *The New York Times*, June 26, 2010, http://www.nytimes.com/2010/06/27/world/asia/27prexy.html?hp.

Chatty, Dawn. "Researching Refugee Youth in the Middle East: Reflections on the Importance of Comparative Research." *Journal of Refugee Studies* 20, no. 2 (2007): 265–280.

Chesnais, Jean-Claude. "Below-Replacement Fertility in the European Union (EU-15): Facts and Policies, 1960–1997." *Review of Population and Social Policy* 7 (1998): 83–101.

"China's Migrant Reforms Will Help Economy." *UPI.com*, December 28, 2009, http://www.upi.com/Top_News/International/2009/12/28/Chinas-migrant-reforms-will-help-economy/UPI-17711262006375/.

Choucri, Nazli. "Migration and Security: Some Key Linkages." *Journal of International Affairs* 56, no. 1 (2002): 97–122.

Choucri, Nazli, and Robert C. North. "Lateral Pressure in International Relations." in *Handbook of War Studies*, edited by Manus I. Midlarsky, 289–326. London: Allen and Unwin, 1989.

Cincotta, Richard P. "Demographic Security Comes of Age." *Environmental Change and Security Program* 10 (2004): 24–29.

Cincotta, Richard. "Review of Bare Branches: The Security Implications of Asia's Surplus Male Population." *Environmental Change and Security Program* 11 (2005): 70–73.

Cincotta, Richard. "Half a Chance: Youth Bulges and Transitions to Liberal Democracy." *Environmental Change and Security Program* 13 (2009): 10–18.

Cincotta, Richard. "Iran's Chinese Future." *Foreign Policy*, June 25, 2009, http://www.foreignpolicy.com/articles/2009/06/25/irans_chinese_future.

Cincotta, Richard, and Eric Kaufmann. "The Changing Face of Israel." *ForeignPolicy.com*.

Cody, Edward. "China Grows More Wary over Rash of Protests." *The Washington Post*, August 10, 2005, http://www.washingtonpost.com/wp-dyn/content/article/2005/08/09/AR2005080901323.html.

Coleman, David. "Why We Don't Have to Believe without Doubting in the 'Second Demographic Transition'—Some Agnostic Comments." *Vienna Yearbook of Population Research* (2004):11–44.

Coleman, David. "Europe's Demographic Future: Determinants, Dimensions, and Challenges." In *The Political Economy of Global Population Change: 1950–2050*, edited by Paul Demeny and Geoffrey McNicoll, 52–95. New York: Population Council, 2005.

Coleman, David. "Immigration and Ethnic Change in Low-Fertility Countries: A Third Demographic Transition." *Population & Development Review* 32, no. 3 (2006): 401–446.

Coleman, Isobel. "The Global Glass Ceiling." *Foreign Affairs* 4, no. 88 (2010): 13–20.

Collier, Paul. "Doing Well out of War: An Economic Perspective." In *Greed & Grievance: Economic Agendas in Civil War*, edited by Mats Berdal and David M. Malone, 91–111. Boulder, CO: Lynne Rienner, 2000.

Collier, Paul. "Economic Causes of Conflict and Their Implications for Policy." Washington, DC: World Bank, 2000.

Copeland, Dale C. *The Origins of Major War*. Ithaca, NY: Cornell University Press, 2000.

"Core Health Indicators." World Health Organization, 2006, http://www.who.int/countries/en/.

"Counterinsurgency." Washington, DC: Headquarters, Department of the Army, 2006.

Crill, M. "The Demobilisation and Reintegration of Former Child Soldiers in the Democratic Republic of Congo." London: Save the Children UK, 2000.

Curtain, Richard. "Where There Are No Jobs." Presented at Youth Exclusion and Political Violence Conference. Oslo: PRIO, December 11, 2008.

Dabelko, Geoffrey D., and Karin R. Bencala. "Water Wars: Obscuring Opportunities." *Journal of International Affairs* 61, no. 2 (2008): 21–33.

Daly, John C. K. "Somalia: Pirates of the Gulf." *International Relations and Security Network,* 2009, http://www.isn.ethz.ch/isn/Current-Affairs/Security-Watch/Detail/?id=97585&lng=en.

Dalziel, Stephen. "Death Rate High in Russian Army." *BBC*, September 13, 2003, http://news.bbc.co.uk/2/low/europe/3106368.stm.

Dandeker, Christopher, and David Mason. "Diversifying the Uniform? The Participation of Minority Ethnic Personnel in the British Armed Services." *Armed Forces & Society* 29, no. 4 (2003): 481–507.

Das Gupta, Monica. "Explaining Asia's 'Missing Women': A New Look at the Data." *Population & Development Review* 31, no. 3 (2005): 529–535.

Daumerie, Beatrice, and Karen Hardee. "The Effects of a Very Young Age Structure on Haiti: Country Case Study." *The Shape of Things to Come Series.* Washington, DC: Population Action International, 2010.

Davis, Diane. "Urban Violence, Quality of Life, and the Future of Latin American Cities: The Dismal Record So Far and the Search for New Analytical Frameworks to Sustain the Bias towards Hope." In *Global Urban Poverty: Setting the Agenda*, edited by Allison M. Garland, Mejgan Massoumi, and Blair A. Ruble, 57–87. Washington, DC: Woodrow Wilson International Center for Scholars, 2007.

de Waal, Alex. "How Will HIV/AIDS Transform African Governance?" *African Affairs* 102 (2003): 1–23.

Democratic Party of Japan. "Creating a Dynamic Japan: Towards a Secure Society." Tokyo: Democratic Party of Japan, 2003.

Department of Defense. "National Defense Strategy of the United States of America." Arlington, VA: US Government Printing Office, 2008.

Department of Defense. "Quadrennial Defense Review Report." Arlington, VA: US Government Printing Office, 2010.

Department of Defense. "2006 Quadrennial Defense Review Report." Arlington, VA: US Government Printing Office, 2006.

Department of Economic and Social Affairs. "United Nations World Youth Report 2005." New York: United Nations, 2005.

Detraz, Nicole. "Environmental Security and Gender: Necessary Shifts in an Evolving Debate." *Security Studies* 18, no. 2 (2009): 345–369.

Dhillon, Navtej Singh. "The Arab Marriage Crisis." *Newsweek*, 2007, http://www.msnbc.msn.com/id/17303203/site/newsweek.

Dhillon, Navtej Singh, and Tarik Yousef. *Generation in Waiting: The Unfulfilled Promise of Young People in the Middle East.* Washington, DC: Brookings Institution Press, 2009.

DiCicco, Jonathan M., and Jack S. Levy. "Power Shifts and Problem Shifts: The Evolution of the Power Transition Research Program." *Journal of Conflict Resolution* 43, no. 6 (1999): 675–794.

Dilley, Maxx, Robert S. Chen, Uwe Deichmann, Arthur L. Lerner-Lam, Margaret Arnold, Jonathan Agwe, Piet Buys, Oddvar Kjekstad, Bradfield Lyon, and Gregory Yetman. "Natural Disaster Hotspots: A Global Risk Analysis, Synthesis Report." Washington, DC: International Bank for Reconstruction and Development/The World Bank and Columbia University, 2005.

Doces, John A. "Feisty Youths and Freedom: The Effect of Youth Populations on Civil Liberties and Political Rights." Presented at *Midwest Political Science Association* Conference. Chicago: 2009.

Dolvo, Delanyo, and Frank Nyonator. "Migration of Graduates of the University of Ghana Medical School: A Preliminary Rapid Appraisal." *Human Resources for Health Development Journal* 3, no. 1 (1999): 45.

Donaldson, Peter J., and Son-Ung Kim. "Dealing with Seoul's Population Growth: Government Plans and Their Implementation." *Asian Survey* 19, no. 7 (1979): 660–673.

Drozdiak, William. "The Brussels Wall." *Foreign Affairs* 89, no. 3 (2010): 7–12.

Dugger, Celia W. "Devastating Exodus of Doctors from Africa and Caribbean Is Found." *New York Times*, October 27, 2005, http://www.nytimes.com/2005/10/27/international/27brain.html.

Dunlop, Imelda. *Business and Youth in the Arab World.* London: International Business Leaders Forum, 2006.

Durch, William J. "Keepers of the Gates: National Militaries in an Age of International Population Movement." In *Demography and National Security*, edited by Myron Weiner and Sharon Stanton Russell, 109–153. New York: Berghahn Books, 2001.

Dyson, Tim. "A Partial Theory of World Development: The Neglected Role of the Demographic Transition in the Shaping of Modern Society." *International Journal of Population Geography* 7, no. 2 (2001): 67–90.

Easterlin, Richard A. "Easterlin Hypothesis." In *The New Palgrave: A Dictionary of Economics, Volume 2*, edited by John Eatwell, Murray Milgate, and Peter Newman, 1–4. New York: Stockton Press, 1987.

Eberstadt, Nicholas. "Drunken Nation: Russia's Depopulation Bomb." *World Affairs,* Spring 2009, http://www.worldaffairsjournal.org/articles/2009-Spring/full-Eberstadt.html.

Ehrlich, Paul R. *The Population Bomb.* New York: Ballantine Books, 1968.

Elbe, Stefan. "Should HIV/AIDS Be Securitized? The Ethical Dilemmas of Linking HIV/AIDS and Security." *International Studies Quarterly* 50 (2005): 119–144.

Ellingsen, Tanja. "Colorful Community or Ethnic Witches' Brew?" *Journal of Conflict Resolution* 41, no. 4 (2000): 509–528.

England, Robert Stowe. *The Fiscal Challenge of an Aging Industrial World.* Washington, DC: The CSIS Press, 2002.

European Defence Agency. "An Initial Long-Term Vision for European Defence Capability and Capacity Needs." Brussels: European Defence Agency, 2006.

European Defence Agency. "Defence Data 2007." Brussels: European Defence Agency, 2007.

Fagen, Patricia Weiss. "Iraqi Refugees: Seeking Stability in Syria and Jordan." Institute for the Study of International Migration, Georgetown University, and Center for International and Regional Studies, Georgetown University School of Foreign Service in Qatar, 2007.

Fargues, Philippe. "Demographic Islamization: Non-Muslims in Muslim Countries." *SAIS Review* 21, no. 2 (2001): 103–116.

Faulconbridge, Guy. "Russia Says Population Up for First Year since 1995." *Reuters India*, January 19, 2010, http://in.reuters.com/article/idINTRE60I2KM20100119.

Fearon, James D., and David D. Laitin. "Sons of the Soil, Migrants, and Civil War." Draft chapter dated January 8, 2004. Forthcoming in *World Development Review*. Cited with author's permission, iicas.ucsd.edu/papers/GTCconf/soil11.pdf.

Fenech, Frederick F. "The Factor of Ageing in International Development Co-operation." *BOLD* 15, no. 3 (2005): 3–10.

Feng, Wang, and Andrew Mason. "Demographic Dividend and Prospects for Economic Development in China." Presented at *UN Expert Group Meeting on Social and Economic Implications of Changing Population Age Structures*. Mexico City: United Nations, 2005.

Figueiredo de Souza, Francisco. "IBSA: A Brazilian Perspective." In *Emerging Powers: India, Brazil and South Africa (IBSA) and the Future of South–South Cooperation*, edited by the Barzil Institute, Woodrow Wilson International Center for Scholars, 8-13. Washington, DC: Woodrow Wilson International Center for Scholars, 2009.

Filkins, Dexter. "Afghans Offer Jobs to Taliban Rank and File If They Defect." *The New York Times*, November 28, 2009, http://www.nytimes.com/2009/11/28/world/asia/28militias.html.

Finer, Jonathan, and Omar Fekeiki. "Tackling Another Major Challenge in Iraq: Unemployment." *The Washington Post*, June 20, 2005, A10.

Florida, Richard. *Who's Your City? How the Creative Economy Is Making Where to Live the Most Important Decision of Your Life*. New York: Basic Books, 2008.

Friedlander, Dov. "Fertility in Israel: Is the Transition to Replacement Level in Sight?" In *Completing the Fertility Transition*, edited by United Nations Department of Economic and Social Affairs, 440–447. New York: United Nations Department of Economic and Social Affairs, 2002.

The Fund for Peace. "Failed States Index Scores 2007." The Fund for Peace, 2007, http://www.fundforpeace.org/web/index.php?option=com_content&task=view&id=229&Itemid=366.

Fuller, Gary, and Forrest R. Pitts. "Youth Cohorts and Political Unrest in South Korea." *Political Geography Quarterly* 9, no. 1 (1990): 9–22.

Fuster, Joaquin M. "Frontal Lobe and Cognitive Development." *Journal of Neurocytology* 31, no. 3–5 (2002): 373–285.

"FY 2007–2008 Annual Report." Department of Defence, Republic of South Africa, 2008.

Gall, Gerald L. "Québec Referendum (1995)." In *The Canadian Encyclopedia*. The Historica Foundation, 2010, http://www.thecanandianencyclopedia.com.

Gallardo, Eduardo. "Chile's Private Pension System Adds Public Payouts for Poor." *The New York Times*, March 10, 2008, http://www.nytimes.com/2008/03/10/business/worldbusiness/10iht-pension.4.10887983.html.

Gardener, Cassie. "The Beat on the Ground: Ethiopia's Bale Mountains." *The New Security Beat*, April 14, 2010, http://newsecuritybeat.blogspot.com/2010/04/beat-on-ground-ethiopias-bale-mountains.html.

Gardner, Richard N. "The Politics of Population: Blueprint for International Cooperation." In *The Population Crisis: Implication and Plans for Action*, edited by Larry K. Y. Ng and Stuart Mudd, 285–297. Bloomington: Indiana University Press, 1965.

Garland, Allison M., Mejgan Massoumi, and Blair A. Ruble, eds. *Global Urban Poverty: Setting the Agenda.* Washington, DC: Woodrow Wilson International Center for Scholars, 2007.

Garrett, Laurie. *HIV and National Security: Where Are the Links?* New York: Council on Foreign Relations, 2005.

Gates, Robert M. "A Balanced Strategy: Reprogramming the Pentagon for a New Age." *Foreign Affairs* 88, no. 1 (2009), www.foreignaffairs.org/20090101faessay88103/robert-m-gates/how-to-reprogram-the-pentagon.html.

Gates, Robert M. "Helping Others Defend Themselves." *Foreign Affairs* 89, no. 3 (2010): 2–6.

Gay, Robert. "From Popular Movements to Drug Gangs to Militias: An Anatomy of Violence in Rio de Janiero." In *Megacities: The Politics of Urban Exclusion and Violence in the Global South*, edited by Kees Koonings and Dirk Kruijt, 29-51. London: Zed Books, 2009.

German Federal Ministry of Defence. "White Paper on German Security Policy and the Future of the Bundeswehr 2006." Berlin: German Federal Ministry of Defence, 2006.

Gilbert, Alan. "Urbanization and Security." *Comparative Urban Studies Occasional Paper Series.* Washington, DC: Woodrow Wilson International Center for Scholars, 1999.

Giles, Keir. "Review: Russia's National Security Strategy to 2020." *Russia Review Series*, edited by Andrew C. Monaghan. Rome, Italy: NATO Defense College, 2009, http://www.ndc.nato.int/research/publications.html.

Gilpin, Raymond. "Counting the Costs of Somali Piracy." *Working Paper.* Washington, DC: United States Institute of Peace, 2009.

"Global 500." *Fortune*, July 20, 2009, http://money.cnn.com/magazines/fortune/global500/2009/countries/SouthKorea.html.

Goldstone, Jack A. "Demography, Environment, and Security: An Overview." In *Demography and National Security*, edited by Myron Weiner and Sharon Stanton Russell, 38–61. New York: Berghahn Books, 2001.

Goldstone, Jack A. *Revolution and Rebellion in the Early Modern World.* Berkeley: University of California Press, 1991.

Goodwin, Liz. "Arizona Official Threatens to Cut Off Electricity to L.A. in Retaliation for Boycott." *Yahoo! News*, May 19, 2010, http://news.yahoo.com/s/ynews/20100519/pl_ynews/ynews_pl2133.

Gorman, Christine. "Sex, AIDS and Thailand." *Time.com*, July 12, 2004, http://www.time.com/time/magazine/article/0,9171,662826,00.html.

Goujon, Anne, Vegard Skirbekk, Katrin Fliegenschnee, and Pawel Strzelecki. "New Times, Old Beliefs: Projecting the Future Size of Religions in Austria." in *Vienna Yearbook of Population Research*, 237–270. Vienna: Vienna Institute of Demography, 2007.

Gräf, Bernhard, and Marc Schattenberg. "The Demographic Challenge." In *Current Issues: Demography Special*, edited by Stefan Schneider. Frankfurt: Deutsche Bank Research, 2006.

Gray, Colin S. "The 21st Century Security Environment and the Future of War." *Parameters* Winter (2008): 14–26.

Green, Elliott D. "Demography, Diversity and Nativism in Contemporary Africa: Evidence from Uganda." Presented at *ASEN Conference on Political Demography*. London: London School of Economics and Political Science, 2006.

Greener, Robert. "The Impact of HIV/AIDS on Poverty and Inequality." In *The Macroeconomics of HIV/AIDS*, edited by Markus Haacker, 167–181. Washington, DC: International Monetary Fund, 2004.

"The Guiding Principles on Internal Displacement." The Brookings-Bern Project on Internal Displacement, http://www.brookings.edu/projects/idp/gp_page.aspx.

Haas, Mark L. "A Geriatric Peace? The Future of U.S. Power in a World of Aging Populations." *International Security* 32, no. 1 (2007): 112–147.

Hanson, Stephanie. "Backgrounder: Urbanization in Sub-Saharan Africa." Washington, DC: Council on Foreign Relations, Last updated October 1, 2007, http://www.cfr.org/publication/14327/urbanization_in_subsaharan_africa.html, accessed December 22, 2009.

Haq, Husna. "Hispanics Abandon Arizona, Fleeing Economy, Immigration Law." *The Christian Science Monitor*, June 10, 2010, http://www.csmonitor.com/USA/Society/2010/0610/Hispanics-abandon-Arizona-fleeing-economy-immigration-law.

Harding, Luke. "No Country for Old Men." *The Guardian*, February 11, 2008, http://www.guardian.co.uk/world/2008/feb/11/russia.

Harrison, Frances. "Quake Experts Urge Tehran Move." *BBC News*, March 14, 2005, http://news.bbc.co.uk/2/hi/middle_east/4346945.stm.

Hattiangadi, Anita U., Gary Lee, and Aline O. Quester. "Recruiting Hispanics: The Marine Corps Experience Final Report." Alexandria, VA: Center for Naval Analysis, 2004.

Haub, Carl. "Population Change in the Former Soviet Republics." *Population Bulletin* 49, no. 4 (1994).

Haub, Carl. "What Is a City? What Is Urbanization?" Population Reference Bureau, 2009, http://www.prb.org/Articles/2009/urbanization. aspx?p=1.

Haub, Carl, and Mary Mederios Kent. "2008 World Population Reference Sheet." Washington, DC: Population Reference Bureau, 2008.

Haub, Carl, and Mary Mederios Kent. "World Population Data Sheet." Washington, DC: Population Reference Bureau, 2009.

Haupt, Arthur, and Thomas T. Kane. *Population Handbook*. 5th ed. Washington, DC: Population Reference Bureau, 2004.

Hauser, Philip M. "Demographic Dimensions of World Politics." In *The Population Crisis and the Use of World Resources*, edited by Stuart Mudd. The Hague: Dr. W. Junk, 1964.

Hedgpeth, Dana. "U.S. Task Force Commander for Haitian Relief Says Logistics Remain Stumbling Block." *The Washington Post*, January 18, 2010, http://www.washingtonpost.com/wp-dyn/content/article/2010/01/18/AR2010011804059.html.

Hegre, Håvard, Tanja Ellingsen, Scott Gates, and Nils Petter Gleditsch. "Toward a Democratic Civil Peace? Democracy, Political Change, and Civil War, 1816–1992." *American Political Science Review* 95 (2001): 33–48.

Heinecken, Lindy. "Facing a Merciless Enemy: HIV/AIDS and the South African Armed Forces." *Armed Forces & Society* 29, no. 2 (2003): 281–300.

Heinecken, Lindy. "HIV/AIDS, the Military and the Impact on National and International Security." *Society in Transition* 31, no. 1 (2001): 120–128.

Hejoj, Ibrahim. "A Profile of Poverty for Palestinian Refugees in Jordan: The Case of Zarqa and Sukhneh Camps." *Journal of Refugee Studies* 20, no. 1 (2007): 120–145.

Hermalin, Albert I., Mary Beth Ofstedal, and Rebbeca Tesfai. "Future Characteristics of the Elderly in Developing Countries and Their Implications for Policy." *Asian Population Studies* 3, no. 1 (2007): 5–36.

Hirschi, Travis, and Michael Gottfredson. "Age and the Explanation of Crime." *American Journal of Sociology* 89, no. 3 (1983): 552–584.

Homer-Dixon, Thomas. *Environment, Scarcity, and Violence.* Princeton, NJ: Princeton University Press, 2001.

Homer-Dixon, Thomas. *The Upside of Down: Catastrophe, Creativity, and the Renewal of Civilization.* Washington, DC: Island Press, 2006.

Hudson, Valerie M., and Andrea M. den Boer. "A Surplus of Men, a Deficit of Peace: Security and Sex Ratios in Asia's Largest States." *International Security* 26, no. 4 (2002): 5–38.

Hudson, Valerie M., and Andrea M. den Boer. *Bare Branches: Security Implications of Asia's Surplus Male Population.* BCSIA Studies in International Security. Cambridge, MA: MIT Press, 2004.

Hudson, Valerie M., and Andrea M. den Boer. "Missing Women and Bare Branches: Gender Balance and Conflict." *Environmental Change and Security Program* 11 (2005): 20–24.

Hurewitz, J. C. "The Politics of Rapid Population Growth in the Middle East." *Journal of International Affairs* 19, no. 1 (1965): 26–38.

"The Incredible Shrinking People." *The Economist* (November 27, 2008), http://www.economist.com/node/12627956.

India Registrar General. "Census of India, 2001, Series 1: India, Paper of 2001: Provisional Population Totals." New Delhi: India Registrar General, Office of the Registrar General, 2001.

"Indian Navy Escorted 900 Foreign Ships in Gulf of Aden." *The Times of India,* June 18, 2010, http://economictimes.indiatimes.com/news/politics/nation/Indian-Navy-escorted-900-foreign-ships-in-Gulf-of-Aden/articleshow/6065236.cms.

Inter-Agency Information and Analysis Unit, United Nations Office for the Coordination of Humanitarian Affairs. "Iraq Labour Force Analysis 2003–2008." 2009.

Interlandi, Jeneen. "What We Did Wrong." *Newsweek,* January 14, 2010, http://www.newsweek.com/2010/01/13/what-we-did-wrong.html.

Internal Displacement Monitoring Centre. "Global IDP Estimates (1990–2009)." Geneva: Internal Displacement Monitoring Centre, 2009, http://www.internal-displacement.org/8025708F004CE90B/%28httpPages%29/10C43F54DA2C34A7C12573A1004EF9FF?OpenDocument&count=1000.

"Iran Earthquake Kills Thousands." *BBC News*, December 26, 2003, http://news.bbc.
co.uk/2/hi/3348613.stm.

Ismail, Salwa. *Political Life in Cairo's New Quarters: Encountering the Everyday State.*
Minneapolis: University of Minnesota Press, 2006.

Jackson, Richard, and Neil Howe. *The Graying of the Great Powers: Demography and
Geopolitics in the 21st Century.* Washington, DC: Center for Strategic & International Studies, 2008.

Jackson, Richard, and Neil Howe. "The Graying of the Middle Kingdom: The
Demographics and Economics of Retirement Policy in China." Washington, DC:
Center for Strategic and International Studies, 2004.

Japan Ministry of Defense. "Defense of Japan 2008." Tokyo: Japan Ministry of Defense, 2008.

"Japan Seeks to Increase Defense Spending." *DefenseNews.com*, 2005, http://dfn
.dnmediagroup.com/story.php?F=1069707&C=asiapac.

Jennings, Chris. "Accelerated Citizenship Available for Active Duty Personnel." *Navy.
mil*, August 27, 2002, http://www.navy.mil/search/display.asp?story_id=3295.

Jha, Prabhat, Rajesh Kumar, Priya Vasa, Neeraj Dhingra, Deva Thiruchelvam, and Rahim
Moineddin. "Low Male-to-Female Sex Ratio of Children Born in India: National
Survey of 1.1 Million Households." *The Lancet* 367, no. 9506 (2006): 211–218.

"John Hajnal on the Prospect for Population Forecasts." *Population & Development
Review* 35, no. 1 (2009): 189–195.

Johnson, Christopher. "A Turning Point in Thailand." *The Japan Times Online*, May 13,
2010, http://search.japantimes.co.jp/cgi-bin/eo20100513a1.html.

Jones, Ellen, and Fred W. Grupp. *Modernization, Value Change, and Fertility in the
Soviet Union.* Cambridge: Cambridge University Press, 1987.

Kabbani, Nader, and Ekta Kothari. "Youth Employment in the Mena Region: A Situational Assessment." Washington, DC: World Bank, 2005.

Kahl, Colin H. *States, Scarcity, and Civil Strife in the Developing World* Princeton, NJ:
Princeton University Press, 2006.

Kapur, Devesh, and John McHale. *Give Us Your Best and Brightest: The Global Hunt for
Talent and Its Impact on the Developing World.* Washington, DC: Center for Global
Development, 2005.

Katz, Jonathan M. "Armed Thugs Filling Haiti's Security Void." *The Seattle Times*, January 18, 2010, http://seattletimes.nwsource.com/html/nationworld/2010828972_
haitisecure19.html.

Katz, Mark N. "Russia and the Shanghai Cooperation Organization: Moscow's Lonely
Road from Bishkek to Dushanbe." *Asian Perspective* 32, no. 3 (2008): 183–187.

Kaufman, Stuart J. *Modern Hatreds: The Symbolic Politics of Ethnic War.* Ithaca, NY:
Cornell University Press, 2001.

Kaufmann, Eric, and Oded Haklai. "Dominant Ethnicity: From Minority to Majority."
*Nations and Nationalism* 14, no. 4 (2008): 743–767.

Kay, Sean. *Global Security in the Twenty-First Century: The Quest for Power and the
Search for Peace.* Lanham, MD: Rowman & Littlefield, 2006.

Kent, Mary Mederios. "Do Muslims Have More Children Than Other Women in Western Europe?" Washington, DC: Population Reference Bureau, 2008, http://prb
.org/Articles/2008/muslimsineurope.aspx.

Kent, Mary M., and Carl Haub. "Global Demographic Divide." *Population Bulletin* 60, no. 4 (2005): 1–24.

Kershner, Isabel. "Israel's Ultra-Orthodox Protest Schools Ruling." *The New York Times*, June 17, 2010, http://www.nytimes.com/2010/06/18/world/middleeast/18israel .html.

Kim, Woosang. "Alliance Transitions and Great Power War." *American Journal of Political Science* 35, no. 4 (1991): 833–850.

Kirk, Dudley. "Population Changes and the Post-War World." *The American Sociological Review* 9 no. 1 (1944): 28–35.

Kissinger, Henry. "National Security Study Memorandum 200 Directive." Washington, DC: National Security Council, 1974, http://www.population-security.org/ 11-CH3.html#1.

Kornegay, Francis A. "Global Governance & Foreign Policy: The South African Dimension of IBSA." In *Emerging Powers: India, Brazil and South Africa (IBSA) and the Future of South–South Cooperation*, edited by the Barzil Institute, Woodrow Wilson International Center for Scholars, 13–16. Washington, DC: Woodrow Wilson International Center for Scholars, 2009.

Kraske, Marion. "Far Right Benefits from Voter Dissatisfaction." *Speigel Online*, September 29, 2008, http://www.spiegel.de/international/europe/0,1518,581098,00. html.

Krebs, Ronald R., and Jack S. Levy. "Demographic Change and the Sources of International Conflict." In *Demography and National Security*, edited by Myron Weiner and Sharon Stanton Russell, 62–105. New York: Berghahn Books, 2001.

Kritzer, Barbara E. "Chile's Next Generation Pension Reform." *Social Security Bulletin* 68, no. 2 (2008): 69–84.

Kugelman, Michael. "Look beyond Islamabad to Solve Pakistan's 'Other' Threats." *The New Security Beat*, edited by Meaghan Parker. Washington, DC: Environmental Change and Security Program, Woodrow Wilson International Center for Scholars, 2010, http://newsecuritybeat.blogspot.com/2010/05/guest-contributor-mi-chael-kugelman.html.

Kummel, Gerhard, and Nina Leonhard. "Casualty Shyness and Democracy in Germany." *Themenschwerpunkt* 3 (2004): 119–126.

Lake, David A., and Donald Rothchild. "Containing Fear: The Origins and Management of Ethnic Conflict." *International Security* 21, no. 2 (1996): 41–75.

Lamb, Robert D. "Ungoverned Areas and Threats from Safe Havens." Arlington, VA: Office of the Under Secretary of Defense for Policy, 2008.

Leahy, Elizabeth. "Beginning the Demographic Transition: Very Young and Youthful Age Structures." *Environmental Change and Security Program* 13 (2009): 40–47.

Leahy, Elizabeth, Robert Engelman, Carolyn Gibb Vogel, Sarah Haddock, and Tod Preston. *The Shape of Things to Come: Why Age Structure Matters to a Safer, More Equitable World*. Washington, DC: Population Action International, 2007.

Lee, Ronald, and Andrew Mason. "What Is the Demographic Dividend?" *Finance and Development* 43, no. 3 (2006).

Lega Nord. "Siamo a Rischio Di Poverta." Milan: Lega Nord, 2008.

Legault, Roch. "The Urban Battlefield and the Army: Changes and Doctrines." *Canadian Military Journal* Autumn (2000): 39–44.

Levy, Clifford J. "Russian Military Cuts Leave Soldiers Adrift." *The New York Times*, June 11, 2009, http://www.nytimes.com/2009/06/12/world/europe/12russia.html.

Li, Xiaobing. "The Impact of Social Changes on the PLA." In *Civil–Military Relations in Today's China: Swimming in a New Sea*, edited by David Michael Finkelstein and Kristen Gunness, 26–47. Armonk, NY: M.E. Sharpe, 2007.

Lischer, Sarah Kenyon. *Dangerous Sanctuaries: Refugee Camps, Civil War, and the Dilemmas of Humanitarian Aid*. Ithaca, NY: Cornell University Press, 2005.

Livi-Bacci, Massimo. *A Concise History of World Population*. 4th ed. Malden, MA: Blackwell, 2007.

"London Bombers: Key Facts." *BBC News,* Last updated July 21, 2005, http://news.bbc.co.uk/2/hi/uk_news/4676861.stm.

Luttwak, Edward N. "Where Are the Great Powers? At Home with the Kids." *Foreign Affairs* 73, no. 4 (1994): 23–28.

Macunovich, Diane J. "Relative Cohort Size: Source of a Unifying Theory of Global Fertility Transition?" *Population & Development Review* 26 (2000): 235–261.

Malthus, Thomas R. *An Essay on the Principle of Population*. London: Reeves and Turner, 1888.

Martin, Philip, and Gottfried Zurcher. "Managing Migration: The Global Challenge." *Population Bulletin* 63, no. 1 (2008).

Mason, Andrew. "Capitalizing on the Demographic Dividend." In *Population and Poverty, Population and Development Strategies*, edited by United Nations Population Fund, 39–48. New York: United Nations Population Fund, 2003.

Mather, Mark, and Kelvin Pollard. "U.S. Hispanic and Asian Population Growth Levels Off." Population Reference Bureau, http://prb.org/Articles/2009/hispanicasian.aspx.

Mazur, Allan, and Joel Michalek. "Marriage, Divorce, and Male Testosterone." *Social Forces* 77, no. 1 (1998): 315–330.

Mazzetti, Mark. "The Downside of Letting Robots Do the Bombing." *The New York Times*, March 21, 2009, http://www.nytimes.com/2009/03/22/weekinreview/15MAZZETTI.html?pagewanted=1&_r=1.

McCoy, Terry L. "Political Scientists as Problem-Solvers: The Case of Population." *Polity* 5, no. 2 (1972): 250–259.

Mearsheimer, John J. *The Tragedy of Great Power Politics*. New York: W.W. Norton, 2001.

Meijer, Roel. "Introduction." In *Alienation or Integration of Arab Youth: Between Family, State and Street*, edited by Roel Meijer, 1–14. Richmond, VA: Curzon, 2000.

Menegat, Rualdo. "Participatory Democracy and Sustainable Development: Integrated Urban Environmental Management in Porto Alegre, Brazil." *Environment & Urbanization* 14, no. 2 (2002): 181–206.

"Military Accessions Vital to the National Interest Pilot Recruiting Program." *STAND-TO!*, March 10, 2009, http://www.army.mil/standto/archive/2009/03/10/.

Ministério da Defesa. "National Strategy of Defense: Peace and Security to Brazil." Brasil Governo Federal, 2008.

Mitchell, James K. "Megacities and Natural Disasters: A Comparative Analysis." *GeoJournal* 49 (1999): 137–142.

Mockenhaupt, Brian. "The Army We Have." *The Atlantic Monthly*, June 2007, http://www.theatlantic.com/doc/print/200706/mockenhaupt-army.

Moran, Benedict. "US–Ecuador: Luring Migrants Home an Uphill Battle." *IPS*, October 27, 2009, http://ipsnews.net/news.asp?idnews=49015.

Morgenthau, Hans J., and Kenneth W. Thompson. *Politics among Nations: The Struggle for Power and Peace*. 6th ed. New York: Alfred A. Knopf, 1985.

Moutsiakis, Dimitrios. "The European Air Transport Fleet Gets Off to Flying Start." *EDA Bulletin* no. 10 (February 2009): 4–5.

Mubarak, Hosni. "President Hosni Mubarak on Egypt's Population." *Population & Development Review* 34, no. 3 (2008): 583–586.

Mutimer, David. "Beyond Strategy: Critical Thinking on the New Security Studies." In *Contemporary Security and Strategy*, edited by Craig A. Snyder, 34–59. New York: Palgrave Macmillan, 2008.

Myers, Steven Lee. "Youth Groups Created by Kremlin Serve Putin's Cause." *The New York Times*, July 8, 2007, http://www.nytimes.com/2007/07/08/world/europe/08moscow.html.

Nelson, Dean, and Rob Crilly. "Mumbai Attack Masterminds 'Will Never Be Brought to Justice.'" *Telegraph*, April 30, 2010, http://www.telegraph.co.uk/news/worldnews/asia/india/7658529/Mumbai-attack-masterminds-will-never-be-brought-to-justice.html.

Newman, David. "Population as Security: The Arab–Israeli Struggle for Demographic Hegemony." In *Redefining Security: Population Movements and National Security*, edited by Nana Poku and David T. Graham, 163–186. Westport, CT: Praeger, 1998.

Ngwanaamotho, Maranyane. "Botswana: HIV/AIDS Stabilises in Botswana." *allAfrica.com*, October 14, 2009, http://allafrica.com/stories/200910150161.html.

O'Donnell, Kelly, and Kathleen Newland. "The Iraqi Refugee Crisis: The Need for Action." Washington, DC: Migration Policy Institute, 2008.

O'Dwyer, Gerard. "World Military Spending Rose by 5.9% in '09: Sipri." *DefenseNews.com*, June 8, 2010, http://www.defensenews.com/story.php?i=4661977.

Obama, Barack. "National Security Strategy." Washington, DC: US Government Printing Office, 2010.

"Obama, Calderon Blast Arizona Immigration Law during White House Visit." *FoxNews.com*, 2010, http://www.foxnews.com/politics/2010/05/19/mexicos-president-blasts-arizona-immigration-law-white-house-visit-1351636523/.

Office of Management and Budget. "Historical Tables: Budget of the United States Government." Washington, DC: US Government Printing Office, 2009.

Ogawa, Naohiro, Makoto Kondo, and Rikiya Matsukura. "Japan's Transition from the Demographic Bonus to the Demographic Onus." *Asian Population Studies* 1, no. 2 (2005): 207–226.

Organisation for Economic Co-operation and Development. "International Migration Outlook: SOPEMI 2009, Summary in English." Paris: OECD, 2009.

Organization for Economic Co-operation and Development. "OECD Employment Outlook 2010: Moving beyond the Jobs Crisis." Paris: OECD Publishing, 2010, 267–305.

Organski, A. F. K. *World Politics*. New York: Alfred A. Knopf, 1958.

Organski, A. F. K., Bruce Bueno de Mesquita, and Alan Lamborn. "The Effective Population in International Politics." In *Political Science in Population Studies*, edited by

Richard L. Clinton, William S. Flash, and R. Kenneth Godwin, 79. Lexington, MA: Lexington Books, 1972.

Organski, Katherine, and A. F. K. Organski. *Population and World Power.* New York: Alfred A. Knopf, 1961.

Pampel, Fred C., and Elizabeth H. Peters. "The Easterlin Effect." *Annual Review of Sociology* 21 (1995): 163–194.

Paperny, Anna Mehler. "In China, out-of-Work Migrants Destabilizing." *SFGate.com,* January 23, 2009, http://articles.sfgate.com/2009-01-23/news/17199365_1_migrant-workers-pro-democracy-demonstrations-china.

Parkanova, Vlasta. "A Role to Play." *EDA Bulletin* no. 10 (February 2009): 8–9.

Parthemore, Christine. "Promoting the Dialogue: Climate Change and U.S. Ground Forces." Washington, DC: Center for a New American Security, 2010.

Partida-Bush, Virgilio. "Demographic Transition, Demographic Bonus and Ageing in Mexico." Prepared for United Nations Expert Group Meeting on Social and Economic Implications of Changing Population Age Structures. Mexico City: Mexico: Population Division, Department of Economic and Social Affairs, United Nations (2005), 285–307.

Passel, Jeffrey, and D'Vera Cohn. "U.S. Unauthorized Immigration Flows Are Down Sharply since Mid-Decade." Washington, DC: Pew Hispanic Center, September 1, 2010, Accessed September 8, 2010, from http://pewhispanic.org/reports/report.php?ReportID=126.

Pedersen, Peder J., Mariola Pytlikova, and Nina Smith. "Migration into OECD Countries, 1900–2000." In *Immigration and the Transformation of Europe,* edited by Craig A. Parsons and Timothy M. Smeeding, 43-84. Cambridge: Cambridge University Press, 2006.

Pelling, Mark. "Urbanization and Disaster Risk." Presented at *Population–Environment Research Network Cyberseminar on Population and National Hazards.* Palisades, New York: Population-Environment Research Network, 2007.

Peng, Xizhe, and Yuan Cheng. "Harvesting the Demographic Bonus: The Impact of Migration in Shanghai." *Asian Population Studies* 1, no. 2 (2005): 189–205.

Peter, Tom A. "Iraqi Refugees Spill into Jordan, Driving Up Prices." *The Christian Science Monitor,* November 29, 2006, http://www.csmonitor.com/2006/1129/p04s01-woiq.html.

Poggioli, Sylvia. "French Minorities Push for Equality Post-Obama." *NPR.org,* January 14, 2009, http://www.npr.org/templates/story/story.php?storyId=99298290.

Population Action International. "How Shifts to Smaller Family Sizes Contributed to the Asian Miracle." *FACTSheet* Washington, DC: Population Action International, 2006.

"Population and Environment." USAID, http://www.usaid.gov/our_work/global_health/pop/techareas/environment/index.html.

Population Division, Department of Economic and Social Affairs. "International Migration Report: A Global Assessment." New York: United Nations, 2006.

Population Division, Department of Economic and Social Affairs. "The World at Six Billion." New York: United Nations, 1999.

Population Reference Bureau. "World Population Highlights 2007: Migration." Washington, DC: Population Reference Bureau, 2007, http://prb.org/Articles/2007/623Migration.aspx.

Posen, Barry R. "The Security Dilemma and Ethnic Conflict." *Survival* 35, no. 1 (1993): 27–47.

Poston, Dudley L., Jr., and Karen S. Glover. "Too Many Males: Marriage Market Implications of Gender Imbalances in China." (2004). Unpublished work obtained with permission of the author: dudleyposton@yahoo.com.

Preston, Julia. "Mexican Data Show Migration to U.S. in Decline." *The New York Times*, May 14, 2009, http://www.nytimes.com/2009/05/15/us/15immig.html.

Price-Smith, Andrew T. *Contagion and Chaos: Disease, Ecology, and National Security in the Era of Globalization.* Cambridge, MA: MIT Press, 2009.

Prins, Gwyn. "AIDS and Global Security." *International Affairs* 80, no. 5 (2004): 931–952.

Putin, Vladimir. "Vladimir Putin on Raising Russia's Birth Rate." *Population & Development Review* 32, no. 2 (2006): 385–388.

"Q&A: The Chechen Conflict." *BBC News*, July 10, 2006, http://news.bbc.co.uk/2/hi/europe/3293441.stm.

Raspail, Jean. *The Camp of the Saints.* Petoskey, MI: The Social Contract Press, 2007.

"Regions and Territories: Ingushetia." *BBC News*, February 10, 2010, http://news.bbc.co.uk/2/hi/europe/country_profiles/3829691.stm.

Reuveny, Rafael. "Climate Change-Induced Migration and Violent Conflict." *Political Geography* 26, no. 6 (2007): 656–673.

"Robotic Baby Seal Wins Top Award." *BBC News*, December 22, 2006, http://news.bbc.co.uk/2/hi/technology/6202765.stm.

Romero, Simon. "Economies in Latin America Race Ahead." *The New York Times*, June 30, 2010, http://www.nytimes.com/2010/07/01/world/americas/01peru.html.

Ross-Thomas, Emma. "Spanish Youth Unemployment Exceeds 40 Percent." *Bloomberg.com*, October 30, 2009, http://www.bloomberg.com/apps/news?pid=20601085&sid=asUuQSLvVciE.

Roudi, Farzaneh. "Youth, Women's Rights, and Political Change in Iran." Population Reference Bureau, 2009, http://www.prb.org/Articles/2009/iranyouth.aspx.

Russian Federation Ministry of Defence. "Recruitment," http://www.mil.ru/eng/1862/12069/index.shtml.

Sachs, Jeffrey D., "The Strategic Significance of Global Inequality." *The Washington Quarterly* 24, no. 3 (2001): 187–198.

Sagala, John Kemoli. "HIV/AIDS and the Military in Sub-Saharan Africa: Impact on Military Effectiveness." *Africa Today* 53, no. 1 (2006): 53–77.

Sarin, Radhika. "The Enemy Within: AIDS in the Military." Online discussion, 2003, http://www.worldwatch.org/node/1550.

Schaefer, Brett D. and Mackenzie M. Eaglen. "U.S. Africa Command: Challenges and Opportunities." *Backgrounder* no. 2118 (Washington, DC: Heritage Foundation, March 21, 2008): 1–10.

Schonteich, Martin. "Age and AIDS: South Africa's Crime Time Bomb?" *Africa Security Review* 18, no. 4 (1999): 1–4.

Schwirtz, Michael, Anne Barnard, and C. J. Chivers. "Russia and Georgia Clash over Separatist Region." *The New York Times*, August 8, 2008, http://www.nytimes.com/2008/08/09/world/europe/09georgia.html.

Shain, Yossi. *Frontiers of Loyalty: Political Exiles in the Age of the Nation-State.* Ann Arbor: University of Michigan Press, 2005.

Shanghai Cooperation Organization. "Brief Introduction to the Shanghai Cooperation Organisation." Shanghai Cooperation Organization, 2010, http://www.sectsco.org/EN/index.asp.

Silver, Hilary. "Social Exclusion: Comparative Analysis of Europe and Middle East Youth." In *Middle East Youth Initiative Working Paper*. Washington, DC: Wolfensohn Center for Development and Dubai School of Government, 2007.

Simon, Jeffrey. "NATO's Uncertain Future: Is Demography Destiny?" *Strategic Forum* 236 (2008): 1–8.

Singer, P. W. "Robots at War: The New Battlefield." *The Wilson Quarterly* Winter (2009), http://www.wilsonquarterly.com/article.cfm?aid=1313.

Slaughter, Anne-Marie. "America's Edge: Power in the Networked Century." *Foreign Affairs* 88, no. 1 (2009): 94–113.

Sotero, Paolo. "Introduction." In *Emerging Powers: India, Brazil and South Africa (IBSA) and the Future of South–South Cooperation*, edited by the Brazil Institute, Woodrow Wilson International Center for Scholars. Washington, DC: Woodrow Wilson International Center for Scholars, 2009.

"Sovereigntists Pursue Quebec Independence." *CBCNews*, June 21, 2010, http://www.cbc.ca/canada/ottawa/story/2010/06/21/sovereignty-march.html.

"Speak Softly and Carry a Blank Cheque." *The Economist*, July 15, 2010, http://www.economist.com/node/16592455.

Spence, Lorna. "A Profile of Londoners by Country of Birth: Estimates from the 2006 Annual Population Survey." London: Data Management and Analysis Group, Greater London Authority, 2008.

Sprout, Harold, and Margaret Sprout. *Foundations of National Power*. Princeton, NJ: Princeton University Press, 1945.

State of Texas. "Estimates of the Population by Age, Sex, and Race/Ethnicity." San Antonio, TX: State of Texas, 2008, http://txsdc.utsa.edu/tpepp/txpopest.php.

Stedman, Stephen John, and Fred Tanner. "Refugees as Resources in War." In *Refugee Manipulation: War, Politics, and the Abuse of Human Suffering*, edited by Fred Tanner and Stephen John Stedman, 1–16. Washington, DC: Brookings, 2003.

Stork, Adrienne. "Demobilized Soldiers Developing Water Projects—and Peace." *The New Security Beat*, April 9, 2010, http://newsecuritybeat.blogspot.com/2010/04/guest-contributor-adrienne-stork.html.

Struyk, Raymond J., and Stephen Giddings. "The Challenge of an Urban World: An Opportunity for U.S. Foreign Assistance." Washington, DC: International Housing Coalition, 2009.

Tammen, Ronald L., Jacek Kugler, Douglas Lemke, Allan C. Stam III, Mark Abdollahian, Carole Alsharabati, Brian Efird, and A. F. K. Organski. *Power Transitions: Strategies for the 21st Century*. New York: Chatham House Publishers, 2000.

Tavernise, Sabrina. "Pakistan's Islamic Schools Fill Void, but Fuel Militancy." *The New York Times*, May 3, 2009, http://www.nytimes.com/2009/05/04/world/asia/04schools.html.

Taw, Jennifer Morrison, and Bruce Hoffman. "The Urbanization of Insurgency: The Potential Challenge to U.S. Army Operations." Santa Monica, CA: RAND, 1994.

Teitelbaum, Michael S., and Jay Winter. *A Question of Numbers: High Migration, Low Fertility, and the Politics of National Identity*. New York: Hill and Wang, 1998.

"Thirteen Killed in Crime Wave in Mexico's Acapulco." *Reuters.com*, March 13, 2010, http://www.reuters.com/assets/pritn?aid=USTRE62C1ET20100313.

"'Thousands Riot' in China Protest." *BBC News*, March 12, 2007, http://news.bbc .co.uk/2/hi/asia-pacific/6441295.stm.

Tibaijuka, Anna Kajumulo. "Introduction: The Challenge of Slums." In *Global Report on Human Settlements*. Edited by United Nations Human Settlements Programme, London: Earthscan Pulbications, Ltd., 2003, vi-vii.

Toft, Monica Duffy. "Differential Demographic Growth in Multinational States: Israel's Two-Front War." *Journal of International Affairs* 56, no. 1 (2002): 71–94.

Toft, Monica Duffy. "Population Shifts and Civil War: A Test of Power Transition Theory." *International Interactions* 33, no. 3 (2007): 243–269.

Twigg, Judyth. "Differential Demographics: Russia's Muslim and Slavic Populations." *PONARS Policy Memo*, Washington, DC: Eurasian Strategy Project, 2005., https:// gushare.georgetown.edu/eurasianstrategy/Memos/2005/pm_0388.pdf.

UNAIDS. "AIDS and the Military: UNAIDS Point of View." Geneva: Joint United Nations Programme on HIV/AIDS, 1998.

UNAIDS. "2008 Report on the Global Aids Epidemic." Geneva: UNAIDS, 2008

United Nations Department of Economic and Social Affairs. "World Urbanization Prospects: The 2007 Revision, Executive Summary." New York: United Nations, 2008.

United Nations Department of Economic and Social Affairs, Population Division. "World Urbanization Prospects: The 2009 Revision." New York: United Nations Department of Economic and Social Affairs, Population Division, 2010, http:// esa.un.org/unpd/wup/index.htm.

United Nations Development Programme. "Arab Human Development Report 2009: Challenges to Human Security in the Arab Countries." New York: United Nations Development Programme, 2009.

United Nations Educational Scientific and Cultural Organization (UNESCO). "Water and natural disasters in celebration of International Day for Natural Disaster Reduction." *UNESCO Water Portal Bi-monthly Newsletter* No 209, Paris: UNESCO, 2008, http://www.unesco.org/water/news/newsletter/209.shtml.

United Nations. "Youth Development Indicators." United Nations, http://www.un.org/ esa/socdev/unyin/youthindicators2.htm, accessed September 22, 2009.

UN-HABITAT. "State of the World's Cities 2006/7. The Millennium Development Goals and Urban Sustainability: 30 Years of Shaping the Habitat Agenda." London: Earthscan for UN-Habitat, 2006.

UN-HABITAT. *State of the World's Cities 2010/2011: Bridging the Urban Divide.* London: Earthscan for UN-HABITAT, 2010.

UN-HABITAT and United Nations Economic Commission for Africa. "The State of African Cities 2008: A Framework for Addressing Urban Challenges in Africa." Nairobi: UN-HABITAT, 2008.

United Nations High Commissioner for Refugees, Division of Programme Support and Management. "2009 Global Trends." Geneva: United Nations High Commissioner for Refugees, Division of Programme Support and Management, 2010.

United Nations Human Settlements Programme. "China's Rising Cities." Nairobi, Kenya: UN-HABITAT, 2006.

United Nations Human Settlements Programme. "Mumbai's Quest for 'World City' Status." Nairobi, Kenya: UN-HABITAT, 2006.

United Nations Human Settlements Programme. "Slums: Past, Present, and Future." Nairobi, Kenya: UN-HABITAT, 2006.

United Nations Human Settlements Programme. "The Challenge of Slums." Sterling, VA: United Nations Human Settlements Programme, 2003.

United Nations Human Settlements Programme. "The Urban Penalty: New Threats, Old Fears." Nairobi, Kenya: UN-HABITAT, 2006.

United Nations Human Settlements Programme. "Reducing Urban Crime and Violence: Policy Directions." London: United Nations Human Settlements Programme, 2007.

United Nations Integrated Regional Information Networks (IRIN). *HIV/AIDS and the Military*. PlusNews. United Nations Integrated Regional Information Networks (IRIN), www.irinnews.org/pdf/pn/Plusnews-Media-Fact-file-Military.pdf.

United Nations in the Russian Federation. "UN in Russia." New York: United Nations, 2007, http://www.unrussia.ru/en/about.html.

United Nations Office on Drugs and Crime. "The Globalization of Crime: A Transnational Organized Crime Threat Assessment." Vienna: United Nations Office on Drugs and Crime, 2010.

United Nations Population Division, "World Population Prospects: The 2008 Revision Population Database." New York: United Nations, 2009, http://esa.un.org/UNPP/.

United Nations Population Division. "World Population Prospects: The 2006 Revision Population Database." United Nations, 2007.

United Nations Population Fund. "The State of World Population 1996: Changing Places: Population, Development and the Urban Future." New York: United Nations Population Fund, 1996.

United Nations Population Fund. "State of World Population 2007: Unleashing the Potential of Urban Growth." New York: United Nations Population Fund, 2007.

The United Nations Refugee Agency. "UNHCR Concerned over Humanitarian Situation in Lampedusa, Italy." Geneva: The United Nations Refugee Agency, 2009, http://www.unhcr.org/news/NEWS/497991064.html.

United Nations High Commissioner for Refugees. "2010 UNHCR Country Operations Profile–Jordan." Geneva: United Nations High Commissioner for Refugees, 2010. Retrieved 17 September, 2010, from http://www.unhcr.org/cgi-bin/texis/vtx/page?page=49e486566.

United Nations High Commissioner for Refugees. "2010 UNHCR Country Operations Profile–Syrian Arab Republic." Geneva: United Nations High Commissioner for Refugees, 2010. Retrieved 17 September, 2010, from http://www.unhcr.org/cgi-bin/texis/vtx/page?page=49e486a76.

United Nations High Commissioner for Refugees. "Internally Displaced People." Geneva: United Nations High Commissioner for Refugees, 2010, http://www.unhcr.org/pages/49c3646c146.html.

United Nations High Commissioner for Refugees. "Statistical Yearbook 2005." Geneva: United Nations High Commissioner for Refugees, 2007.

United Nations International Strategy for Disaster Reduction. "2009 Global Assessment Report on Disaster Risk Reduction: Risk and Poverty in a Changing Climate." Geneva: United Nations International Strategy for Disaster Reduction Secretariat, 2009.

United States Agency for International Development. "Assistance for Iranian Earthquake Victims." Washington, DC: USAID. Last updated January 16, 2004, http://www.usaid.gov/iran/.

United States Agency for International Development. "Population, Health and Environment (PHE)." USAID, http://www.ehproject.org/phe/phe.html. Accessed April 17, 2010.

United States Agency for International Development. "Unmet Need for Family Planning." *Issue Brief.* Washington, DC: USAID, 2006.

Urdal, Henrik. "A Clash of Generations? Youth Bulges and Political Violence." *International Studies Quarterly* 50, no. 3 (2006): 607–630.

Urdal, Henrik. "The Demographics of Political Violence: Youth Bulges, Insecurity, and Conflict." In *Too Poor for Peace? Global Poverty, Conflict, and Security in the 21st Century*, edited by Lael Brainard and Derek Chollet, 90–100. Washington, DC: Brookings Institution Press, 2007.

Urdal, Henrik, and Kristian Hoelscher. "Urban Youth Bulges and Social Disorder: An Empirical Study of Asian and Sub-Saharan African Cities." In *Policy Research Working Paper.* Washington, DC: The World Bank, 2009.

Vallin, Jacques. "The Demographic Window." *Asian Population Studies* 1, no. 2 (2005): 149–167.

van de Kaa, Dirk J. "The Idea of a Second Demographic Transition in Industrialized Countries." Presented at *Sixth Welfare Policy Seminar of the National Institute of Population and Social Security.* Tokyo, Japan: National Institute of Population and Social Security, 2002.

Vasileva, Katya, and Fabio Sartori. "Acquisition of Citizenship in the European Union." *Population and Social Conditions: Statistics in Focus: Eurostat* 108 (2008).

Vermeer, Eduard B. "Demographic Dimensions of China's Development." In *The Political Economy of Global Population Change, 1950–2050*, edited by Paul Demeny and Geoffrey McNicoll, 115–144. New York: Population Council, 2006.

Vidino, Lorenzo. "Europe's New Security Dilemma." *The Washington Quarterly* 32, no. 4 (2009): 61–75.

Wæver, Ole. "Securitization and Desecuritization." In *On Security*, edited by Ronnie D. Lipschutz, 46–86. New York: Columbia University Press, 1995.

Weiner, Myron, and Michael S. Teitelbaum. *Political Demography, Demographic Engineering.* New York: Berghahn Books, 2001.

Wilson, Jamie. "Ethnic Minorities to Form Majority by 2050." *The Guardian*, August 13, 2005, http://www.guardian.co.uk/world/2005/aug/13/usa.population.

Wolf, Aaron T., Shira B. Yoffe, and Mark Giordano. "International Waters: Identifying Basins at Risk." *Water Policy* 5, no. 1 (2003): 29–60.

Wongboonsin, Kua. "Labor Migration in Thailand." Presented at *International Conference on Migrant Labor in Southeast Asia.* UNE Asia Center and School of Economics. Armidale, Australia: University of New England, December 1–3, 2003.

Wongboonsin, Kua, Philip Guest, and Vipan Prachuabmoh. "Demographic Change and the Demographic Dividend in Thailand." *Asian Population Studies* 1, no. 2 (2005): 245–256.

The World Bank, "Girls' Education," Last updated April 1, 2009, http://go.worldbank .org/1L4BH3TG20.

The World Bank. "Open Data." Washington, DC: The World Bank, 2010, http://data .worldbank.org.

The World Bank. "World's Progress on Maternal Health and Family Planning is Insufficient." Last updated July 9, 2009. Accessed September 8, 2010, from http:// go.worldbank.org/70P0CCPUF0.

The World Bank. *World Development Indicators.* Washington, DC: International Bank for Reconstruction and Development/The World Bank, 2007.

World Intellectual Property Organization. "World Patent Report: A Statistical Review." Geneva: World Intellectual Property Organization, 2008.

Yin, Sandra. "The Plight of Internally Displaced Persons," 2005, www.prb.org.

Zhang, Yuanting, and Franklin W. Goza. "Who Will Care for the Elderly in China? A Review of the Problems Caused by China's One-Child Policy and Their Potential Solutions." *Journal of Aging Studies* 20, no. 2 (2006): 151–164.

Zinnbauer, Dieter, Rebecca Dobson, and Krina Despota, eds. *Global Corruption Report 2009: Corruption and the Private Sector.* New York: Cambridge University Press, 2009.

Zolberg, Aristide. "From Invitation to Interdiction: U.S. Foreign Policy and Immigration since 1945." In *Threatened Peoples, Threatened Borders: World Migration and U.S. Policy,* edited by Michael S. Teitelbaum and Myron Weiner, 123–124. New York: W.W. Norton, 1995.

Zolberg, Aristide R. "Managing a World on the Move." In *The Political Economy of Global Population Change, 1950–2050,* edited by Paul Demeny and Geoffrey McNicoll, 222–253. New York: Population Council, 2006.

Zolberg, Aristide, Astri Suhrke, and Sergio Aguayo. *Escape from Violence: Conflict and the Refugee Crisis in the Developing World.* Oxford: Oxford University Press, 1989.

# Index

## About the Author

**JENNIFER DABBS SCIUBBA** is Mellon Environmental Fellow in the International Studies department at Rhodes College in Memphis, Tennessee. Dr. Sciubba has attended the Max Planck Institute for Demographic Research in Rostock, Germany, and is a former demographics consultant to the Office of the Secretary of Defense (Policy) in Arlington, VA. She received her Ph.D. and M.A. from the University of Maryland and her B.A. from Agnes Scott College.